Quasi-Experimental Research Designs

To Vera,

With love and affection,

Bruce T.

POCKET GUIDES TO
SOCIAL WORK RESEARCH METHODS

Series Editor
Tony Tripodi, DSW
Professor Emeritus, Ohio State University

Determining Sample Size:
Balancing Power, Precision, and Practicality
Patrick Dattalo

Preparing Research Articles
Bruce A. Thyer

Systematic Reviews and Meta-Analysis
Julia H. Littell, Jacqueline Corcoran,
and Vijayan Pillai

Historical Research
Elizabeth Ann Danto

Confirmatory Factor Analysis
Donna Harrington

Randomized Controlled Trials:
Design and Implementation for
Community-Based Psychosocial
Interventions
Phyllis Solomon, Mary M. Cavanaugh,
and Jeffrey Draine

Needs Assessment
David Royse, Michele Staton-Tindall,
Karen Badger, and
J. Matthew Webster

Multiple Regression with Discrete
Dependent Variables
John G. Orme and Terri
Combs-Orme

Developing Cross-Cultural Measurement
Thanh V. Tran

Intervention Research:
Developing Social Programs
Mark W. Fraser, Jack M. Richman,
Maeda J. Galinsky, and Steven H. Day

Developing and Validating Rapid
Assessment Instruments
Neil Abell, David W. Springer, and
Akihito Kamata

Clinical Data-Mining:
Integrating Practice and Research
Irwin Epstein

Strategies to Approximate Random
Sampling and Assignment
Patrick Dattalo

Analyzing Single System Design Data
William R. Nugent

Survival Analysis
Shenyang Guo

The Dissertation:
From Beginning to End
Peter Lyons and Howard J. Doueck

Cross-Cultural Research
Jorge Delva, Paula Allen-Meares, and
Sandra L. Momper

Secondary Data Analysis
Thomas P. Vartanian

Narrative Inquiry
Kathleen Wells

Structural Equation Modeling
Natasha K. Bowen and Shenyang Guo

Finding and Evaluating Evidence:
Systematic Reviews and
Evidence-Based Practice
Denise E. Bronson and
Tamara S. Davis

Policy Creation and Evaluation:
Understanding Welfare Reform in
the United States
Richard Hoefer

Grounded Theory
Julianne S. Oktay

Systematic Synthesis of
Qualitative Research
Michael Saini and Aron Shlonsky

Quasi-Experimental Research Designs
Bruce A. Thyer

BRUCE A. THYER

Quasi-Experimental
Research Designs

OXFORD
UNIVERSITY PRESS

OXFORD
UNIVERSITY PRESS

Oxford University Press, Inc., publishes works that further
Oxford University's objective of excellence
in research, scholarship, and education.

Oxford   New York
Auckland   Cape Town   Dar es Salaam   Hong Kong   Karachi
Kuala Lumpur   Madrid   Melbourne   Mexico City   Nairobi
New Delhi   Shanghai   Taipei   Toronto

With offices in
Argentina   Austria   Brazil   Chile   Czech Republic   France   Greece
Guatemala   Hungary   Italy   Japan   Poland   Portugal   Singapore
South Korea   Switzerland   Thailand   Turkey   Ukraine   Vietnam

Published by Oxford University Press, Inc.
198 Madison Avenue, New York, New York 10016
www.oup.com

Oxford is a registered trademark of Oxford University Press

Library of Congress Cataloging-in-Publication Data

Thyer, Bruce A.
Quasi-experimental research designs / Bruce A. Thyer.
p. cm. — (Pocket guides to social work research methods)
Includes bibliographical references and index.
ISBN 978-0-19-538738-4 (pbk. : alk. paper)
1. Social sciences—Research—Methodology.
2. Research—Methodology. I. Title.
H62.T49 2012
001.4'34—dc23   2011036983

Printed in the United States of America
on acid-free paper

Contents

Preface   vii

1 The Role of Group Research Designs to
   Evaluate Social Work Practice   3

2 Pre-Experimental Research Designs   29

3 Quasi-Experimental Group Designs   77

4 Interrupted Time Series Designs   107

5 Evaluating and Reporting Quasi-Experimental Studies   127

Glossary   179

References   187

Index   201

Preface

It has been argued that research which focuses on evaluating the outcomes of social work programs, on those services provided to individuals, groups, couples, families, organizations, and communities, or aimed at empirically evaluating the effects of various social welfare programs, are among the most scientifically valuable contributions that can be made by our discipline's researchers. Regardless of whether or not one subscribes to this appraisal, it is clear that the formal research method that is most often used in the evaluation of social work practice is the general type called *quasi-experimental design*. Practice outcomes can, of course, be evaluated using a diversity of approaches, including clinical judgment, narrative case histories, single-case studies, randomized controlled trials, meta-analyses, and systematic reviews. Each of these has its strengths and limitations. However, the adaptability of quasi-experimental designs for use in field settings—those naturalistic environments in which real social work services are provided to real clients, under clinically representative conditions—renders them particularly suitable for use by social work researchers.

In this work, I review the history and background of quasi-experimental designs as used by social workers, and I walk the reader through an increasingly complex array of these designs. I begin with studies of the outcomes obtained by a single group of clients, studies that are sometimes collectively labeled as pre-experimental designs. A variety of these designs are described, with their strengths, limitations, and practical uses. I next move to a discussion of designs involving evaluating the outcomes of two or more groups of clients, with one group receiving an intervention that is the focus of investigation, and the other(s) receiving either no treatment, standard care or treatment-as-usual, and/or a group receiving an innocuous intervention that serves as a control for nonspecific placebo influences (which are ubiquitous in the human services, sometimes powerfully and positively so). The final category of designs presented are various time-series designs, most often used in policy evaluation studies. Each design is illustrated with a description of its application in one or more previously published articles authored by social workers. The concluding chapter addresses how the data from quasi-experimental designs can be statistically evaluated, reviews some ethical standards and guidelines relating to the protection of human subjects from risk, and describes some contemporary standards that are recommended to be followed when reporting the results of quasi-experimental investigations.

There are, of course, other texts available that cover the methodology of the design and conduct of quasi-experimental studies, but none do so from the particular perspective of the profession of social work. Such a disciplinary focus, I hope, represents the unique contribution of the present volume. I would like to express my gratitude to the four reviewers of this book in manuscript form, and for their many(!) helpful suggestions, which greatly strengthened it. I would also like to thank my collaborators at Oxford University Press, Maura Roessner and Nicholas Liu, whose patience was extensively tested as this volume developed. My spouse, Dr. Laura Myers, as always, was a recurring source of support and inspiration. At one point in the past year, she was busy coauthoring her own social work research textbook and our late-night sessions propped up in bed together, surrounded by laptops, books, and papers, were a source of amusement to our four children.

This book is respectfully dedicated to William Shadish, whose exemplary work in exploring the limits and strengths of quasi-experimental and experimental research designs has inspired a generation of researchers in the human service professions. Over the years, I have followed his continuing oeuvre with admiration, respect, and humility. I was delighted to find him a warm, engaging, and friendly soul when we attended a conference together at the Lejondals Slott, near Stockholm, Sweden, in the winter of 2011. He has my thanks for his professional contributions.

Bruce A. Thyer, Ph.D., LCSW, BCBA-D
Tallahassee, FL

Quasi-Experimental Research Designs

The Role of Group Research Designs to Evaluate Social Work Practice

Social work as a professional discipline has defined itself from its earliest years as a scientifically grounded field. Initially, its conceptions of "science" were relatively simplistic, consisting of tabulating descriptive information about social problems and of individual clients. The social survey movement of the late 1800s and early 1900s almost defined what was then meant by scientific research within our field, and was very useful in setting the stage for social reform legislation by revealing the extent and seriousness of social problems in urban areas (Gordon, 1973; Bales, 1996). To gain a sense of the magnitude of these efforts, recall that Charles Booth's survey of the *Life and Labour of the People of London* (Booth, 1902–1903) required more than a decade to complete and ultimately comprised some 17 volumes! The Pittsburgh Survey (Devine, 1908) is the closest U.S. counterpart to Booth's massive project, and W. E. B. DuBois' (1899) *The Philadelphia Negro* represents one of the earliest empirical studies of the psychosocial and economic life of African Americans. Jane Addams and her staff at Hull House, in Chicago, devoted considerable effort to the graphic depiction of social conditions through the construction of the Hull House maps (Residents of Hull House, 1895), again a purely descriptive project aimed at illuminating social pathologies and suggesting possible ways to alleviate them. The contemporary Hull House museum provides reproductions of these impressive Hull House maps (see http://www.uic.edu/jaddams/hull/urbanexp/geography/geography.htm). Such descriptive surveys and studies were of immense value, even if the naïve assumption that solutions would somehow become self-evident once social problems were sufficiently identified and quantified turned out to be overly optimistic.

Later in the 20th century, social science in general, including social work, became more interested not only in describing social work conditions, but in attempting to more accurately understand their causes and correlates. Such research became technically feasible through the development of more sophisticated methods of statistical description, analysis, and inference. Correlational statistics and inferential tests were developed that helped social and behavioral scientists make more legitimate assertions about apparent associations, differences, and changes observed in the heretofore purely descriptive quantitative data they gathered. As sampling techniques and statistical methods of analysis improved, so did research methods themselves, to the point at which it became possible to undertake systematic evaluations of the outcomes of social work services. For example, Carl R. Rogers, the founder of person-centered therapy, was employed early on in his career as a social worker, and he conducted a small-scale evaluation of a foster home involving 10 boys. These were tough cases. "In spite of the fact that not one of the whole group was over the age of 11 years of age, sex misconduct of every variety was represented—masturbation, attempted sexual intercourse, filthy language, incest, extreme sexual curiosity, sex perversions of every sort" (Rogers, 1933, p. 21). He was able to present data on the IQ scores of the boys obtained when they initially entered the foster home and again some 3 years later, showing "a slight, but significant increase in mentality" (Rogers, 1933, p. 37). Rogers noted that the effects were small and that it was not possible to conclusively assert that the positive changes observed were *caused* by the foster home's beneficial effects. Despite these limitations, his study was considered sufficiently exemplary to be worthy of being reprinted in Lowry's (1939) *Readings in Social Casework: 1920–1938*.

Similar small-scale investigations, now known as pre-experimental studies, involving the more or less systematic assessment of clients before they received a social work program and again some time later, provided crude efforts to see if clients really *were* getting better following participation in our discipline's services, began to accrue during the 1930s and 1940s. These, in turn, were supplemented by somewhat more sophisticated studies involving naturally occurring control or comparison groups (such studies became known as quasi-experiments). By being able to *compare* the outcomes of clients receiving special social work services with those receiving either no such services or some alternative form of intervention, it is possible to have a stronger sense of the actual impact of the special social work services. Later, added to the mix, emerged a small number of true experimental studies, ones in which the control or comparison groups were created using random assignment procedures. This helps to ensure that the groups were essentially equivalent on most significant variables, including demographic features, problem severity, the possession of strengths, and any personal or social assets that may impact how a treatment could improve someone's situation.

F. Stewart Chapin, then Director of the School of Social Work at the University of Minnesota, wrote favorably on this topic in 1949, in his article titled *The Experimental Method in the Study of Human Relations*. According to Chapin:

> In the interest of clear thinking about this problem it is helpful to distinguish, first, the trial-and-error "experiments" of social legislation as a means to achieve some desired end; . . . second, the operations of natural social forces that produce an effect; . . . and, third, the use of experimental designs as a method of the study of the first two, in order to determine the degree of success in the attainment of a desired social end, or to measure the effect of some social force. . . . (Chapin, 1949, p. 132)

> There are three general patterns of experimental design in the study of human relations: . . . first, a cross-sectional design in which comparison is made for a given date between an experimental group which receives a social program, and a matched control group denied this program; second, a projected design in which before and after measurements are made upon an experimental group which received a program over an interval of time, and a matched control group denied this program; and, third, what may be called the ex post facto design, in which a present situation is taken as an effect of some assumed and previously operating causal complex of factors, and, depending on the adequacy of accessible records, an experimental group and a matched control group are traced back to an earlier

date when the forces to be measured began functioning upon the experimental group but not upon the control group. (Chapin, 1949, p. 133)

Chapin then went on to describe examples of using such designs in the evaluation of various social work and welfare interventions (e.g., the Boy Scouts, the federal Works Progress Administration, public housing, juvenile delinquency intervention, the effects of education on income, etc.). As we shall see later in this book, Chapin's description of posttest-only controlled group designs, and of pre- and posttest controlled group studies are distinctions that remain major forms of what are now called quasi-experimental research designs and whose inferential logic remains largely unchanged through to the present. He was optimistic about the potential for utilizing research methods in the appraisal of the results of social work, unabashedly claiming it to be possible to identify causal relationships in human affairs:

The experimental method has contributed in large measure to the striking achievements of modern science. This method allows us to analyze our relations of cause and effect more rapidly and clearly than by any other method. It permits verification by many observers. It has substituted for unreasonable prejudice a definite sort of proof that has attained sufficient certainty to justify prediction. . . . Experiment is simply observation under controlled conditions. When observation alone fails to disclose the factors that operate in a given problem, it is necessary for the scientist to resort to experiment. The line between observation and experiment is not a sharp one. Observation tends gradually to take on the character of an experiment. Experiment may be considered to have begun when there is actual human interference with the conditions that determine the phenomenon under observation. (Chapin, 1917, p. 133)

The reader may have noted the 42-year gap between these two lengthy quotes by Chapin.

In the 1970s, social worker Joel Fischer (1973, 1976) completed a comprehensive review of quasi and experimental studies on the outcomes of what was then labeled "social casework," services largely provided by workers holding master's degrees in social work (MSWs). He found one such study that had been published during the 1940s, two during the 1950s, and 11 that had been published during the 1960s.

Fischer found that when all these prior studies were examined, and the original authors' conclusions summarized, there was very little evidence that clients benefited from receiving conventional social casework services, and considerable evidence showed that a significant percentage were harmed as a result of their receipt of social services. Fischer's review was buttressed by other similar but independent analyses of the same literature, conducted about the same time, which arrived at equally dismal conclusions (e.g., Segal, 1972; Grey & Dermody, 1972). This was very bleak news indeed, and Fischer's conclusions provoked a storm of controversy, with some reactions being largely defensive in nature, others consisting of personalized criticism of Fischer's motivations for conducting these reviews, and some claiming that the effects of social work were simply not amenable to scientific investigations (e.g., Pharis, 1976). Fortunately, this latter view was not widely held.

One reaction to the Fischer assessment was a recognition that evaluation studies needed to employ more scientifically legitimate outcome measures, finally taking seriously the early recommendations of Mary Macdonald:

> The first essential, then, for evaluative research on practice is to make explicitly, specific, and concrete the objectives towards which practice is directed.... The essence of research is that the findings relate to that *which is observed and not to the individual observer.* This is the criterion of objectivity, or reliability, and it is one to which until recently such evaluative research as we had in social casework has given little or no attention. In research, the burden of proof is on the investigator, and he is expected to show that his results are not a matter of personal whim. One step in this direction has been taken when success is defined in specific and concrete terms. (Macdonald, 1952, p. 136, emphasis added)

Other positive reactions to the Fischer report were to focus on more narrowly circumscribed issues and problems addressed using interventions that could be operationalized well, thus enabling others to replicate those essential elements of the social work services possibly deemed effective in producing positive change. A further improvement was to adopt research designs of greater scientific credibility, thus permitting a clearer determination of the effects of social work. Within a decade following Fischer (1973), the picture had changed considerably, and for the better.

Reid and Hanrahan (1982) published a further review of more recently conducted outcome studies on social work, finding largely positive results, as did a number of other reviewers (Thomlison, 1984). In 1988, Lynn Videka-Sherman undertook the largest effort to date at tracking down outcome studies on social work, and conducted what is called a *meta-analysis* on these studies, a method of integrating the findings of disparate studies. Videka-Sherman claimed to find largely positive effects for social work services provided across a wide array of practice domains. Although Videka-Sherman's analysis regrettably included a large number of non-social work studies and included some other significant mistakes that clouded the conclusions that could be drawn about social work per se, the overall report was seen as important and served to bolster the profession's claim that it was indeed capable of assisting clients in a meaningful manner. Although each of these newer outcome studies can be and were legitimately criticized as overly optimistic and insufficiently critical (e.g., Hogarty, 1989; Epstein, 1990), it is fair to say that, in terms of methodological sophistication and results, the 1980s brought to light an increasing array of evaluation studies that improved the evidentiary foundations and justification for social work services. Subsequent systematic reviews and meta-analyses have reinforced this conclusion (e.g., de Schmidt & Gorey, 1997; Gorey, Thyer, & Pawluck, 1998; Grenier & Gorey, 1998). At present, more quasi-experiments and randomized controlled trials of social work services are published in a given year than occurred during entire decades prior to 1980. This reflects the discipline's maturation as a legitimate profession based on credible knowledge derived from high-quality social and behavioral science.

THE ROLE OF QUASI-EXPERIMENTAL STUDIES

Pre-experimental and quasi-experimental research designs are often used to try to evaluate the effects of a social program, a particular type of psychotherapy or some other form of psychosocial intervention, or the results of public policy. They are also widely used in medicine to evaluate the effects of medications. The term *design* in its broadest sense refers to all the elements that go into creating and conducting a research study, features such as forming a broad research question; creating a specific, directional, and falsifiable hypothesis; deciding upon a unit of analysis (e.g., individuals, groups of persons, organizations, communities, counties, states, countries, etc.); selecting a sample of clients or other units of analysis; choosing one or more outcome measures; developing a way to deliver the intervention in a credible manner; figuring out how to assess client functioning following (and sometimes before) receipt of the intervention; analyzing the results; and integrating the findings back into any relevant body of theory that the hypotheses were based upon (recognizing that not all hypotheses are based on an explicit behavioral or social science theory). Although this book discusses each of these elements of an outcome study to some extent, our primary focus will be upon the *logical or comparative* aspects of a research project, those features that comprise the most commonly understood meaning of the term "design."

Traditionally, research designs used in outcome studies have been broadly categorized into three types. Those which involve the analysis of a single group of clients have traditionally been called *pre-experimental designs*. Those that involve comparing the outcomes of one group receiving a treatment that is the focus of evaluation to one or more groups of clients who receive either nothing or an alternative real treatment, or to a group receiving a placebo-type treatment, have been called *quasi-experimental designs*. And the third type, *true experiments*, are characterized by creating different groups (those receiving "real" treatment vs. those receiving nothing, alternative treatment, or placebo) by randomly assigning clients (or other units of analysis) to those various treatment conditions. It is with these distinctions in mind that traditional research textbooks have used the terms pre-experimental designs, quasi-experimental designs, and true experimental designs (e.g., Campbell & Stanley, 1963; Cook & Campbell, 1979; Rubin & Babbie, 2008; Thyer, 2010a; Yegidis, Weinbach, & Myers, 2011). Some authorities have classified pre-experimental designs as quasi-experiments (Shadish, Cook, & Campbell, 2002), and it is with this sense in mind that the title of the present book is derived. However, given the continuing widespread understanding of the traditional distinction between pre- and quasi-experimental designs, these designs will be addressed in separate chapters in this volume.

When a researcher has access to a relatively large number of people who have or will receive a particular type of social work intervention, and she wishes to try to figure out what the effects of that intervention may have been, then pre- and quasi-experimental group research designs can be an excellent approach. For many years, authorities in social work have claimed that the design and conduct of outcome studies on social work is one of the most, if not *the* most valuable type of research project that can be undertaken, given social work's applied interests (see Chapter 1 in Royse, Thyer, & Padgett, 2010, which reviews this position). I tend to agree with this perspective (Harrison & Thyer, 1988).

A very large proportion of social work services and programs are undertaken with no systematic efforts made to evaluate the outcomes of these services. This is despite language found in the Code of Ethics of the National Association of Social Workers (2008), as in Standard 5.02 for dealing with Evaluation and Research:

(a) Social workers should monitor and evaluate policies, the implementation of programs, and practice interventions.
(b) Social workers should promote and facilitate evaluation and research to contribute to the development of knowledge.

It is clear that practice evaluation studies are not only the purview of the academic social worker but of all professional practitioners in our discipline. Relatedly, social work's accreditation organization, the Council on Social Work Education, provides guidelines as to what is required to be taught within the bachelor of social work (BSW) and MSW programs. Among the policies found in the social work Educational Policy and Accreditation Standards (Council on Social Word Education, 2008) is the following:

Educational Policy 2.1.6—Engage in research-informed practice and practice-informed research.
Social workers use practice experience to inform research, employ evidence-based interventions, evaluate their own practice, and use research findings to improve practice, policy, and social service delivery. Social workers comprehend quantitative and qualitative research and understand scientific and ethical approaches to building knowledge. Social workers
• use practice experience to inform scientific inquiry and
• use research evidence to inform practice.

The content of this book, relating to using quasi-experimental designs to evaluate the outcomes of social work, is core information needed by all social work students and practitioners to critically evaluate our discipline's research literature. It is obvious that research studies should include practitioner participation in order for such evaluations to be effectively designed, executed, and completed. And, competent research methodologists are necessary to help practitioners to design credible evaluations of their services. Perhaps the ideal scenario occurs when an experienced social worker goes on to obtain his or her research-based Ph.D., with a focus on acquiring skills in intervention research in social work (Harrison & Thyer, 1988). Most social workers will not actually undertake empirical research of any kind, and few will apply the types of designs described in this book in the context of evaluation studies. But *all* social workers need to have the ability to digest and understand such studies, regardless of whether they are presented in the form of a journal article, book chapter, books, governmental report, or organizational monograph. This book is intended to facilitate the student's and practitioner's ability to be an effective consumer of the research literature across the human services.

SOME QUESTIONS QUASI-EXPERIMENTAL STUDIES CAN ANSWER

These pre-experimental and quasi-experimental designs can be usefully employed to provide legitimate answers to fundamental questions such as the following:

1. *What is the status of clients after they have received a given course of treatment?*

Treatment can refer to a specific form of psychotherapy, a school or community-based intervention, a new social policy, or the like. And clients can refer to not only individuals, but also to other units of analysis, such as couples, families, small groups, organizations, communities, counties, states, or even nations. If a program or intervention really *is* effective, those clients assessed when it is completed should have good outcomes. For example, if 100 families provided a new home via the Habitat for Humanity program were assessed 3 years later, and all 100 families continue to reside in the Habitat homes they were provided, this would be a very good outcome, However, if only 30 families were found to have maintained ownership of their homes after 3 years, with 70 being unable to afford the minimal payments, then the Habitat program would not be seen as very effective in terms of providing long-term housing for the poor. Recently, I (Thyer, 2010b) reported on the pass rates of MSW graduates taking the licensed clinical social worker (LCSW) examination using this type of simple design. It can also be used to examine, for example, client satisfaction with social work services, or to evaluate how social workers attending a continuing education seminar viewed the quality of the instruction they received.

2. Do clients improve after receiving a given course of treatment?

This question is an incremental increase in sophistication over the first, in that it requires some sort of formal appraisal of the functioning of a group of clients *prior to* their receipt of social work services. It then systematically compares the posttreatment outcomes with the results of the pretreatment assessment. Both assessments must be conducted in a very similar manner for this type of comparison to be legitimate. If improvements are found, and they are meaningful, such a result is consistent with the hypothesis that treatment caused the group of clients to improve. Of course, there are other reasons why the clients could have gotten better, so it is not usually permissible to claim that treatment caused the improvements, only that improvements *happened*. If improvements are not found, and the study was conducted properly, the results would be consistent with the hypothesis that the treatment is not effective. Both results can be useful to know.

3. What is the status of clients who have received a given treatment compared to those who did not receive that treatment?

If the answers to questions 1 and 2 are positive, the next increasingly sophisticated question relates to determining if the positive changes can be reasonably attributable to the passage of time alone. This requires comparing the outcomes of the treated clients to a similar group of clients who did not receive the intervention. If treated clients end up better off than untreated ones, such results are consistent with the hypothesis that treatment produces more improvements than no treatment or the passage of time alone. This is good to know since many types of client problems wax and wane in severity over time, either in response to the natural history of the problem itself, in response to environmental changes, or in response to both influences. Intrinsic or environmental influences may be presumed to equally affect clients in the treatment and no-treatment groups. With these influences partially controlled for, the remaining possible source of posttreatment differences may be more credibly presumed to be due to the social work intervention received by the treatment group. Of course, other possible confounds remain, such as placebo influences, social desirability bias in client reports, nonspecific relationship effects, and the like.

4. *What is the status of clients who have received a novel treatment compared to those who received a credible placebo treatment?*

If it is shown that treated clients have high levels of functioning, that they actually improved following the receipt of social work services, and that they are better off than clients who did not receive a social work intervention, a further question of interest consists of finding out if clients who received a novel or experimental treatment fared better that clients who received an inert or placebo-type therapy. Any given social work intervention consists of at least three distinct elements that could possibly be responsible for therapeutic change. One important factor consists of the *therapeutic relationship*, which is known to be powerfully influential. A second important factor consists of the specific treatment techniques that are provided, within the context of the therapeutic relationships. The third important factor consists of the positive expectations for change induced simply by the experience of receiving a credible treatment method delivered by a warm and caring therapist. This latter mechanism of change can be called the *placebo factor*, of which more will be said later. Needless to say, placebo influences are ubiquitous in the delivery of interpersonal services in social work and other health care professions. Truly professional social work services consist of the creation of positive changes in clients induced by relationship factors *and* specific therapies, positive changes that are more powerful than placebo factors alone. One does not need years of graduate training to provide placebo treatments, and one would hope that the profession of social work provides treatments that are considerably more powerful than placebo. One very good way to help determine if this is the case is to compare the outcomes of clients who received a real experimental social work treatment with the results of clients who received a placebo or sham therapy. This is not as uncommon as you might think. Over a dozen nomothetic studies of social work intervention have used credible placebo groups in an effort to tease out the specific effects of treatment from those induced by relationship or placebo factors.

Almost 50 years ago, the distinguished social work researcher Margaret Blenkner (1962) authored a very important article titled "Control-groups and the Placebo Effect in Evaluative Research," an article that appeared in our profession's flagship journal, *Social Work*. Blenkner reviewed the salience of placebo effects in the provision of social work services and of the need for evaluation studies to control for placebo effects by using control groups providing apparently credible but actually innocuous therapies. Although concerns exist about providing placebo therapies to clients in need, circumstances can arise wherein providing a placebo-like therapy is both ethical and methodologically legitimate. For example, Wolf and Abell (2003) conducted a controlled study on the effects of a specific form of meditation on client psychosocial functioning. The meditation technique involved providing half the clients with a "real" mantra of Sanskrit words ("hare Krishna, hare Krishna. . . .") whereas half received a fake mantra of meaningless Sanskrit words ("sarva dasa, sarva dasa . . ."). Clients received otherwise identical instructions on how to meditate, and their psychosocial functioning was assessed before and after 4 weeks of meditation practice. Clients who received the real meditation method reported lower levels of stress than did the clients who received placebo medication practice. Afterward, those clients who initially received the fake mantra were debriefed and taught the real technique. Similarly, Pignotti (2005) evaluated the effects of a psychotherapy called thought field therapy (TFT). Thought field therapy involves a supposedly crucial treatment technique involving the client tapping on his or her body in very specific positions and timing sequences. In a test of this therapy, Pignotti arranged for half the clients to receive real TFT, with accurate instructions on where to tap their body. The other half were instructed (without their being aware of it) to tap on randomly chosen parts of their body. The real TFT group experienced modest improvements, but so did the placebo TFT group, thus demonstrating that TFT is essentially a technique that primarily relies on placebo influences to bring about its benefits, not anything specific to the tapping technique. Hyun, Lee, Kang, and Choi (2008) treated smokers with two forms of acupuncture: "real" acupuncture, involving real needle placement according to the acupuncture theory of meridians and invisible bodily energies unknown to science; and fake acupuncture, in which needles were placed on sites supposedly unrelated to the theory behind acupuncture. Subjective nicotine craving was measured posttreatment and found to be reduced in all clients but not to differ between the groups receiving real and fake acupuncture. This suggests that any beneficial effects of acupuncture are attributable to placebo factors, not to any technique-specific effects.

In a final example, two social workers conducted a study of the effects of eye-movement desensitization and reprocessing therapy (EMDR) on women prisoners with a history of being physically abused. The clients first received a treatment that the researchers were sure would not be helpful—relaxation training (RT), something not known to help persons with posttraumatic stress disorder (PTSD) symptomatology. After a period of receiving RT, all clients then received EMDR. Generally speaking, there were few to no differences between the small improvements observed following RT or EMDR. Given that EMDR is claimed by its proponents to produce dramatic improvements above and beyond placebo influences, this small-scale study suggested the opposite: that EMDR has effects similar to those induced by a placebo treatment (Colosetti & Thyer, 2000).

Currently, however, placebo-control conditions are not a common feature of social work outcome studies that make use of quasi-experimental designs. Given the seriousness of the conditions that our clients bring us, and the general paucity of evidence that clients are helped at all by what is routinely provided, few intervention research programs have advanced to the stage of needing to control for placebo influences. As our disciplinary outcomes-research endeavors mature over the ensuing decades, the use of credible placebo-control groups will become more evident.

5. What is the status of clients who have received a novel treatment compared to those who received the usual treatment or care?

Treatment innovations occur all the time in social work, and it can be useful to compare the outcomes of clients who receive a new intervention, relative to clients who receive standard care or treatment as usual. Early on in social work outcomes research, studies were undertaken comparing the results of standard, longer-term social casework against the results obtained from clients who received time-limited intervention or other forms of briefer therapies (e.g., Reid & Shyne, 1969). Some might even contend that it is ethically important to compare any new treatment against standard accepted care—and to demonstrate that the innovative approach is both safe and effective—prior to the new therapy being adopted on a wide scale.

This list of five fundamental questions could be extended a good deal by asking about additional practical issues, such as the durability of any initial effects observed during follow-up periods of various lengths, about possible side effects (good and bad) seen following receipt of treatments, of the costs of care relative to the benefits apparently received, and more. But, for now, we will limit our discussion to these five initial and incrementally more complex questions.

Notice the cautious language presented in Questions 1–5. We are not making any claims about treatment *causing* any observed outcome or improvement; rather, we are seeking answers to more modest questions. The question *Do clients get better following treatment?* is much easier to answer than is the question *Did the treatment cause the clients to get better?* Questions 1–5 may be answerable using the pre-experimental and quasi-experimental designs presented in this book, because questions regarding the causal effects of intervention usually require more rigorous designs, called *randomized controlled trials* (RCTs), as discussed in Solomon and Draine (2009) and in Cnaan and Tripodi (2010), among many other sources. Nevertheless, we believe that Questions 1–5 are worth investigating. Few social work programs, and few therapies, can provide definitive answers, in a scientifically credible manner, to Questions 1–5. Providing such answers can be a useful preliminary to conducting the more complex and difficult RCTs described elsewhere. For example, if simple investigations using pre-experimental and quasi-experimental designs reveal that clients who received treatment X did not get better, or that X is followed by results no better than standard care or a placebo treatment, then it makes little sense to conduct a more complex and expensive RCT to further evaluate treatment X. In that sense, the simpler designs described in this chapter can be a useful screening method to distinguish *potentially* effective treatments from ineffective ones. Caution is warranted here in the possible case of a therapy that slows deterioration, but does not enhance clients' absolute levels of functioning. A quasi-experimental study might find that clients are worse following therapy; but, absent proper comparison groups, the researcher might not know that the treated clients were actually better off than if they had not received treatment.

It was said earlier that the designs described in this chapter are widely used. How widely? Well, Rubin and Parrish (2007) reviewed every issue of two major journals that tend to report more outcome studies than do other social work journals, *Research on Social Work Practice* and *Social Work Research*, published during a 6-year period (2000–2005). They categorized the articles according to the type of design used in empirical outcome studies. They found a total of 28 quasi-experimental studies of social work practice and 21 pre-experimental studies (using the one-group pretest–posttest design described below), making a total of 49 published studies using the methods described in this book. In contrast, they found only 16 studies that used a randomized experimental design, nine used single-system research designs, 11 were correlational investigations, and one was a qualitative article. In a related study, Holosko (2010) examined 3 years' (2005, 2006, and 2007) worth of articles published in three major social work journals (*Research on Social Work Practice, Social Work Research, Journal of Social Service Research*), with a focus on the designs used in evaluating the outcomes of practice. He found a total of five randomized controlled trials, but 53 studies making use of pre- and quasi-experimental research designs. Clearly, these latter approaches are the designs most frequently used to evaluate the outcomes of social work practice, at least as reflected in these three selective and highly cited journals.

PURPOSES OF QUASI-EXPERIMENTAL STUDIES

Some contend that the highest or most sophisticated type of knowledge is *causal knowledge*, information that allows us to accurately predict what will happen to people who receive a particular social work intervention. As a result, less sophisticated research is sometimes minimized, seen as not worth doing, or as relatively unimportant. In this section, my hope is to disabuse the reader of such notions by describing some ways in which quasi-experimental designs can be useful in social work research.

Initial Screening of Treatments

The design and conduct of an intervention study can be a massive undertaking, expensive in terms of time, money, and other resources.

Many treatments, sadly, will ultimately prove to not be genuinely helpful. It is possible through small-scale quasi-experiments to identify interventions that clearly *do not work*. This information can be of considerable value—clients can subsequently avoid being exposed to ineffective interventions, and researchers can move on to devote their attentions to more promising lines of treatment. An example from the field of medicine can help convey this point. Suppose it is predicted that a new strain of influenza will emerge next year, and the Snape Potions Company has prepared a special vaccine that is supposed to protect those immunized with it from contracting this new strain of flu. It would be relatively simple to recruit a sample of 100 healthy volunteers, immunize all of them, then expose them to the new flu virus. If 100% of the sample, all 100 patients, subsequently came down with the new type of flu, this would be pretty convincing evidence that the new vaccine was not worth pursing. With this simple study used as a preliminary screening test, the company could avoid the expense of a much larger-scale study involving many hundreds of patients, various control groups, and the like.

We could envision something similar used in the human services. Suppose a novel psychotherapy called rectification therapy (a term I made up for the purposes of this book) was claimed to be very highly effective at preventing relapse (defined as subsequent attempts to kill oneself) among persons with major depression who attempted suicide for the first time. To test this prediction, we could provide rectification therapy to a consecutive series of depressed patients who had recently made their first suicide attempt and follow-up on their incidence of reattempting suicide over the next 12 months. If 100% were determined to have tried to kill themselves again, then rectification therapy would rather convincingly have been shown not to be very effective in achieving its intended goal of preventing all further suicide attempts. With proper comparison groups, it might be possible to demonstrate whether clients treated with rectification therapy had *fewer* suicide attempts than untreated clients, as well. It can be a mistake to undertake, as an *initial* appraisal of the effectiveness of a new treatment, a very complex design with hundreds of clients. Most therapies will, in the fullness of time, turn out to be not very useful. This finding can be determined with very simple studies. Do small-scale studies first as a screen, and only pursue more ambitious ones if the intervention passes the preliminary trials presented by the simpler studies and show at least *some* promise as useful.

Testing and Advancing Theory via Corroboration or Falsification of Hypotheses

Another useful function of quasi-experiments is to provide preliminary tests of hypotheses or answers to questions that are not about practice outcomes, but that address other potentially important issues, say, related to the causes or etiology of selected psychosocial problems. Take a clinical observation of Sigmund Freud, related to the etiology of agoraphobia:

> In the case of agoraphobia etc., we often find the recollection of an anxiety attack and what the patient fears is the reoccurrence of such an attack, under the special circumstances in which he believes he cannot escape. (Freud, 1962/1894, p. 81)

Based on his work with a number of agoraphobic patients, Freud came to believe that the agoraphobia stemmed from their experiencing a panic attack. Notice that he said this for persons with agoraphobia, not persons who are depressed, schizophrenic, or otherwise afflicted. Thus, this is a specific and easily falsifiable hypothesis. You could test it via a highly controlled quasi-experiment by systematically looking at several groups of clients (agoraphobics, depressed, schizophrenic, etc.) and assessing them via a reliable and valid history-taking of their experiences with panic attacks. If such experiences were very prevalent among those with agoraphobia and *not* among those with other disorders, then Freud's hypothesis could be said to be corroborated or supported (we rarely say "confirmed" in the behavioral sciences). Such a study would be a complex undertaking. However, you could do a simpler test. Ask a number of persons with agoraphobia to complete a simple questionnaire about their experience with panic attacks. If the incidence is high, then you have provisional or preliminary support for Freud's hypothesis and thus some justification for undertaking a larger-scale investigation. But if, contrary to his hypothesis, you found that very few persons with agoraphobia reported such a history, then you might decide that this is a line of etiological research that will likely prove to be a dead end, and thus opt to do something else. In such an instance, this very simple research design is quite valuable.

Developing Generalizable Knowledge

In many areas of psychosocial and health research, it is simply not possible to conduct true experiments, experimental studies that afford the best opportunity to develop true knowledge about the causes of problems and the real effects of interventions. Sometimes these difficulties are logistical. It may not be possible to gain access to a sufficiently large number of subjects to make a large-scale study feasible. People presenting with some issues, such as sex offenders, sex workers, prisoners, members of visible minorities, substance abusers, and the like may be reluctant to voluntarily participate in any kind of research project. And, perhaps most commonly, it may not be practical to develop and implement procedures to randomly assign clients to experimental versus standard versus placebo versus no-treatment conditions. Ethical considerations may preclude random assignment methods, or one's institutional review board may not approve of randomly assigning clients in need to control or comparison conditions. In such instances, true experiments may simply not be possible, and one must, perforce, rely on an array of research designs of lesser potential validity. This need not doom one's quest for developing causal knowledge, however. Take the case of smoking and lung cancer.

No one has ever designed a randomized controlled study wherein young children were assigned to a condition requiring them to smoke cigarettes from an early age into late adulthood, while others were strictly prohibited from ever smoking, and then having researchers look at the incidence of lung cancer in the two groups. Such a horrible study would be a very good way, scientifically, to see if smoking causes lung cancer; but fortunately, absent such research, there are other lines of evidence we can use to investigate possible associations. One could retrospectively look at the smoking histories of people who do and do not have lung cancer. If a smoking history is disproportionally present in the backgrounds of the lung cancer patients, this correlational evidence points in the direction of concluding that smoking causes cancer. It *points* to this conclusion but does not prove it to be true. One could look at the lung cancer rates among groups of people with high rates of smoking (e.g., the poor, or the French) versus those with lower rates of smoking (the well-to-do, or Mormons), and see if the incidence of lung cancer is higher among those who smoke more. One can look at lung cancer rates in countries with high and low rates of smoking and see if country-wide lung cancer rates systematically vary across these countries. One can examine the incidence of newly diagnosed lung cancer and see if it varies as the prevalence of smoking changes. For example, in the United States, new cases of lung cancer have declined, roughly proportionately with the declines in the numbers of people smoking. And one can look at animal research, examining the emergence of lung cancer in laboratory animals exposed to tobacco smoke versus clean air for long periods of time. If (as it so happens), over time, across research groups, and across countries, the nonexperimental research consistently points in the direction favoring the hypothesis that smoking causes lung cancer, and absent credible counterfactual evidence, the scientific community eventually concludes that there is a true causal association, and we thus have warning labels on cigarettes telling us that smoking causes lung cancer.

The lesson here is that an array of quasi-experimental, correlational, and epidemiological studies have the potential to provide our field with relatively plausible causal knowledge about the true effects of certain psychosocial interventions. If quasi-experimental study after quasi-experimental study points to the same conclusion (e.g., rectification therapy helps people with problem X) then, even in the absence of true experimental evidence, the field can provisionally accept this hypothesis, always being ready, of course, to revisit this conclusion as more evidence accumulates. This illustrates another manner in which quasi-experiments can be useful—in the development of generalizable knowledge.

Obtaining Pilot Data in Support of Research Grant Applications

In many circles, the acme of academic success is getting a large-scale federal research grant funded. Many research proposals are prepared in response to a federal request for proposals, for areas of research the government particularly wishes addressed. Others are unsolicited applications. In either case, grant applications proposing to conduct a large-scale randomized true experiment can be considerably strengthened by including information from previously conducted quasi-experiments—pilot studies, if you will—preliminary to a more rigorous investigation. One of social work's most successful recipients of large-scale federal research funding is

Dr. Gail Steketee, Dean of the Boston University School of Social Work. Here is what she and her colleague Scott Geron have to say on this topic:

> Pilot data are important because they demonstrate the applicant's expertise in a target area and serve as a basis from which the proposed research is built. Pilot data are essential for obtaining most federal funds and show the investigator's capacity to complete the study . . . the investigator should highlight the results from pilot studies that illustrate the need to conduct the proposed research, including the relevance of the findings to specific hypotheses, the proposed sample size and methodology, and the likelihood that study hypotheses will be supported. The investigator seeking larger-scale funding will need more substantial pilot data illustrating good effects in the predicted direction. Key points to consider in describing pilot studies include the following:
>
> Complete pilot studies before submitting federal grant proposals.
>
> Refer only to pilot studies . . . that clearly demonstrate one's technical skills and expertise in the proposed research area.
>
> Note how the pilot data are promising but insufficient and that, therefore, more data are needed. (Geron & Steketee, 2010, p. 626)

Rubin and Babbie (2008, p. 262) echo this advice:

> [I]f you seek funding for a more ambitious experiment or quasi-experiment, your credibility to potential funding sources will be enhanced if you can include in your proposal for funding evidence that you were able to successfully carry out a pilot study and that its results were promising.

Quasi-Experimental Studies As a Teaching Tool

The design and conduct of outcome evaluations in social work and other human service disciplines is a sophisticated skill, and like all sophisticated skills, they are unlikely to spring forth fully formed, like Athena from the forehead of Zeus. It is more likely that advanced skill development will be based on learning preliminary skills by doing simpler tasks, completed a number of times to the point of mastery, prior to undertaking more technically difficult projects. In my career as an academic, I have frequently worked with master's- and doctoral-level students on completing simple pre- or quasi-experiments as a preliminary to undertaking more ambitious ones. Dorothy Carrillo, for example, conducted a pre-experimental outcome study on training students in interviewing skills (Carrillo, Gallant, & Thyer, 1993) and subsequently completed a more sophisticated quasi-experiment as her Ph.D. dissertation project on the same topic (Carrillo & Thyer, 1994). Betsy Vonk was involved in conducting two quasi-experimental studies of relatively simple design (Thyer, Vonk, & Tandy, 1996; Vonk, Zucrow, & Thyer, 1996), prior to undertaking her more complex dissertation project (Vonk & Thyer, 1999). Similarly, Patrick Bordnick worked on two small-scale pre-experimental outcome studies (Capp, Thyer, & Bordnick, 1997; Crolley, Roys, Thyer, & Bordnick, 1998) to help acquire the skills he needed to do a larger-scale RCT of various inpatient therapies for cocaine addicts (Bordnick, Elkins, Orr, Walters, & Thyer, 2004). It can be a mistake for an inexperienced researcher to undertake an exceedingly ambitious outcome study without having acquired the necessary preliminary experience and skills to successfully pull off the larger project. Working on pre- and quasi-experimental outcome studies serves the dual functions of modestly contributing to disciplinary knowledge and in helping the graduate student to develop advanced skills in intervention research.

I hope that this section has persuaded the reader that the design and conduct of quasi-experimental outcome studies in social work can be of significant value. They can provide an initial screening of the possible effectiveness of interventions. If the results are positive, then the intervention *may* be effective and worth further investigation. If the results are negative, then the intervention is pretty certain to *not* be effective, and you may shortcut a potentially futile line of inquiry. Quasi-experiments testing particular treatments, especially if a series of such studies reach conclusions that consistently point in a similar direction, may yield conclusions you can be pretty confident in. As Rubin and Babbie (2008, p. 255) note "Despite the lack of random assignment, well-designed quasi-experiments can have a high degree of internal validity." Studies by research methodologist William Shadish and others have examined the conclusions reached via high-quality quasi-experiments compared to the same interventions evaluated using randomized controlled experiments.

He has found "substantial cause for optimism that conditions do exist under which nonrandomized experiments can yield accurate answers" (Shadish, 2011, p. 641; see also Shadish & Ragsdale, 1996; Shadish, Clark, & Steiner, 2008; Shadish, Galindo, Wong, Steiner, & Cook, 2011). This is not to say that quasi-experiments are always essentially equivalent to true experiments in their rigor at arriving at valid conclusions, but neither should they be cavalierly dismissed as inadequate for evaluation purposes. There are also simple pragmatic considerations, as set forth by Ottenbacher:

> Cronbach (1983) suggested that outcome studies should be guided by attempts to construct designs that meet situational needs, rather than focusing strictly on the requirements of an idealized true experiment. Creating the best research design, in this view, involves multiple considerations, including the purpose of the investigation, the specific setting, and the available resources. Cronbach (1983) argues that there is no single ideal standard for designs in clinical or applied environments. Any design is an interplay of resources, possibilities, creativity, and personal judgments. (Ottenbacher, 1997, p. 233)

These quasi-experimental designs can also serve a useful role in providing pilot data to be included in research grant applications, in addition to being published in their own right. Grant applications are considerably strengthened via the inclusion of solid pilot data and may pave the way to receive the funding necessary to conduct stronger evaluation studies. The final function mentioned was the pedagogical role of participation in quasi-experimental research projects for doctoral students and others new to the evaluation research field. Practical participation in such projects is often much more valuable than reading about research designs in a textbook.

THE THEORETICALLY NEUTRAL ASPECT OF QUASI-EXPERIMENTAL DESIGNS

One of the strengths of quasi-experimental designs is that they are sufficiently versatile as to be useful in the evaluation of virtually any psychosocial or medical intervention, regardless of the theoretical basis of that treatment. Whether an intervention is derived from social learning theory or psychodynamic principles, transactional analysis or hypnosis, the strengths perspective or a personal deficit orientation, so long as a treatment is hypothesized to produce real improvements in clients' lives, quasi-experimental designs may be usefully employed to empirically ascertain if those improvements occurred or not, and in some cases, to permit tentative causal inferences as to the effects of treatment. It is in this sense that these designs are atheoretical.

Quasi-experimental designs are, of course, based upon certain philosophical assumptions about the nature of the world (ontology) and how we come to arrive at legitimate knowledge of that world (epistemology), but these assumptions are those shared by conventional scientific inquiry as a whole. Among these foundational positions are empiricism, realism, operationalism, scientific skepticism, naturalism, determinism, parsimony, pragmatism, and the like. Although these fundamental philosophical assumptions may be enjoyably debated by philosophers, such discussions are to some extent fruitless since the issues are not capable of being satisfactorily resolved (which is why they continue to be endlessly argued). Those who accept the philosophical assumptions of mainstream science will find the application of quasi-experimental designs to be a very useful tool to answer questions and to test hypotheses. Those who do not accept these assumptions may find quasi-experimental designs to be an unsatisfactory approach to creating knowledge. It certainly seems reasonable that social scientists have the latitude to adopt any set of philosophical assumptions and research methodologies they deem appropriate. The ultimate validation of the usefulness of these competing approaches to research will reside in their ability to produce knowledge that helps prevent and solve the serious psychosocial problems that social work clients bring to members of our discipline.

Radical feminist and qualitative researcher Liane Davis wryly noted that when she was asked by the National Association of Social Workers' National Committee on Women's Issues to examine gender disparities within the profession of social work itself, she

> [O]btained a large data-set and was cranking out statistic after statistic on my office computer. Using this quantitative research method I was once again demonstrating that female social workers earn less than male social workers, even when controlling for important relevant variables. . . . Clearly this is a task that can only be accomplished with quantitative methodology. (Davis, 1994, p. 73)

Apart from quantitative statistics, Davis also used a quasi-experimental design, with gender as an independent variable. This research anecdote illustrates the principle that one should adopt the research method that will provide the best, most accurate, and credible answer to one's questions. If a self-described radical feminist and assertive advocate of qualitative research methodologies like Liane Davis can comfortably make use of quasi-experimental designs, what better proof do we have of the ubiquitous value of these latter approaches?

NOMENCLATURE, SYMBOLS, AND ASSUMPTIONS IN DESCRIBING QUASI-EXPERIMENTS

Both pre-experimental and quasi-experimental designs use some simple nomenclature and symbols to provide an outline or sketch of what was done. The typical symbols and their meaning are described below:

- O means a period of time in which clients were assessed (or *Observed*).
- O_1 means the first time clients were assessed, O_2 the second time, O_3 the third, and so forth. The measures used in the assessment of research participants are often called *dependent variables* in behavioral and social science, but in this book we will call them outcome measures, since we are focusing on evaluating the results of intervention.
- X usually means a novel treatment, the service that is the primary focus of an interventive study. In much social and behavioral science research, an intervention such as X may be called the *independent variable*, that which is manipulated (e.g., some clients get a therapy, and others do not). While keeping this usage in mind, this book will usually refer to these conditions more simply as "treatments" since most of the illustrations will involve evaluating social work practices or programs. Obviously, when the factor under investigation varies and we examine its presumed effects (which is not done in the context of an outcome study), the phrase "independent variable" is more accurate.
- Y, Z, or other letters mean other conditions or therapies received by a group of clients. Y might mean, for a given study,

treatment as usual (also known as TAU), Z might refer to a placebo treatment, and so forth. Such designations have no standard usage (e.g., Y = treatment as usual), so the meaning of these symbols may vary.

- $X_1 X_2$ means the same intervention given on different occasions.
- R means that the group was composed using random assignment methods.
- n means the size of a group or sample.
- N means the size of the population from which n was obtained.

The designs used in this chapter are founded on the traditions of what is called *nomothetic research,* that is, research using large numbers of people. In the case of outcome studies of social work practice, it is more respectful to refer to the people involved in our research as clients, since they are, after all, often real-life social work clients. This is in contrast to most other behavioral and social work science research projects that use people to test hypotheses derived from theories solely for the purposes of knowledge development, to advance knowledge for its own sake. In the latter instances, the people being studied are usually called *subjects* or perhaps, more recently, research *participants.*

To properly assess the results of one's observations of large numbers of clients, social work evaluators usually use one or more of several methods commonly called *inferential statistics,* statistical tests which, when used properly, help us in making correct inferences about the status of clients after treatment, whether or not a single group of clients appreciably changed following treatment, or whether two or more groups of clients differ at a given point in time (e.g., after receiving an intervention). Such outcome measures are rated or scored in such a way as to produce aggregated information expressed in the form of arithmetic averages, or mean scores and their associated standard deviations. These measures are usually analyzed by a class of inferential statistics called *parametric inferential statistics,* statistical tests based in part on the assumption that the large amounts of data involved would approximate a normal or bell-shaped curve, when plotted on a graph. Parametric tests can be used, for example, to see if the mean scores of a single, large group of clients have changed, posttreatment, compared to their pretreatment status. They can also be used to see if, posttreatment, the clients who received Treatment X significantly differ from the clients who received Treatment Y, and the like.

Some outcome measures involve simple yes-or-no categorizations, or may be expressed in terms of numbers, frequency, or percentages. In such cases, the inferential statistics involved in the analysis of the data are often *nonparametric tests,* ones *not* based on the assumption that the data are roughly normally distributed. For example, if at pretreatment 100% of the clients met the diagnostic criteria for panic disorder, and after participating in a treatment for anxiety, posttreatment only 60% (or 90%, or 80%, or 30%, etc.) were so diagnosed, a simple nonparametric test could tell you if this was a statistically significant (e.g., reliable, or not likely due to chance) change. One's choice of an inferential statistic should be driven by the type of data obtained and the research design employed, and *not* by a researcher's desire to use a familiar or novel method of statistical analysis. Let the tools fit the job. Do not arrange the job to be assessed by a particular tool. There will be further discussion on the use of inferential statistics in the final chapter of this book.

SUMMARY

Group research designs have long been used in the evaluation of social work programs and policies, and to produce more basic scientific knowledge. One type of group design, known as quasi-experiments, possesses particular advantages when conducting intervention research in real-life agency and other practice settings. Quasi-experimental designs are capable of answering some very important and fundamental questions about how clients fare after receiving social work services. All too often, practitioners and agencies do not possess systematic information on client outcomes and follow-up status. Quasi-experimental studies can provide this data. These studies are also useful for screening out ineffective treatments, identifying potentially effective therapies, testing theories and producing generalizable knowledge, as a teaching tool for graduate students, and in producing pilot data to accompany grant applications.

2

Pre-Experimental Research Designs

This chapter reviews the design and conduct of the simplest of nomothetic (involving relatively large numbers of clients) quasi-experimental research designs. These designs involve looking at only *one group* of people, those who received a given social work intervention that is the focus of the study, referred to here and in later chapters as the *treatment group*. The prerequisites to conduct this type of study are straightforward. You need clients, of course, ideally folks experiencing a similar problem, and they should have received a similar program of social work treatment. Without *both* of these two features, you have a jambalaya of ingredients that form an indigestible recipe, and it is very difficult to draw any legitimate conclusions about the effects of treatment when you have very diverse client problems addressed with an array of different interventions. Clients can, and usually do, present with many disparate problems, sometimes concurrently.

For the purposes of evaluation research, one of the lessons learned from Fischer's (1973, 1976) assessment is that intervention should focus on a fairly narrow range of problems. In mental health, it might be clients who meet the diagnostic criteria for a particular disorder, say major depression or obsessive-compulsive disorder (OCD). With the very poor, it might be unemployment only. With substance abusers, it might be individuals who primarily abuse one particular type of drug, say cocaine. By restricting your initial evaluation efforts to a fairly narrowly defined clientele, you actually enhance the likelihood of finding a positive effect. Take mental health as an example. Few psychotherapies or medications can be expected to help with *every type* of disorder. Rather, therapies are often tailored for particular conditions. Thus, we have, for example, the treatment called exposure therapy and response prevention useful in helping folks who meet the criteria for OCD; we have assertive community treatment (ACT) for individuals with schizophrenia, Alcoholics' Anonymous (AA) for alcoholics, and social worker Myrna Weissman's interpersonal psychotherapy (IPT) or Aaron Beck's cognitive therapy for persons with depression. We would not expect ACT to be helpful for someone with OCD or for AA to help people with schizophrenia (unless they also abused alcohol). Prozac notwithstanding, we have yet to develop any true panacea treatments. Imagine having a widely varying mix of clients whose primary diagnosis involves dozens of mental disorders, applying a single intervention to them, and expecting to see overall positive results. It is extremely unlikely. But, if we can do a study of the effects of AA alone on persons only suffering from alcohol abuse, the chances of seeing a clear effect are greatly enhanced, *if* the treatment is genuinely useful.

In some ways, the situation is like that of the chemist who wishes to control for extraneous effects by using only very pure chemicals combined at conditions of standard temperature and pressure. Keep your research picture as pure as possible—successfully isolate an effect—replicate (e.g., reproduce) that effect, *then* and only then, introduce greater variability into the picture. If you can demonstrate that rectification therapy seems to help the pure alcoholic, then do further studies of people who abuse alcohol, as well as another drug, say cocaine. If you find the therapy is still beneficial with this more complex clinical picture, consider adding another complicating element or variable, say marijuana. And so on, gradually approximating research clients who resemble more and more the "typical" substance-abusing client seen by social workers in agency-based practice.

Psychologists in particular are known for conducting such "pure studies" on various types of psychotherapies. These studies utilize carefully chosen clients presenting with only one major problem, carefully trained psychotherapists with sterling clinical credentials receiving expert supervision while they treat clients during the study, therapy conducted in controlled surroundings, and the like. Such studies are often critiqued, and legitimately so, for not reflecting representative clinical conditions;

that is, clients with multiple and complex problems, clinicians with limited training and less than adequate supervision, shabby offices, limited time, etc. The answer to such critiques is not to repudiate undertaking therapy research but to gradually conduct outcome studies under conditions that increasingly reflect everyday clinical realities, to see if the original positive results obtained under "ideal" circumstances hold up under less than perfect situations. In this way, such replication studies provide us with greater confidence regarding the usefulness of a new treatment under clinically representative conditions and can be more effectively promoted in mainstream practice.

Such work is being undertaken. Stewart and Chambless (2009) recently published a review of cognitive-behavioral therapies (CBTs) for adults with anxiety disorders. These treatments were initially developed under very tightly controlled conditions using carefully screened clients and supervised therapists. Such experiments are called *efficacy studies* and are basically intended to see if an intervention works under *ideal* circumstances. Once such efficacious treatments are identified, they can then be put into practice under clinically realistic conditions and their effects reevaluated—these studies are then labeled *effectiveness studies*. In this case, Stewart and Chambless found that the CBTs found useful in helping adults with disabling anxiety disorders in tightly controlled efficacy studies were also very effective in everyday practice, not just in university and hospital clinics, but in public agency practice. This conclusion is the results of many years of patient research, involving hundreds of clinicians and researchers, and thousands of clients, but the end result is very rewarding in determining that we do indeed have some highly effective therapies to help seriously handicapped clients (see also Shadish, Matt, Navarro, and Phillips, 2000).

All right, let us review some of the simpler group outcome studies and see how they may be of value.

ONE GROUP POSTTREATMENT-ONLY DESIGN

Take a look at the following design, and see if you can figure out what it means:

$$X - O_1$$

If you said something along the lines of "A group of social work clients received a treatment, labeled X, and afterward they were assessed on some outcome measure," you would be exactly right. This design is called the *one group post-treatment-only design* and can be exceedingly useful in attempting to answer Question 1 from Chapter 1: *What is the status of clients, after they have received a given course of treatment?* Noting the simplicity of this design, you may be tempted to be rather skeptical as to its value. Let me see if I can persuade you otherwise.

Supposed a group of middle school students are provided a comprehensive drug education program aimed at deterring drug use. These students were able to be followed-up 5 years later, and it was found that 90% of them admitted to regularly using drugs. What would this tell you about the effectiveness of the drug education program? Obvious, it is not *highly* effective. Suppose another group of middle school students received a school-based abstinence-oriented sex education curriculum, and 5 years later, 90% anonymously admitted to having regular sexual intercourse outside of marriage? Would this be useful (if disappointing) information to know, especially for a school system contemplating adopting the same abstinence-oriented sex education program? If you are a master's degree social work (MSW) student, you may run across advertisements for persons or firms selling social work licensing examination preparation programs, workshops, manuals, or online tutorials said to enhance your likelihood of passing your state's licensing test. Would it make a difference to you to learn that 95% of MSWs who completed a given proprietary licensed clinical social worker (LCSW) test preparation program passed the licensing test? And that another program's "graduates" only had a pass rate of 60%? Which preparation program would you want to pay for and complete? Perhaps the $X – O_1$ design has some potential value after all? Here are some published examples of this type of simple design.

Do Children on Medicaid Receive Required Preventive Screening Services?

Medicaid, the federal- and state-funded medical insurance program for the poor, requires early and periodic screening, diagnostic, and treatment examinations for children and youth under the age of 21. The theory is that these preventive tests will detect health problems early on and, in doing so, will result in improved health for poor children. These required evaluations are in the areas of a comprehensive health and developmental history, an unclothed physical examination, immunizations, laboratory tests, and health education. Staff within the Department of Health and Human Services reviewed the medical records for 345 children receiving Medicaid in nine different states to assess the extent to which these young persons were receiving required screenings. Fully 75% of the children did not receive all required medical, vision, and hearing screenings, and 41% did not receive *any* required medical screenings. When young people did receive such screenings, they were often incomplete (Levinson, 2010). This finding has rather important implications. First, taxpayers are paying for health services from which poor people obtain little benefit, primarily because of their lack of contact with health care providers. The issue is not cost, since these services are free to the patients. It also bears on the potential for planned national health care to significantly impact the access of the poor to physicians and other health care providers. Apparently, simply making free health care available does not ensure ready access, at least not for poor children. This is a very important finding and was brought to the attention of policy-makers by a simple post-test-only group design.

Do Families Follow-Through with Referrals?

MSW student intern Wendy Pabian was placed in a large diagnostic and evaluation agency serving clients with serious developmental disabilities and their families. The major purpose of the agency was to not only provide a solid diagnostic assessment in heretofore difficult-to-diagnose cases, but also to provide an array of medical and psychosocial treatment recommendations to the families, so that their children with developmental disabilities could be provided the services most likely to facilitate their growth and development to the greatest possible extent. As her faculty liaison, in conversations with Wendy, I asked her if the agency's clients were actually following through on the treatment recommendations so laboriously and expensively provided by the agency's interdisciplinary treatment teams. She said she did not know. I asked her to check it out at the agency itself, and a week's inquiries confirmed her impression—no one at the agency really knew if families were obtaining the recommended services. I suggested that doing a post-service assessment of this issue would be a valuable MSW intern project that would be useful to the agency. She agreed, as did her on-site field instructor and agency staff.

Wendy obtained a list of clients and families seen during a given time frame some months earlier, and then contacted them by phone, asking the parents about their seeking or obtaining each of the services recommended by Wendy's agency. Happily, it turned out that most *were* obtaining most recommended services, suggesting that the agency was indeed providing a useful service to clients with developmental disabilities and their families. Wendy prepared an internal report for the agency, as well as a more formal journal article that was subsequently published (Pabian, Thyer, Straka, & Boyle, 2000).

Are State Medicaid Application Enrollment Forms Readable?

Medicaid is a state- and federally funded program that provides health insurance to poor individuals, primarily among families whose annual income is below the federal poverty level, and to poor pregnant women. For persons to receive Medicaid benefits, they must first apply for them via a written or computer-based application form. Individuals who are poor disproportionately suffer from illiteracy or low-literacy, and/or represent persons whose primary language is not English. The readability of the application materials used to enroll persons in Medicaid can be a significant barrier for such individuals to qualify for this benefit to which they may be legitimately entitled. If the reading level is too high, the application attempt may be incomplete or abandoned entirely, resulting in a lack of benefits. In an attempt to determine if this may be a problem for the poor, Wilson, Wallace, and DeVoe (2009) obtained Internet-based Medicaid enrollment applications from 49 states (excluding Kentucky, which was unavailable online) and the District of Columbia. The readability of these forms was assessed using a standardized format widely used in the measurement of this construct (readability) as it pertains to health-oriented materials. The readability of the Medicaid applications ranged from the 11th to the 18th grade level. The authors believed these levels to be excessively high, exceeding the reading levels recommended for patient education in health literature and the actual reading levels of the average American.

Language excerpts from the actual Medicaid forms were presented along with examples of how this same content could be rewritten to a 6th-grade level, thus permitting the poor to more readily comprehend the language used in these forms. A very similar posttest-only design was used by Zite, Philipson, and Wallace (2007) to evaluate the readability of the Consent to Sterilization form used within the Medicaid system; this form is used when a person requests that he or she be sterilized as a voluntary method of birth control. Obviously, it is very important that the application forms and consent materials used in welfare eligibility determinations and requests for voluntary sterilization be easy to understand by the members of the population for whom they are intended. This simple design is an appropriate—indeed excellent—approach to see if the poor are being discouraged from applying for and receiving birth control via application materials using an excessively high reading level.

Do Adults Raised as Children in Orphanages Fare Well in Life?

In another example, social worker Laura Myers collaborated with a traditional orphanage located in Florida to conduct a follow-up study of the psychosocial well-being of the adults who had been raised in the orphanage many years ago. The orphanage maintained a mailing list of all of its "alumni," and Laura crafted a mailed written survey combined with some standardized and previously published measures of life satisfaction and quality of life to send to these alums. The research question generally dealt with how these individuals fared, later on in life, as assessed on educational, financial, familial, and social variables. There are actually very few studies that have been conducted on this topic, even though traditional orphanages have always played a major role in the country's child welfare system of care. The orphanage mailed out the surveys and an explanatory cover letter, which were returned directly to the orphanage by the alums who completed it. After personally identifying information was removed, the orphanage staff forwarded the completed surveys on to Laura, who analyzed the results. Retrospective appraisals of the care the alums received at the orphanage were quite positive, and they were, overall, doing quite well as adults in terms of education, income, life satisfaction, and other indicators. These results also yielded a respectable journal publication (Myers & Rittner, 2001) and have important implications for foster care and adoption services.

Are Consumers of Mental Health Services Satisfied with Their Treatment?

Social worker Jan Ligon was a senior administrator with the state mental health services program in Atlanta, Georgia. He helped design and conduct a consumer satisfaction study for the clients of a crisis and stabilization program providing services to clients with a serious mental health or substance abuse program and their families. He used a previously published, reliable, and valid measure of client satisfaction, and surveyed some 54 clients and 29 family members in the program, finding generally high levels of satisfaction, which is of course a good thing (see Ligon & Thyer, 2000).

Does a Coalition-building Program Promote Integrated Services?

MSW student Grace Smith was undertaking her internship at an agency that provided workshops called *coalition-building forums*, to service providers in the fields of developmental disabilities (DD), aging services, and mental health and substance abuse treatment—service providers who typically had little contact with each other in their professional roles. The purpose of these forums was to promote person- and family-centered care for older persons with developmental disabilities and their families. Information was provided on the services available through the aging, mental health, and DD networks, and a presentation was made by an older consumer with a developmental disability (or a family member). A networking session among the service providers and small-group activities related to integrating services across the three service programs were also provided. The purpose of these day-long meetings was to promote networking, collaboration, and increased political activities among the service providers in the months following the networking forums, so that services could be more effectively integrated with this high-risk population.

Ms. Smith contacted a sample of about 20% (n = 64 people) of all those who participated in these networking sessions several months later and asked them ten standardized questions regarding the possible impact of the forums on their daily practice. About half (47%) indicated that they had made professional contact with people they had met or heard about through attending the networking sessions. In general, respondents indicated improvements in their knowledge, awareness, and attitudes relating to older persons with developmental disabilities but relatively few (15%) indicated that they had engaged in lasting collaborative activities with service providers in other areas to serve such persons. This "bottom-line" result was disappointing and suggested that the networking sessions were not an effective mechanism to promote the long-term integration of services, which was the actual aim of the program (see Smith, Thyer, Clements, & Kropf, 1997). If you were the manager or administrator of the agency providing these networking forums, would you find it useful to learn whether or not your participants were undertaking the activities your sessions were intended to promote? Of course you would. Lacking this information, you might go on continuing to deliver the same old format, month after month, and have little incentive to try to improve your ability to really promote better integrated services.

Do Individual Developmental Accounts Help the Poor Achieve Financial Goals?

On a more macro scale, we can look at evaluations of individual development accounts (IDAs). IDAs are a widely used mechanism to provide incentives for the poor to save toward achieving one or more of several very limited goals—save for a house down payment, save for college, save to start a new business, or save to pay for significant home improvements. IDAs work by providing financial education and a match (often 2:1 or 3:1; i.e., for every dollar you place in your IDA account, it is eventually matched by $2 or $3), which poor individuals are able to set aside toward one of these goals. There are over 500 IDAs programs in the United States. Do IDAs help the poor achieve these goals? How could we find out? Well, one simple way would be to create a group of poor persons who enrolled in an IDA program and examine their attainment of one of these targeted goals after a reasonable period of time had elapsed, say 5 years. If, for 1,000 participants saving for a home down payment it was found, 5 years later, that 800 had been able to buy their own home using their IDA savings, this would likely be seen as a good outcome. If only 100 had done so, then the outlook for the effectiveness of IDAs would be less positive. See Richards and Thyer (2011) for a review of the evidence on IDA effectiveness, most of which uses relatively simple quasi-experimental designs.

This $X - O_1$ design has many merits. It is a great way to initially evaluate programs that have not had the advantages of formal pretreatment assessments; it can be used to help screen out obviously ineffective treatments; and positive results can encourage further, more sophisticated appraisals of an intervention initially seen as promising through this initial, simple, evaluation. However, this design is seriously limited in that, without any systematic assessment of the clients' functioning *before* they received the intervention, it is logically difficult to make any legitimate inferences regarding whether the group of clients receiving treatment actually had *changed*. And, without any kind of comparison group that did not receive intervention X, it is difficult to make any conclusions as to how the group that received X might have changed if they had not received X. Shadish, Cook and Campbell (2002, p. 107) do note:

> However, the design has merit in rare cases in which much specific background knowledge exists about how the dependent variable behaves. For example, background knowledge of calculus is very low and stable in the average high school population in the United States. So, if students pass a calculus test at levels substantially above chance after taking a calculus course, this effect is likely due to the course. . . . But for valid, descriptive causal inferences to result, the effect must be large enough to stand out clearly, and either the possible alternative causes must be known and be clearly implausible or there should be no known alternatives that could operate in the study context.

This posttest-only design has, in prior years, been labeled the "one-shot case study." This language is no longer recommended because of the confusion the term engenders with the similarly named qualitative method widely used in the psychotherapy literature, the narratively presented "case study" of an individual client (e.g., Brandell & Varkas, 2010). Simple though it is, there are a number of methodological refinements that can be added to the basic design $X - O_1$ that can strengthen it as an evaluation method. Some of these techniques are described below.

WAYS TO STRENGTHEN THE POSTTEST-ONLY GROUP DESIGN

Use Outcome Measures Known to be Reliable and Valid

All outcome measures are not alike. Some have strong psychometric properties—they are internally consistent and have high test–retest reliability. Their face and content validity is evident, their internal factor structure is robust, and they have strong concurrent and predictive validity. They are easy to complete, score, and interpret, and are low in cost and readily available. Use such measures whenever possible, in lieu of surveys or rating scales especially developed for a particular study and not previously demonstrated to be reliable and valid. Outcome measures must also be sensitive, in that they are capable of detecting small but meaningful differences and changes.

Use Several Different Outcome Measures

A client's level of functioning, strengths, deficits, or psychopathology may be capable of being concurrently measured in several different ways. In the measurement of depression, for example, the Beck Depression Scale (BDI) is intended to be completed by depressed clients themselves and is widely considered to be among the best measures of depression available. The Hamilton Rating Scale also is used to assess depression, but it is intended to be completed by a health care professional or caregiver, thus providing another perspective on a client's depression. A third potential way to assess depression would be to ask the client to complete a sleep log, indicating the times at which he or she fell asleep, woke up, and total duration of sleep each night. A posttest-only study with three somewhat distinct measures of depression, each legitimate in its own right yet tapping into different aspects of depressive phenomenology, can yield a stronger assessment of a client's depressive status than may be obtained by using only one measure. In research, this approach is known as *triangulation*—using different, perhaps imperfect, measures to more adequately capture some outcome variable.

Use Larger Samples of Clients

In nomothetic research, size matters (20 is better than 10, 50 is better than 20). The larger the sample size, the more persons you have to draw conclusions from and the more likely it is that your sample reflects some larger population of interest. Now, to be sure, using a randomly selected sample, one wherein every person in a population has the same likelihood of being selected, is the most solid way to ensure having a sample that accurately represents a larger population of interest. This ideal is often not feasible however, especially in research settings such as social service agencies. If your agency sees 300 new cases a year, you can see how a sample of 100 of these clients, albeit nonrandomly selected, will yield a more representative sample of your 300 cases than would having only 20 nonrandomly selected individuals. Also, as we shall see in Chapter 5, using larger sample sizes increases what is known as *statistical power*, the ability to detect true differences or changes when they really exist. And this is a good thing. However, be aware that simply having a larger sample size alone is no guarantee that the sample is more representative of the larger population of interest. A very large sample of persons chosen in some biased manner can still be unrepresentative, even if the bias is unintentional. For example, suppose you wished to sample "telephone users," and you used the local white pages to select your sample. Well, no matter how big a group you contacted, you would still largely leave unsampled cell phone users (who are not listed in the white pages) and those who do not have a landline registered in their names.

Use Multiple Posttreatment Assessments

Assessing client functioning once after receipt of services is a good start. But to do this again after, say, 3 months have elapsed from the termination of treatment is even better, and 6 months better still. Providing services that produce a strong effect immediately after treatment is great, but if these improvements evaporate after a month or two, we will be much less excited about the effectiveness of our program. The only way to make this determination is to conduct suitable follow-up assessments. If gains are maintained months or years down the road, this is of far greater import to clients and social work services.

The posttest-only design with repeated measures can be diagrammed as follows:

$$X - O_1 - O_2 - O_3$$

By adding one or more additional posttreatment assessments, this design is strengthened by permitting an appraisal of how well any initial effects (e.g., improvements) have been maintained, or if any other effects emerge over time. It may be that, immediately posttreatment, the clients' status was not very good, perhaps leading to the conclusion that treatment could not have possibly had any beneficial effects. But a further post-treatment assessment, perhaps weeks or months after the first one, could disclose that folks were doing very well indeed. The delay in observing any effect complicates inferences about the possible effects of treatment, since the closer in time a presumed effect occurs after exposure to a presumed cause (e.g., treatment), the stronger is the logical warrant to link the apparent results to the treatment.

The elements of theory and plausibility also need to be taken into account in trying to make a causal inference. Someone who takes aspirin for a headache expects an effect (e.g., pain relief) in an hour or two, not days later. However, persons with an earache will not display any improvements immediately after taking an antibiotic medication; improvements can be predicted to begin only a day or two later. Similarly, some interventions may also be predicted (ideally in advance) on the basis of clinical observation, prior research, or even of theory, not to produce immediate changes, and only to have improvements become evident some time following receipt of treatment. For example, certain psychotherapies that aim at symptomatic improvement on the basis of the client developing "insight" could reasonably be expected to not yield any improvements for the first month or so. If this is the case, then the social work researcher can deliberately arrange for posttreatment assessments to take place only after the interval of time supposedly needed for improvements to become evident.

Other treatments could be predicted to have an additive effect, wherein treatment benefits accrue over time, even after intervention has been discontinued. Say that treatment X consists of intensive tutoring in reading provided to low-income elementary school students. One might expect a certain level of reading proficiency when reading ability is measured immediately after the tutoring program is discontinued, say at time 1, or $X - O_1$. It would be reasonable to anticipate that at time 2, say 3 months later, reading proficiency would have gotten even better, or $X - O_1 - O_2$, and so forth, with the group of children's reading scores progressively improving as they gain practice in reading.

Use These Designs Prospectively

These designs are best used *prospectively*; that, is planned for and with data gathered after the study has been planned. This is opposed to using them *retrospectively*, a method that looks at data after the fact, without having had any plans to use the data for evaluation services when the data were initially gathered.

Look for Generalized, Positive Outcomes or Potential Negative Ones

It is common in therapy outcome studies to include one or more measures related to a client's primary issue, such as depression, marital discord, abuse of a given substance, or domestic violence. This is, of course, important. If the intervention may be predicted to produce other broader-ranging effects, these too might be measured. For example, in the instance of an intervention designed to reduce spousal battering, obtaining credible measure of the episodes of abuse is crucial, but including additional measures, say, of *quality of life* or of *life satisfaction*, could also be important. One would hope that a reduction in marital violence would also improve quality of life or life satisfaction, even though these may not have been among the client's primary complaints when initially seeking treatment. If a therapy is effective in alleviating the dysfunctional mood swings associated with bipolar disorder, but the client's level of life satisfaction declines, this is obviously not as satisfactory an outcome as one with a treatment that reduces mood swings and promotes life satisfaction. Some therapies can have negative side-effects (even non-drug-related interventions), and screening for these negative side effects is also a valuable adjunct to assessing changes in focal problems.

You can probably think of many other ways in which the basic $X - O_1$ design could provide useful information. For example, if you are a BSW or MSW student, do you have the opportunity to complete a course evaluation at the end of each class? Some universities make this information publicly available, for each professor. Suppose you learn that Dr. Thyer consistently earns high ratings on his students' course evaluations. Or that he usually earns very low ratings? Would this information be of any use to you in deciding whether or not to take Thyer's classes? Student course evaluations, client satisfaction studies, follow-ups on prevention and other service programs, studies on the natural history of disorders—these are all types of inquiry in which the $X - O_1$ design can provide very useful information. Do not dismiss them as scientifically useless. If you have a simple question (e.g., *What is the status of clients after they received a social work intervention?*), these simple designs can help answer it.

But if you have a more complicated question, you may need more complicated studies, such as those described below.

THE ONE-GROUP PRETEST–POSTTEST DESIGN

If you would like to answer the second question mentioned Chapter 1, *Do clients improve after receiving a given course of treatment?*, you can add a pretreatment assessment to the basic $X - O_1$ design and end up with an approach that can be diagrammed as follows:

$$O_1 - X - O_2$$

Clients are assessed twice, and their responses are aggregated (often using an average score for all clients) at the pretest and again after they complete treatment, with this second assessment called the posttest. Not surprisingly, this design is called the *one-group pretest–posttest design*. As before, you need to make use of one or more reliable and valid outcome measures that assess some aspects of client functioning. These can be diagnostic measures or an assessment of a problem, a deficit, or a strength. Clients are assessed, subsequently participate in a social work treatment program or intervention, and are then assessed again, in the same manner as during the pretest phase of the study. You can then compare their aggregated posttest scores or measures with their pretest scores and see if things have changed, overall, for that group of clients. Ideally, they have, and for the better. Either way, you can at least partially answer Question 2: "Yes, they are better following Treatment X," or "No they are not better after Treatment X," or "They are worse off, following Treatment X," or, least satisfactorily, "The data are too unclear to say if they have changed." It is not usually enough to *simply look* at the aggregated scores pre- and posttreatment when assessing a sample of clients. You usually need to "test" the changes using one or more inferential statistical tests to rule out random fluctuations in the data as being responsible for any noted differences. Such tests will be briefly discussed in Chapter 5.

This design is often feasible, even in conventional agency-based settings without many resources, and can be undertaken by individual social workers who lack advanced degrees and research training (although these can obviously be of help!). The These designs can be done *retrospectively*, in circumstances wherein clients complete some sort of pretreatment and posttreatment assessments as a part of routine agency or clinical practice, and the data are later accessible to a given social worker or research team. Simply (!) obtain agency permission to extract the desired information, comply with oversight by any pertinent institutional review board, place the data in a spreadsheet or statistical package database, and look at the results. There are many opportunities to conduct such retrospective studies, as agencies are often sitting on a gold mine of data gathered in this manner, data which often just sit there, unanalyzed, unused, and not contributing to the expansion of knowledge so desperately needed by the field.

As this book is being written, I am working with a doctoral student in social work who is in charge of a substance abuse treatment program at a state women's prison. Prisoners who are known to have a history of drug abuse are assigned to this residential drug abuse program (RDAP) within the prison. Although the RDAP is a widely used intervention sponsored by the Federal Bureau of Prisons to treat substance abusers, little appears to be known as to whether it is truly effective at deterring substance abuse (see http://www.bop.gov/inmate_programs/substanceabuse_faqs.jsp). We could find no published outcome studies evaluating RDAPs. As a part of the RDAP, prisoners complete several outcome measures pertaining to knowledge about illegal drugs and their health consequences, as well as their attitudes about drug abuse. And they do this again after several months of participation. This information is available to my student within her work role via the prison records for several hundred RDAP participants, and it has not been analyzed. Such data can be characterized as "low-hanging fruit," easy to harvest, and I am urging my doctoral student to gain access and analyze these data as her Ph.D. dissertation research project. In this instance, the average scores on, say, an attitudinal measure related to substance abuse could be assessed when the prisoners are initially enrolled in the RDAP program—the O_1 assessment. Then, the enrollees begin the RDAP and remain in it for 3 months, after which they complete the same attitudinal measure, or O_2. This results in the complete design being diagrammed as $O_1 - X - O_2$. This *would be* adequate to test the predictive hypothesis that "RDAP participants will display statistically significant improvements related to attitudes about drug abuse, following 3 months of participation in the program."

If the average score on a measure of attitudes at time 2, or O_2 were significantly improved relative to the average score for the entire group at time 1, or O_1, then we could legitimately claim that the hypothesis was supported or corroborated. It would be very rare for one to be able to say that the hypothesis was *confirmed*, as this is generally too strong a position to take with results obtained from nonexperimental research designs. Given the limited empirical evidence that the RDAP program really works, a relatively simple pretest–posttest study of this nature would be a useful addition to the professional literature on the drug rehabilitation of incarcerated offenders.

These designs may also be *prospectively* undertaken, planned in advance by an individual or research team to improve or refine the evaluation. Sometimes prospectively designed studies can make use of more valid outcome measures than those routinely used by agencies, or steps can be taken to ensure that the treatment is provided to the clients in a manner that promotes adherence to the best practices appropriate to the model of treatment being evaluated. A prospective study may opt to use independent evaluators to assess clients pre- and posttreatment, to try to partially control for the bias engendered by having the therapists who delivered the treatment be the ones who assess whether the clients benefited from the treatment. Or, steps can be taken to ensure that the posttests are really administered in a manner equivalent to the pretests, to partially control for possible changes in how clients were assessed, pre- and posttreatment. For these reasons, prospectively designed outcome studies are usually seen as more rigorous tests of a treatment's effectiveness than are retrospectively designed ones, which are limited to existing data that may not have been gathered with formal research purposes in mind. But, having said that, retrospectively undertaken investigations are also very worthwhile in their own right. Here are some examples of social workers using the $O_1 - X - O_2$ design.

Evaluating Group Therapy for Children After Homicide

Traumatic grief reactions are common among children who witness homicide and other forms of violence, and clinical social workers and other mental health professionals are often called upon to provide therapeutic services to them. Obviously, we wish to deliver care that is genuinely helpful, without adverse side effects, that produces lasting change and is low in cost.

There are not many treatments like this, and social workers delivering services that lack a strong evidence base are understandably interested in evaluating the programs they do deliver, to help assure that children are not being harmed (see Lilienfeld, 2007; Barlow, 2010) and perhaps are receiving benefit. Such were the circumstances faced by mental health workers in the city of New Orleans, who developed a "Loss and Survival Team" to provide services to homicide victims and children exposed to violence. Each child received a semi-structured group therapy program consisting of eight to ten sessions, and completed a previously published, reliable and valid posttraumatic stress disorder (PTSD) assessment at the beginning of group therapy and again when it ended. Over time (October 1997–December 2001), some 21 groups were completed in ten different public schools, involving a total of 102 African American children. All the group therapists were MSWs or MSW interns. Symptoms of PTSD dropped statistically significantly for the 102 children as a whole, and various subgroup analyses were also performed (boys vs. girls, younger vs. older, etc.). This was a very nice illustration of using the one-group pretest–posttest design, as well as of the efforts of social workers providing clinical services to children systematically evaluating outcomes following treatment. Question 2 was answered nicely, and the answer was an agreeable "Yes!" The authors appropriately discuss the limitations of their study in their conclusions and also present suggestions to enhance future research with this clinical group and problem situation (see Salloum, 2008).

Evaluating Abstinence-based Sex Education

This design was also used to evaluate an abstinence-oriented empowerment program for public school youth. The problem area was teenage pregnancy, and the issue was the possible effectiveness or ineffectiveness of the widely used approach called *abstinence education,* aimed at deterring the teenage initiation of sexual intercourse. A total of 130 public school children in grades 5 through 9 participated in 18 eight-week group interventions. The psychoeducational program was theoretically based and designed to be consistent with recommended "best practices" in this area. Outcome measures included a previously published and widely used measure of children's self-esteem, a knowledge measure of coping with peer pressure, a measure of intention to abstain from sex, and a measure of parent–adolescent communication, all given pre- and posttreatment.

All measures showed improvements that were statistically significant, and the authors discussed the strengths and limits of their study (see Abel & Greco, 2008). Abstinence-only sex education is a controversial approach to sex education, and it reflects favorably on the providers of this program that they were willing to subject it to this type of evaluation. The basic elements of the pretest–posttest design in the above example were augmented by using several, not just one, reliable and valid outcome measures. Your conclusions are obviously strengthened if you use several measures of what you are trying to change and all these measures consistently point, posttreatment, to changes in the desired direction.

Evaluating Cognitive Behavior Therapy for Depression

Chen, Jordan, and Thompson (2006) used this design to evaluate the possible outcomes of CBT on depression among 30 clients receiving intensive outpatient services at a psychiatric hospital in a Texas city. Clients completed standardized self-report measures of depression and of their problem-solving ability at the beginning of outpatient treatment and again when the daily group therapy program (each session lasting about 2.5 hours per day!) was concluded. Posttreatment depression scores significantly improved, compared to the group's pretreatment mean scores, when pretreatment problem-solving ability scores were controlled for (this is a methodological twist we need not get into here). This is a modest study, but one that can and should be used as an instructive example by social workers seeking guidance on how they can integrate simple research methods to evaluate their own practice.

Evaluating School Social Work

Like the posttest-only design, the pretest–posttest single-group design can be improved by using more than one reliable and valid outcome measure and by conducting repeated posttreatment assessments. This was done by Diehl and Frey (2008), in the evaluation of a community–school model of social work practice. The study involved 12 schools located in one school district in the Midwest. The intervention consisted of referring youth with behavior problems to the local school social worker, who provided a standardized system of case management and direct intervention involving individual counseling and home visits, sometimes with group and family therapy sessions added. Upon referral, the child completed a standardized problem behavior scale, and the parents and teachers completed forms measuring their behavioral concerns about the child. The program evaluation occurred for all kids referred from August 2000 to December 2002, a total of 154 youth. Assessments were completed not only at intake but also 3 and 6 months following treatment, resulting in the following design:

$$O_1 - X - O_2 - O_3$$

There were statistically significant improvements in the kids' behavior at 3 months (O_2) and 6 months (O_3) compared to the children's assessment when they were initially referred (O_1). This is good thing, overall. However, there were some problems. Data were not available on all 154 kids at the 3-month follow-up assessment. In fact, it was only available for about half of them, and for only 29% at 6 months. Can you see how this problem of *client attrition* complicates making any conclusions about the possible effectiveness of the school social work program? We will return to this issue of attrition, also known as *mortality*, later on in this book.

Evaluating Internet-based Treatment for PTSD

Knaevelsrud and Maercker (2007) conducted a randomized controlled trial of Internet-based treatment for 96 participants with PTSD. About half (n = 41) were randomly assigned to a 5-week, ten-session cognitive-behavioral writing program that included exposure work, social sharing, and cognitive reappraisal. The remaining participants were initially assigned to a waiting list control condition. Three distinct measures were given at the pretest: a measure of PTSD symptomatology (the Impact of Event Scale), a measure of mood (the Brief Symptom Inventory), and a measure of health (physical and mental). After the treated clients completed their program, they and the waiting list control participants were reassessed using the same measures, and it was found, basically, that the treated group had marked improvements on all measures except physical health, whereas the waiting list control group did not change much. These results clearly favored the Internet-based treatment. At this point, the initial phase of the project was completed, and the wait-listed clients were provided the Internet-based therapy. Knaevelsrud and Maercker (2010) later went back and recontacted the original group of 41 clients who were initially treated and asked them to take the assessment measures again at 3 months posttreatment and for a fourth time 18 months posttreatment. A total of 34 of the original 41 clients were assessed at 18 months (an attrition of 7 out of 41, or 17%). This later aspect of their study could be diagrammed as follows:

$$O_1 - X - O_2 - O_3 - O_4$$

with the posttreatment assessments corresponding to the initially treated group being evaluated immediately after treatment (O_2), 3 months after treatment (O_3), and 18 months after treatment (O_4). Because these follow-up data are reported for only the one group, the initial randomized controlled trial had been broken down to a quasi-experimental pretest–posttest study with repeated follow-up assessment. It is still a good study, especially since multiple outcome measures were used and the results were consistently favorable during all posttreatment measures, even 18 months after treatment was discontinued. Many studies only undertake a single posttreatment evaluation of client functioning, usually immediately after treatment, so having three evaluations, with the relatively lengthy follow-up period of 18 months, is a real strength. Providing services for persons with PTSD via the Internet appears to provide a promising approach for extending the availability of therapy beyond the confines of the consulting room, which would be helpful.

Post-Psychiatric Hospitalization Follow-up of Adolescents

Welner, Welner, and Fishman (1979) conducted a follow-up study of the disposition of 77 adolescents (average age at treatment was 16 years) who had been psychiatrically hospitalized. Follow-up was conducted some 8–10 *years* after discharge. Subgroup analyses were completed, looking at rates of suicide and rehospitalization among patients with various initial diagnoses. These found that adolescents with a diagnosis of bipolar illness faired particularly poorly, as did those with adolescent-onset schizophrenia. This study, whose third author was a social worker, was not so much an evaluation of the effects of treatment as a study in the prognosis of serious mental illness among the young. Still, it is a good example of answering Question 1, and took place over a remarkably long time frame. It appeared in one of the premier psychiatric journals.

There are some other ways to enhance the usefulness of the pretest–posttest single-group design. One is to use more than one pretreatment assessment, as in:

$$O_1 - O_2 - X - O_3$$

Having more than one pretest provides more credible evidence regarding the clients' problem status prior to intervention, just as having more than one posttest enhances our sense of the client's long-term status after treatment. However, most researchers using the pretest–posttest design only make use of one pretest and one posttest assessment, not several. If you employ a whole series of pre- and posttests, your design begins to segue into another conceptually similar evaluation method called the *time series design*, which will be covered in Chapter 4.

Another refinement in trying to more legitimately figure out the effects of a given treatment is to add additional elements to your basic $O_1 - X - O_2$ design through use of a subsequent period of time during which treatment is *removed* and the client's status assessed again. This can be diagrammed as:

$$O_1 - X_{introduced} - O_2 - X_{removed} - O_3$$

In terms of logical inference, this design modification only makes sense if you have reason to believe that the effects of X are likely to be temporary. Here is an example. A group of kids (say n > 20) diagnosed with hyperactivity disorder is assessed using a reliable and valid measure of hyperactive behavior. They are then treated early the next day with a short-lived medication intended to reduce hyperactivity; in the middle of the day, they are reassessed as before. The following day they do *not* receive the medicine for hyperactivity, and in the middle of that day, they are assessed a third time. The logic of this design is that if the drug really improves behavior, this will be evident at the second assessment, O_2. If positive effects are indeed observed at O_2 for the group of kids as a whole, this is tentative evidence that the drug had its intended effect. If it is true that the drug caused the kids to improve, and the drug is deliberately withheld the next day, at the third assessment, their behavior should return to close to that observed at O_1. If such outcomes are forthcoming at O_3, you have stronger logical grounds for concluding that X (the drug) was causally responsible for the changes in comportment. This is pretty nifty in terms of trying to make causal inferences, but not a good result clinically, of course.

There are many psychosocial interventions you can conceive of that would have immediate but short-lived effects and could be amenable to being studied in this manner. For example, many classrooms use some sort of point system to reward good behavior and deter misbehavior. Do these really work as intended? The question is not a moot one. Point systems take time to devise, implement, and run. If they work well, they may be a blessing. But if they are not really useful, then why go to all the bother? So, imagine the following study. A class of kids is assessed during one day with no particular program in place to encourage on-task academic behavior. The next day, a token or point system is explained and put into place, and at the end of the day, rewards are provided to the kids who performed well. Behavior is assessed all during this day as in the previous day. The third day, the point system is not in operation, and behavior is assessed again. If you saw improvements during the day when the point system was in place, improvements over the first day's behavior, and a restoration to the original level of functioning on the third day, most teachers (and social workers) would be pretty convinced that the point program was effective in promoting on-task behavior and reducing misbehavior. You may be able to think of other psychosocial interventions that could be evaluated using this type of design. For example, the use of a token economy on the behavior of psychiatric inpatients, the effects of daily attendance at Alcoholics Anonymous meetings on one's craving to drink, the effects of a day treatment program on the mood of people with clinical depression, and more. Basically, any intervention whose effects are expected to be immediate but *temporary* can be evaluated using this approach.

SUMMARY ON STRENGTHENING THE ONE-GROUP PRETEST–POSTTEST DESIGN

All those methods listed above for use in strengthening the posttest-only design apply here. In addition, you may do the following.

Use Multiple Pretreatment Assessments

Client problems may wax and wane in response to the ebb and flow of naturally occurring life events, via their own natural history (e.g., bipolar disorder, depression), or in response to biological changes occurring within clients (e.g., changes in diet, sleeping, exercise, medication use, use of food supplements and herbal products, menstrual cycle, etc.). This can complicate making any inferences about meaningful changes following receipt of social work services. Using two or more preassessment periods permits a more informed appraisal of true changes, relative to measuring a group at a single point in time. If problems are seen to be tending upward or downward during these pretreatment assessments, or if they are relatively stable, one is better able to detect any true changes by comparing the several pretreatment values with the posttreatment one (or several posttreatment evaluations, which is even stronger). Clearly a

$$O_1 - X - O_2$$

design is greatly improved upon by using the design below:

$$O_1 - O_2 - O_3 - X - O_4 - O_5 - O_6$$

For example, suppose in the first example immediately above (the $O_1 - X - O_2$ Design), the average pretest score was 60 and the average posttest score was 40 (the meaning of these numbers is unimportant here), with higher scores meaning greater problems. This would look pretty good, with problems decreasing from 60 to 40 points following treatment. It would indeed look good if this was all the information you had. But suppose you used the second design, and the three average pretest scores were 100, 80, and 60, with the three average posttest scores being 40, 20, and 0. Would having this additional information change how you viewed the originally presented average pretest score of 60 and posttest score of 40? Most likely it would, since you could see that the three pretreatment scores were tending downward, and the posttest scores simply reflected this pretreatment trend extended over time. In other words, in the second instance, it looks as if treatment had *no effect*. This possibility could only be ascertained by using multiple pretests and posttests.

Use a Removal or Withdrawal Phase

During a removal or withdrawal phase, clients' are reassessed after the treatment is deliberately removed. This approach is viable when the effects of treatment are short-lived. Assess the group, treat the group, reassess. If you see a positive change, terrific. Then, withhold the treatment and reassess. If you see a relapse when treatment is not provided, your ability to infer that the original positive changes were the results of treatment is enhanced. Not perfect, just enhanced. And, of course, it is not desirable to terminate a study at this point, but you may, if feasible, reinstate the original treatment condition on an enduring basis.

Use These Designs Prospectively

Use these designs prospectively; that is, in a way that is planned for and with data gathered in advance, as opposed to using them *retrospectively*—looking at data after the fact, without having had any plans to use the data for evaluation services when the data were initially gathered.

These designs are widely used across the human services and health professions, and regularly appear in some of the world's most prestigious journals. It is ill-informed to simply dismiss them as unworthy of consideration because of their frequently low internal validity.

Some additional social worker examples of using these designs can be found:

- Raskin, Johnson, and Rondestvedt (1973) evaluated the pretest–posttest changes that occurred among ten patients who suffered from chronic anxiety, and who were treated with muscular relaxation-based biofeedback. Outcome measures included a measure of anxious mood, sleep difficulties, headaches, and sense of relaxation. This simple study appeared in a leading journal, the *Archives of General Psychiatry*.
- A novel form of comprehensive care for troubled youth has been developed, known as *wrap-around services*. Wrap-around is a family-centered and strengths-based program involving interdisciplinary team treatment with elements of educational, mental health, child welfare, and juvenile justice services being provided in a coordinated manner. Many hundreds of millions of dollars have gone into the federal funding for wrap-around,

with relatively little evidence that it really helps kids. Copp, Bordnick, Traylor, and Thyer (2007) conducted a pretest–posttest evaluation of the first 15 youth who received wrap-around in a pilot program initiated in Georgia, for whom complete baseline and 6-month follow-up information was available. No significant changes were found on any of the outcome measures. This was disappointing. As the authors pointed out, these negative results may have been due to the relatively small sample size and to some concerns that the newly initiated wrap-around model may not have been implemented as recommended.

• Holly Bragg Capp, a MSW intern, arranged to have newly admitted inpatients on a psychiatric unit complete a reliable and valid measure of psychiatric symptoms, and for them to complete the same measure again, just prior to their discharge. Over the course of one semester, she was able to obtain pretest–posttest data on 78 consecutively admitted patients. After examining the data, she was able to conclude that the patients' reported symptoms improved both statistically and clinically. Very few programs can answer the question "Did our patients improve?" with empirical data, and Holly's study was a nice step in providing a preliminary answer to this question. Can she assert that they improved because of the inpatient program? No. But still it is useful to undertake simple studies like this. Certainly, the program's administrators were happy with the result! See Capp, Thyer, and Bordnick (1997) for a full report of this project.

Some non–social work examples of using the pretest–posttest design include the following:

• Spinelli (1987) used a pretest–posttest design with 13 participants to evaluate possible effects of interpersonal psychotherapy on a group of clients with which it had not been previously used. This study was published in one of the world's leading psychiatric journals, the *American Journal of Psychiatry*.
• Whitt-Glover, Hogan, Lang, and Heil (2008) evaluated a faith-based physical activity program to promote exercise among

sedentary African Americans. This appeared in a well-respected public health journal.

- Schneider et al. (2006) evaluated the outcomes of a large-scale community-based program aimed at promoting the consumption of fresh fruits and vegetables among school children. This appeared in the prestigious *Journal of the American Medical Association.*
- Novak, Cusick, and Lowe (2007) evaluated the impact of an occupational therapy program provided in the homes of Australian children with cerebral palsy.
- Keller et al. (2009), psychologists, evaluated a statewide suicide prevention program delivered to 416 providers of child welfare services.

Clearly, these designs have usefulness in evaluating a wide array of social care and health services, and, if well-conducted and circumspect in drawing causal inferences, are capable of being published in very prestigious professional journals. They should not be cavalierly dismissed as useless or unimportant.

SOME LIMITS OF THE PRE-EXPERIMENTAL DESIGNS

You will probably have noticed that even the best of the pre-experimental designs are generally only capable of answering Questions 1 and 2 from those introduced in Chapter 1. They are not very good at answering the other three questions. This is because Questions 3–5 all involve trying to compare outcomes from a group of clients who received an intervention of interest with the outcomes of clients who received no treatment, standard treatment, or placebo treatment. Because the pre-experimental designs have no other groups to evaluate treated clients against, any comparisons between groups are not possible. It is this feature, the lack of any comparison or control groups, which has traditionally separated the pre-experimental designs from the so-called quasi-experimental designs. The latter designs *do* involve comparison groups. But the quasi-experimental designs do not rise to the level of sophistication of true experiments because they lack a further refinement; namely, the deliberate random assignment of clients to various conditions or groups.

You can use the bulleted points below to help distinguish among these three types of nomothetic research designs, as they are often traditionally construed:

- *Pre-Experimental designs.* Looks at a group of clients posttreatment only, *or* compares posttreatment outcomes with pretreatment observations, obtained from the same group.
- *Quasi-experimental designs.* Compares a treated group against other groups of clients who received no treatment, standard treatment, another treatment, or placebo treatment.
- *Experimental designs.* Includes the elements of pre- and quasi-experimental designs, *plus* the added feature of creating these groups through random-assignment methods.

Do keep in mind that, in this book, pre-experimental and the traditional quasi-experimental designs are collectively referred to as quasi-experimental designs. A specific type of experimental design used in more tightly controlled social work intervention research, the *randomized controlled trial* (RCT), is covered in another volume in this series (Solomon, Cavanaugh, & Draine, 2009), as well as in a number of other similarly excellent books (Shadish et al., 2002; Nezu & Nezu, 2008), and is often covered in separate chapters in general social work research textbooks (e.g., Cnaan & Tripodi, 2010; Pignotti & Thyer, 2009). The virtue of RCTs resides in their stronger potential ability to permit true causal inferences, to be able to say with some degree of confidence that a given effect was the result of a given treatment. This is obviously important because if we cannot sort out legitimately effective interventions from ineffective ones, those that fail to produce positive effects above and beyond those induced by placebo effects, or those that are harmful to clients, in some ways the rationale for the existence of the profession of social work is called into question. Quasi-experimental designs are an attempt to build upon the methods of the pre-experimental designs by adding some type of control groups or conditions, for the purposes of strengthening our ability to test causal hypotheses of a more complicated nature than those implied in Questions 1 and 2.

For example, take something fairly new to our field, called *narrative therapy*. The specifics of it are not important. It would be a nice thing to show that clients who received narrative therapy were very satisfied with their treatment, or were functioning very well. But this does not prove that narrative therapy is genuinely effective. It would be an improvement to show that clients who received narrative therapy were better off after narrative therapy than they were before receiving this treatment. But even this level of evidence is insufficient to prove that narrative therapy is genuinely effective. However, if we could show that clients who received narrative therapy were truly better off afterward, compared to a group of clients who got no treatment at all, this would greatly add to the credibility of narrative therapy as an effective intervention. And, if we could show that narrative therapy produces better results than treatment as usual, or compared to a credible placebo treatment, this would be better still. And this is the purpose of quasi-experiments, to conduct such studies to provide stronger evidence of the effectiveness (or ineffectivenss) of various social work interventions. Ideally, intervention researchers maintain a studiously neutral stance by not attempting to prove that something does or does not "work." Rather, they aim to empirically determine a treatment's effectiveness, whatever the outcomes. Seeking after "truth" is the foremost agenda, not supporting one's preferences.

The ability to make legitimate causal inferences requires more than simply demonstrating change. One must have some confidence that other factors potentially responsible for these changes have been effectively ruled out, and it is for this purpose that quasi-experiments make use of various comparison or control groups. Next, we will review some of the more common reasons, apart from Treatment X, which might be responsible (at least in part) for client improvement. These alternative explanations are collectively called *threats to internal validity*. We will then examine how various quasi-experimental designs try to control for these confounding effects.

SOME THREATS TO INTERNAL VALIDITY

Placebo Effects

Placebo effects can be defined as:

> Any therapy or component of therapy (or that component of any therapy) that is intentionally or knowingly used for its nonspecific, psychological, or psychophysiological effect, or for its presumed therapeutic

effect on a patient, symptom, or other illness but is without specific activity for the condition being treated. (Bausell, 2007, p. 29)

or, similarly,

Changes in a dependent variable that are caused by the power of suggestion among the participants in an experimental group that they are receiving something special that is expected to help them. These changes would not occur if they received the experimental intervention without that awareness. (Rubin & Babbie, 2008, p. 642)

Placebo effects can be assumed to be present to some degree whenever a client believes he or she is receiving a credible treatment or intervention of some sort. The credibility of an intervention may involve not only the features of the treatment itself, but also the appearance, manner, and confidence of the social worker providing the therapy; the physical surroundings associated with treatment (a well-appointed office in a nice part of town vs. shabby digs on the wrong side of the tracks); the legitimate and perhaps not-so-legitimate degrees, credentials, and certifications possessed by the social worker; the therapist's reputation; and more. For two different treatments to be legitimately compared in terms of their effectiveness, both interventions must possess equivalent credibility. If treatment X seems highly credible, and treatment Y much less so, a study comparing X and Y is automatically biased in favor of X from the onset of the study. Hence, well-designed outcome studies attempt to ensure that the placebo-engendering features surrounding X and Y are roughly the same. It is sad but true that if therapy X is provided by Dr. George Clooney, and therapy Y by Dr. Quasimodo, clients may respond as much to *who* provided the treatment, as to the essential features of the treatment itself.

Regression to the Mean

It is not uncommon for clients to seek treatment, even to participate in clinical trials of psychosocial intervention, when their problems are at their peak. Many of the psychosocial and health disorders for which social work clients seek assistance have a natural tendency to wax and wane on their own. This is obviously true for conditions such as moderate depression and bipolar disorder, but also true for spousal abuse, alcoholism, and schizophrenia. This ebb and flow of symptom severity can be said to fluctuate around a general trend or average (mean) level. Thus, clients who enroll in treatment studies when their problems are particularly bad may experience a lessening of symptom severity over the ensuing weeks or months, an apparent amelioration that has little to do with the actual effects of treatment but more to do with the natural history or progression of their difficulties. This reversion back to the more general level of severity is called *regression to the mean*. In these instances, it is natural for such individuals to often ascribe their improvements to their participation in a treatment and, if actual improvements are measured, it is equally natural for therapists, even those participating in research projects, to similarly attribute these improvements to treatment, rather than to natural (temporary) remission. This however, commits the logical fallacy of *post hoc ergo propter hoc*, Latin for "after this, therefore because of this," by reasoning along the lines of "Since that event *followed* this one, that event must have been *caused* by this one."

Maturation

Maturation refers to developmental changes that occur over time in some client populations. Young children, adolescents, and the elderly are client groups in which maturational changes are particularly salient. In outcome studies transpiring over long periods—months, perhaps even years—clients may change rather dramatically for reasons that have nothing to do with their receipt of therapy. Children may make striking advances in social or cognitive development in a surprisingly brief period, and the elderly may experience rapid changes in the opposite direction, toward more impairment, cognitive abilities, or senescence.

Passage of Time

A number of the specific threats to internal validity mentioned thus far involve the element of time—time is required to elapse before factors such as maturation, regression to the mean, concurrent historical influences, mortality, etc. become potentially operative. There is another element in which time poses a threat, and it refers to simple changes induced by one's experience with a condition or disorder. Over time, the morale-eroding influence of a problem may become more or less impactful. Think of common phrases of everyday speech such as *time heals all wounds, the tincture of time,* or *one day at time.* With time, one's craving for cigarettes may decline after stopping smoking. The pain of being newly unemployed may diminish, or, conversely, the misery of living with severe obsessive-compulsive disorder may lead to thoughts of suicide. One may adapt to living with a verbally abusive spouse by withdrawing, and so reduce the psychological anguish of feeling unloved. These are all changes that can operate in the context of an evaluation study and give rise to improvements or deterioration that may superficially look like the results of an intervention but are actually a function of a far simpler accounting—the mere passage of time alone. It is not biologically mediated maturation, nor the statistical artifact of regression, just time alone.

Mortality/Attrition

Although the term *mortality* usually connotes death, in social work intervention research it more often refers to the problem of clients dropping out of treatment. If you begin a simple pretest–posttest study with a client sample of 100 and 3 months later, following intensive treatment, you only have 70 clients continuing to participate in the study, the threat to internal validity called mortality may be present. Suppose you had an outcome measure that consisted of scores on a rapid assessment instrument, and you looked at the group's mean pretest score and compared it with the group's mean posttest score. The first mean was based on the original sample of 100 clients, whereas the second was based only on the remaining 70 clients still participating in your study. It is possible that the 30 folks who dropped out differed in meaningful ways from the 70 "survivors." Perhaps the 30 had more severe problems? If so, the mean for the remaining 70 will display improvements at the posttest assessment *not* because of the effects of participating in therapy, but because the mean score for the remaining clients is no longer dragged down by the scores of the more seriously impaired ones who dropped out. But mortality may not be due to symptom severity. More prosaic problems may be operative, such as a lack of access to reliable transportation among the clients who dropped out, or a lack of adequate child care needed for clients to attend clinic appointments. It can be difficult to know why people dropped out of a study. Even if you compare demographics and symptom severity of the dropouts versus survivors and find no difference, there may be undetected or unassessed variables at work that are responsible for mortality. Thus, this would make it unwise to claim that, since the clients who dropped out were similar to those who survived, you can safely ignore your study's high mortality as a potential threat to internal validity. A practical example of this problem occurred in the study evaluating school social work services conducted by Diehl and Frey (2008) described above.

Differential Attrition

Imagine you are comparing the effects of two treatments, X and Y. X makes many demands on clients and is psychologically stressful, a treatment such as primal scream therapy (PS, invented by a social worker, Arthur Janov). Treatment Y, on the other hand, is much less upsetting, say, narrative therapy (NT, invented by a social worker!). In fact, Y is so reinforcing that the clients look forward to their sessions. Say you began your study with two groups receiving these two treatments, with 50 clients in each group. After some months, 20 of the 50 folks receiving PS therapy had dropped out, whereas only three of those enjoying NT stopped participating. At the end of the study, instead of comparing 50 clients to 50 clients, you compared 30 clients to 47 and found that, on average, those who received NT were dramatically better off compared to those who got PS therapy. Could you legitimately conclude that NT is a more effective treatment than PS? Not really, since the confounds associated with mortality noted above are now differentially present between your two groups, and these complicate your ability to make causal inferences.

Concurrent History

The threat known as *concurrent history* refers to impactful events taking place in clients' lives outside the context of their participation in a treatment outcome study. Sometimes these can be very conspicuous things, such as 9–11, Hurricane Katrina, or the election of a very popular president. Such events can broadly affect the mood and well-being of research participants, and these effects may be reflected in your posttreatment outcome measures and complicate your ability to make any inferences about the effects of treatment per se. Macdonald noted this threat early on, urging us to "take cognizance of the possibility that the patients might have improved if left untreated.... We should never lose sight of the possibility that the improvement of the patient is not related to our efforts" (Macdonald, 1952, p. 137).

Nonblind Assessments

If outcome measures used in a treatment study involve the judgments of others, such as therapists' ratings of their own clients or the ratings of independent observers, and these raters/judges are aware of which phase of a study (pre- vs. posttreatment) is being rated or which treatment condition the client received (experimental therapy, treatment as usual, placebo treatment), it can introduce an element of bias into their appraisals. Suppose, as a part of a study on treating depressed clients, the therapists themselves were asked to determine if the clients met the diagnostic criteria for major depression before they began therapy and then again, after the clients' completion of a treatment program administered by the therapists themselves. You can see that using the treating therapists to determine if the clients still met the criteria for major depression after they were treated would incur a strong tendency for the therapists to be biased in favor of detecting clinical improvements. After all, who would want to judge their own clients as *unimproved* following treatment? A more rigorous approach would be to have specially trained diagnosticians assess the clients; these raters would be uninvested in the outcomes of the study, have no allegiance to any particular type of therapy being evaluated, and not be aware of whether the client was beginning treatment or had completed therapy. Knowing that you are assessing someone at the *end* of a treatment outcome study may also create a bias toward a more favorable assessment. Having these independent diagnosticians be unconnected with the actual treatment would help ensure their independence, as they would have less of an investment in detecting improvements.

Also, if you have clients receiving different treatments, with one group receiving a novel therapy and a second receiving treatment as usual, if at the time of the posttreatment evaluations the assessors are aware of which treatment the clients had received, this may bias their judgments. Thus, really well designed outcome studies have assessors who do not know if the client they are evaluating is at the beginning or end of a treatment program, nor do they know which treatment condition the client received. An even more rigorous technique is to ask, after the assessments have been completed, the assessors to *guess* if the client was pre-treatment or posttreatment, or if posttreatment, which treatment they had received (novel treatment, treatment as usual, placebo treatment, etc.). If the assessors can guess no better than chance, then the "blindness" of the ratings has been maintained. If they do guess better than chance, then blindness has been compromised, and the study should not be reported as having made use of truly blind evaluators.

Multiple Treatment Interference

Sometimes—indeed, most times—psychosocial treatments contain multiple elements. Most therapies, except perhaps bibliotherapies or Internet- or computer-based self-help programs, contain important client–therapist relationship elements, features separate from the specific *techniques* that may be the manifest focus of treatment. Narrative therapy involves the telling of stories, solution-focused treatment is based on envisioning life without a given problem or issue, dynamic psychotherapy involves recounting childhood experiences, behavior therapy involves arranging for certain desired behaviors to be reinforced, and so on. And within each therapeutic model may be found many different components. A program of behavior analysis could involve reinforcement, modeling, shaping, manipulation of antecedent stimuli, and the like. Dynamic psychotherapy could involve recounting childhood memories, the interpretation of dreams, the analysis of resistance, and free association. And sometimes clients receive different treatments at the same time, as in interpersonal psychotherapy combined with receiving an antidepressant medication. This receipt of multiple or combined treatments makes it problematic to assert that only *one* element of a therapeutic regiment is causally responsible for any observed improvements. In such instances, one may at best conclude that a given *combination* of treatments was followed by certain changes, but one cannot legitimately assert that only one or more elements of that combination were responsible for these improvements. Such a design could be diagrammed along the following lines:

$$O_1 - (X + Y) - O_2$$

with (X + Y) reflecting the fact that clients got two discrete interventions. It is commonly understood, however, that X implies all of the particular therapeutic elements that go into X, given the complexities of social work intervention. Once X has been shown to be genuinely helpful, subsequent studies may be used to isolate the active ingredients of X, compared to the inactive one.

Assessment/Treatment Interactions

In a treatment study, clients may be formally evaluated prior to beginning therapy, then receive therapy, and then be reevaluated. It is both possible and plausible that the act of being assessed *combined with* the subsequent receipt of treatment exerts an effect different from that to be obtained if a client received the treatment alone. For example, if a client, as a part of a weight reduction program was asked, prior to treatment, to weigh himself for a number of days prior to beginning formal treatment, and then at the conclusion of the program was weighed again, the act of consciously weighing himself could, *by itself*, motivate him to begin some efforts at losing weight. The outcome of people receiving this combination of assessment and treatment would be different relative to a group of clients who got the formal treatment alone, without a formal preliminary period of self-monitoring, and who were weighed only at the conclusion of formal treatment. Such self-monitoring effects are not uncommon in the world of therapy, and many times these efforts produce modest changes irrespective of other formal treatments. In treatment outcome studies of people with specific phobias (to say dogs, cats, birds, snakes, etc.), one assessment method is called a *behavioral approach test* (BAT), wherein the phobic person is asked to approach the restrained, feared animal as closely as possible, with the closest distance obtained being one measure of the severity of fear (more phobic persons approach less closely). Repeated BATs themselves can produce mild improvements, even in the absence of formal therapy. Thus, if you designed a study involving a preliminary BAT, then provided a completely useless therapy, followed by a posttreatment BAT, you might see small reductions in avoidance. It would be very tempting to conclude that "treatment" produced these gains, when in reality it was simply the act of being assessed by a BAT.

It is also known that individuals taking certain standardized tests, such as the Graduate Record Examination (GRE), tend to improve their scores the second time they take the test. Some commercial firms provide test preparation programs for the GRE and similar exams, a component of which involves taking practice tests very similar to the real examinations. They then report the pass rate or scores of those who took the commercial test preparation program and compare those scores to national test scores (usually favoring the people who enrolled in the test prep course). A more legitimate comparison is to compare the test scores of those who took the test preparation class with the scores of those who simply practiced taking the test an equivalent number of times on their own, not those taking the real test for the first time. Such an evaluation would likely show a much narrower gap in pass rates between those who completed a prep class and those who simply practiced taking the test an equivalent amount.

Instrument Change

The term *instrument* refers to the methods used to assess client functioning. This may involve a wide variety of approaches, including client self-reports; ratings of others such as caregivers, teachers, or family members; direct behavioral observations; formal or informal interviews; the client's completion of various tests, rating scales, or rapid assessment instruments, and the like. To compare the posttest scores of one group of clients with their pretest scores requires that the assessment methods or instruments used be similarly conducted, ideally identically, at the two points in time, pre- and posttreatment. If the assessment method differs in some meaningful manner, then you cannot legitimately compare the two sets of scores and make any valid conclusion regarding real changes in client functioning. Similarly, if you wish to compare assessments of two groups of clients, at pretest, at posttest, or both, then not only must the assessments at pretest and posttest be similarly conducted, but they must also be similarly provided *between* the two groups.

Instrument change may not be much of a threat when clients do something simple, such as complete an easy-to-read scale or self-rating form. In this case, they can be given the form, read the simple directions, and fill out the form; then the forms are collected and later analyzed. But when more complex assessments are used, the threat of changes in instrumentation may arise. For example, lets say that at the beginning of a study a clinician is asked to conduct a structured diagnostic interview to determine if a client meets the criteria for a particular psychiatric condition such as PTSD. The clinician interviews a large number of clients (say, >30) in the context of a pretest–posttest study. At the beginning of the study, she interviews potential client #1 at pretest, determines that he does meet the criteria for PTSD, and the client is duly enrolled in the study. She then interviews client #2, finds that this person also meets the criteria for PTSD and is eligible to participate in the study, and so on. Eventually, a sufficient number of participants are enrolled and therapy begins. A few months later, therapy is terminated and posttreatment interviews are conducted by the same clinician, who again determines whether or not the client meets the Diagnostic and Statistical Manual (DSM) criteria for PTSD. At the beginning of the study, 100% of the participants were judged to meet the criteria for PTSD; at the end, only 30% were, thus giving an apparent outcome that 70% of the clients no longer "had" PTSD and raising the possibility that the treatment is a highly effective cure for this serious condition!

One possible confound or threat to internal validity here is the clinician-diagnostician's changes in diagnostic skill over the course of the study. It is very likely that her interviewing skills and ability to apply the DSM criteria with the first five clients assessed pretreatment were considerably different from her skills applied to the last five clients assessed posttreatment. Simply put, she may have experienced a considerable improvement in her diagnostic acumen during the course of applying the structured clinical interview over 60 clients. Practice may make one perfect. Or, she might have gotten bored with the repetitiveness of the process and began to cut some corners by leaving out some questions, resulting in a less accurate diagnostic determination. In other words, the "instrument" used to assess clients (the diagnostician) changed over the course of the pretreatment and posttreatment assessment process, and the possibility exists that it is this confounding factor that resulted in the apparent decline in the numbers of clients meeting the criteria for PTSD, *not* the curative powers of the presumptive therapy.

How can this confound be controlled for? One approach is to train evaluators to some criterion prior to really using their appraisals in a study. Don't use someone new to a complex assessment method—use highly experienced people. Another approach, when using human raters, interviewers, or observers, is to use *two* independent evaluators and calculate the extent to which they agree. For example, in the PTSD study just described, the potential research participant could be evaluated by two clinicians acting independently of each other. Each determines if potential client #1 did or did not meet the DSM criteria for PTSD, and only those clients who were determined by *both* raters acting independently are enrolled in the study. And, when therapy was completed, it required *both* raters to judge the client as no longer meeting the DSM criteria for PTSD in order for the client to be tabulated in the "cured" category. This raising of the methodological bar makes for better science, but it is costly in terms of time and money.

In a study on changes in clinical interviewing skills found among MSW students taking a social work methods course, Carrillo, Gallant, and Thyer (1993) used two independent raters to judge the MSW students use of facilitation, questioning and clarification, and support and empathy during structured interviews with a simulated client. The raters' scores had very high reliabilities, and it was found that, by the end of the class, the MSW students' scores on these skills had improved. This sounds good, but something problematic happened in the course of the study. The simulated client used in the mock interviews at the beginning of the term became unavailable, and a different person had to be recruited to portray a client at the end of the term, for the posttraining mock interview. The improvements observed at the end of the class *may* have reflected not only genuine enhancements in the students' interviewing skills, but also changes in the ease with which the different simulated client used at the end of the class could be interviewed. It is possible that this second, different person was simply easier to interview compared with the person portraying the mock client at the beginning of the class. In other words, the instrument (in this case, the simulated client) used to assess client functioning (in this case, the MSW students) was significantly changed, making it very difficult to strongly claim that taking the class really improved interviewing skills. Of course, that is what the authors would like to have believed, but they recognized that this change in the person serving as the simulated client introduced the possibility that their students' improvements were the results of changes in instrumentation, and so noted this in the published article. This is honest reporting, but simply recognizing the problem as a possible confound does not adequately control for it.

Differing Treatment Credibility

Some therapies seem, on their face, to be highly credible and indeed make sense. The gradual real-life desensitization of phobic persons to their feared object, animal, or situation is one example of a common-sense–based therapy. The degree of credibility people perceive with respect to the treatment they receive in the context of a treatment outcome study can affect clients' responses to the treatment. If, in the name of therapy, you are asked to do something that makes no sense, or may even seem silly, the crucial element of the positive placebo effect is reduced and less improvements may be forthcoming. If you are exposed to a treatment that seems highly credible, then placebo effects are maximized and greater improvements may be elicited, relative to those caused by less credible therapies. Really good psychotherapy outcome studies ask clients at the beginning and end of treatment how much they expected to benefit from the treatment they were going to, or had, received. Or, clients are asked how "believable" the treatment seems/seemed to them. To make a legitimate comparison of the true effects of treatment X versus treatment Y, X and Y should have equivalent credibility or believability on the part of the clients. Otherwise, you are not comparing the true effects of X versus Y, but rather, for example, a seemingly legitimate treatment X versus a silly-seeming treatment Y, and this is not a genuine comparison of the real effects of X and Y, relative to each other, independent of credibility issues.

The costs of treatment, oddly enough, may affect how effective services may be. It has long been believed that clients who pay money for psychotherapy services tend to benefit more than do clients who receive free services, a belief stemming from both psychoanalytic and cognitive dissonance theory (Shipton & Spain, 1981; Wood, 1982, Yoken & Berman, 1984; Herron & Sitkowski, 1986). And, paying higher fees induces a greater benefit than does paying lower fees. Recently, Waber, Shiv, Carmon, and Ariely (2008) exposed healthy volunteers to a painful task, receiving a series of electric shocks to the wrist of increasing intensity, and had them rate the pain induced by each individual shock received. All participants were given a pill before the task and, when given the pill, half of the subjects were informed that it cost of $2.50 and the other half were told that it cost 10 cents. The pill was supposedly an analgesic (pain reliever) but in reality it was a placebo. The researchers examined the pain intensity ratings of the two groups and found that those subjects who received the pill supposedly costing $2.50 reported significantly lower pain ratings than did those who received the pill costing 10 cents. In other words, the person's perceptions of the cost of a treatment apparently affected how well the treatment performed. Similar influences may effect the outcomes of psychosocial interventions as well.

Selection Bias

There are two ways in which selection bias may complicate the results of your evaluation study. In the first, you may conduct a study on a group of clients that possess characteristics that render them particularly susceptible to either positive or negative responses to a given intervention, leading to a false conclusion about the treatment's presumptive positive (or negative) effects. If your sample consists of particularly high-functioning persons, the results may not be generalizable or relevant to the larger population of people with a particular problem. Hence, your conclusion that therapy X helps clients with that problem may be incorrect. For example, if a program that was intended to help the unemployed find work only enrolled persons with a college degree into an intervention study, and it was later found that a very high proportion did indeed obtain good jobs, this would not mean that the program was an effective method for helping the vast majority of persons (who are less well educated) obtain work. Conversely, if a program of assertive community treatment (ACT), a complex intervention requiring intense daily monitoring by a treatment team of the functioning of persons with chronic mental illness, only was tested on persons meeting the criteria for schizophrenia of the paranoid subtype, the intervention may meet with great resistance, given the particularities of that form of schizophrenia. The negative result may lead to a conclusion that ACT does not work, when in reality it does not work with this particular type of client, but may well be very effective for persons with other forms of schizophrenia.

Selection bias also refers to the possibility that two or more groups in a quasi-experimental study may have unrecognized preexisting treatment differences that only became evident following treatment, with these differences then being incorrectly ascribed to the differing impacts of the treatment conditions. Suppose a social work researcher wanted to determine if clients who received group therapy at her agency improved as much as those who received individual treatment. In this hypothetical example, the normal agency practice is for an intake clinician to conduct all initial evaluations of new clients and to suggest treatment options (in this case group or individual therapy), with most clients following the recommended course of action. Clients begin treatment, say for 3 months of *either* individual or group therapy, and are then formally assessed using one or more reliable and valid outcome measure(s). This design could be diagrammed as:

$$X - O_1$$

$$Y - O_1$$

With X indicating clients who received individual therapy, Y being those clients who received group therapy, and O_1 the posttherapy assessment scores.

The social work researcher gathers the data and finds out that clients who received group therapy had much higher scores on functioning compared with those clients who received individual treatment. This could lead an unsophisticated researcher to the conclusion that group therapy was more effective than individual care. But such a conclusion would not take into account the possibility of selection bias in the composition of the two groups. It is possible that the intake clinician unknowingly (or perhaps knowingly) assigned more seriously disturbed clients to receive individual treatment, believing that this was somehow more intense therapy. Thus, at the beginning of treatment, the two groups of clients— those getting group therapy and those getting individual treatment—were *already different* in that the individual therapy clients were more seriously impaired. Thus, when the posttreatment evaluations were made, what was revealed were these *preexisting* difference in the two groups of clients, not the results of group therapy being more effective at helping people.

How can this threat be controlled for? One common way is to conduct *pretreatment* assessments of clients, so that their scores on relevant measures of functioning, strengths, or psychopathology can be ascertained to determine if they are equivalent or not. Showing that they are similar goes some way toward reducing the possibility that selection bias resulted in nonequivalent groups from the beginning. And, apart from formal assessment of functioning, it is also very useful to compare the two (or more) groups of clients on a variety of important demographic variables, with age, race, socioeconomic status, and gender being among the most important in this regard. Showing that your groups are equivalent demographically helps alleviate the possibility that any posttreatment differences may be due to some inherent differences in the groups due to their demographic composition. Men and women, whites and blacks, young and old, rich and poor, may all react differently to receiving certain social work services. If one group is composed predominantly of men and the other of women, posttreatment differences may reflect how the two genders react to the treatment differentially (maybe men do not get as much benefit from a given intervention). By being able to show that the groups are pretty much the same on important demographic variables, this threat can be partially controlled for. But only partially, because there may be some unrecognized feature that distinguishes the two (or more) groups and that is not measured but that nevertheless exerts an impact on response to treatment. Such latent differences may never be able to be detected, yet they may influence outcomes. This is why the methodological refinement of creating treatment and control groups on the basis of random assignment is considered by research methodologists to be one of the best safeguards against groups not being equivalent on virtually all relevant factors. More on this later.

Diffusion/Contamination of Treatments

This threat refers to a breakdown in the essential features supposedly distinguishing one treatment condition from others in a quasi-experiment. Suppose you have two groups of clients, about half of whom are assigned to receive group therapy alone and the other half individual counseling during the normal process of agency operations. A social work researcher wishes to see if the two groups of clients had differing outcomes. If they did, then one approach to treatment might be seen as more effective than another. Diffusion or contamination of treatments could occur if it transpired that a number of persons supposedly receiving only group therapy were later found to have sought out and obtained individual counseling on their own, perhaps through a local church, independent of the services your agency provided. This would compromise the researcher's ability to compare the outcomes of group versus individual counseling since, in reality, you are comparing group therapy *plus* individual counseling versus individual counseling alone, not individual versus group therapy alone. Sometimes clients assigned to one treatment condition encounter and share information and experiences they have had with clients assigned to another treatment or to a control condition. This may inadvertently contaminate the "purity" of your supposedly differing treatments.

Therapist Bias/Allegiance Effects

Individuals who evaluate social work services are often heavily personally invested in the services they provide. If you have centered your professional life around a given form of service or therapy, be it psychodynamic treatment, behavior therapy, solution-focused brief treatment, narrative therapy, group work, family treatment, cognitive therapy, multisystemic treatment, or other, it is understandable that your efforts at evaluating these services could be biased by your preexisting investment in your favored approach. This is a simple fact of life and not intended as a personal criticism of therapy researchers. This is why, when the founder of eye-movement desensitization and reprocessing (EMDR) Francine Shapiro published astonishingly positive outcome studies on EMDR; when the founder of cognitive therapy, Aaron Beck, did the same with cognitive therapy; or when the promoter of facilitated communication, Douglas Biklen, claimed that seriously developmentally disabled people could type with a high level of fluency, the scientific community wanted to see if these initial reports of success undertaken by a new treatments' advocates could be successfully replicated by independent researchers lacking the personal and perhaps financial investments in these novel approaches. This is not to imply that a therapy's enthusiasts are somehow lacking in honesty, but merely to recognize that all of us have our biases and preferences and that, when potential conflicts are obvious, more stringent standards of evidence may be called for. Sometimes, initially promising treatment results cannot be replicated by independent researchers, giving rise to concerns that the initial results were a fluke or perhaps contaminated by misguided zeal. At other times, independent researchers repeatedly corroborate the effectiveness of new therapies, which is the best possible outcome.

A particularly egregious threat pertaining to allegiance effects is the rising practice known as *ghost authorship*. Ghost authorship occurs when scientific writers who are employees of a corporation (e.g., a pharmaceutical company, a tobacco firm, etc.) actually write up a complete journal article, and the completed article is then offered to various respected authorities in that particular field for their editing or reviewing. In return, their name is appended to the article as an author or co-author; sometimes, the industry ghost writers who actually wrote the study do not appear anywhere on the list of authors, or even in footnotes. This gives rise to an independent-appearing paper apparently originating from respected authors at a prestigious academic institution. However, this is basically fraudulent in terms of authorship, and presents possibly questionable scientific findings, since the results were filtered through an industry with a significant financial investment in the product being evaluated. For example, one influential study that found that tobacco advertising bans had little effect in reducing tobacco consumption was "authored" by a respected marketing professor. In reality, the study was ghost-written by tobacco associations (see Davis, 2008), who paid the professor to present the study at conferences and before the U.S. Congress. The ghost-authorship and payments were not disclosed as conflicts of interest at the time. Similar conflicts have emerged in the reporting of drug trials (see DeAngelis & Fontana, 2008). These are serious threats to the integrity of research reporting and have led to more stringent editorial policies relating to the mandatory disclosing of possible conflicts of interest. Many journals, including *Research on Social Work Practice*, now require the authors of accepted papers to describe all such potential conflicts of interests, including factors such as receipt of grant funding, consulting fees, or providing paid trainings in the treatments under investigation.

Lack of Treatment Fidelity

Treatment fidelity refers to the extent to which services are delivered to clients in the manner in which they were intended. Important aspects to fidelity include the adherence of the therapists to the proper services model, as well as the competence of the service providers. Unfortunately, good adherence to prescribed therapies delivered by an incompetent therapist fails to provide a fair test of a given service. Similarly, a highly competent therapist who inadvertently blurs treatment techniques and fails to adhere to assigned treatment protocols also compromises a study's treatment fidelity. Treatment fidelity can be enhanced through various prospective methods. These include using well-proceduralized treatment manuals, if these are appropriate to the clinical situation and available;

developing these if they are not; utilizing as therapists only those individuals who are appropriately credentialed (e.g., licensed or certified, if appropriate) and skilled in the particular treatment method they are being asked to deliver (many persons possess generic credentials as a psychotherapist, but that does not mean they are necessarily competent in providing very specific forms of treatment); building into the delivery of services careful, regular supervision by a supervisor experienced in the treatment being provided; and providing some practice sessions with live supervision, prior to unleashing "treatment" therapists on real clients enrolled in the study.

Some other methods include audio- or videotaping treatment sessions and having these immediately reviewed by supervisors to ensure that therapists are delivering therapy as planned and taking corrective supervisory actions if it is not, and using any of a number of existing measures of therapist adherence or treatment fidelity (see Nezu & Nezu, 2008, pp. 263–281 for a review of some of these).

Concluding Remarks on Threats to Internal Validity

This review of some common threats to internal validity need not be overwhelming. If you would like a more light-hearted approach to trying to understand how these factors can complicate your ability to conclude that a given treatment is effective, go to the *YouTube* website and look up some of the videos of the comedic magician team of Penn and Teller (e.g., http://www.youtube.com/watch?v=MzjoKhBklYg) who demonstrate the power of placebo therapies and alternative medicine treatments by setting up bogus health clinics in which fake doctors offer to treat people with magnets, kazoo music, snail mucus (!), and toilet plungers. These videos are really hilarious.

Keep in mind that one needs to control for *plausible* controlling factors, not every conceivable potential confound. For example, if you use a no-treatment control group or a treatment-as-usual comparison group, it is a useful practice to demonstrate that your two groups are statistically equivalent at pretreatment on important demographic and clinical factors, on variables such as age, race, gender, education, socioeconomic background, severity of clinical symptomatology, etc. But you need not examine essentially irrelevant factors such as clients' astrological signs, phases of the moon when treatment is administered, and the like.

The designs described in the next chapter illustrate how social work researchers attempt to introduce various controls for some of these legitimate threats by using quasi-experimental methods. All the threats to internal validity mentioned in this chapter as potentially impacting the interpretation of results from studies using pre-experimental research designs also apply to the quasi-experimental designs presented in the next chapter.

SUMMARY

This chapter has provided an overview of the logical and design features of those approaches to evaluation that have been traditionally labeled as pre-experimental, in that they involve the assessment of only a single group of clients. These designs may assess clients only after they have received an intervention, or they may assess client functioning before and after exposure to a treatment. A variety of ways were presented to potentially strengthen these pre-experimental designs, and numerous examples were described, taken from the published social work journal literature, describing how each of these designs has been used to evaluate the outcomes of social work services. Also provided was a review of various threats to internal validity, factors that can complicate one's ability to conclude that a given treatment *caused* any apparently positive outcomes.

3

Quasi-Experimental Group Designs

In Chapter 1, a series of five questions was presented, questions which required an increasingly more stringent level of evidence in order for them to be credibly answered. Question 1, which asks, *What is the status of clients after they have received a given course of treatment?* can be answered using the $X - O_1$ design, and Question 2, *Do clients improve after receiving a given course of treatment?* can be addressed with the $O_1 - X - O_2$ design, with O referring to a point in time when clients are systematically assessed using some reliable and valid outcome measure and X depicting the individuals' receipt of some form of social work intervention. However, Question 3, *What is the status of clients who have received a given treatment compared to those who did not receive that treatment?* cannot usually be answered with a pre-experimental design because the question involves not comparing the same group posttreatment with its pretreatment level of functioning, but instead requires looking at the results for a group of clients versus a similar group who did not receive the treatment. Thus, some sort of comparison group is required. As noted before, it is this element of having some sort of comparison or control group that has traditionally distinguished the quasi-experiments from the pre-experiments.

The terms *control group* and *comparison group* have somewhat different meanings. A control group is one that does not receive any kind of formal treatment at all. Generally, the sole contact that members of a control group may have as a result of their participation in this type of study is via the process of being assessed. A comparison group refers to individuals who receive some sort of alternative treatment. This may be treatment as usual (TAU), which is some other legitimate intervention used when trying to see if one treatment is superior to another or to a placebo treatment. A *placebo control group* occurs when clients receive a seemingly credible treatment, which in reality the researchers presume to be ineffective in terms of helping improve the problem or situation being presented by the clients. Sometimes, placebos are otherwise legitimate practices, like relaxation therapy or hypnosis, which may have their place in the effective treatment of some problems, but not in others. Relaxation training may have a role in helping people with generalized anxiety disorder, but when used to treat persons with schizophrenia, a condition for which it has no discernible value, it would be considered a placebo therapy. At other times, a placebo may be a frankly bogus or fake treatment, a condition that is either deceptive or simply known to be useless. For example, audiotapes or CD recordings containing supposedly subliminal messages have been marketed to help people lose weight or stop smoking, but extensive research has shown that they do not work; other placebos may include sham needle placement in acupuncture studies, eye movements conducted in ways that the treatment theory suggests should not have any effect, administering homeopathic pills that actually contain no trace of an active ingredient, and the like. If presented in a believable manner, all these can make a useful placebo treatment for comparison purposes. The term *experimental group* usually refers to those clients who received the actual, legitimate, or novel treatment under formal investigation.

The next sections describe some common variations of more sophisticated control and comparison group quasi-experimental designs.

DESIGNS WITH CONTROL GROUPS AND POSTTESTS ONLY

The Posttest-only No-treatment Control Group Design

Moving incrementally, the simplest of the quasi-experimental designs can be diagrammed as follows:

Group 1 Received Treatment	$X - O_1$
Group 2 Did Not Receive Treatment	O_1

Some researchers might pose a formal predictive hypothesis, such as *Clients who received social work treatment X will have higher functioning than will clients who did not receive treatment X*, and use this design to see if this hypothesis is supported or not. The inferential logic is simple: If the group who received X differs significantly from those who did not receive X, this would support the hypothesis that X produces certain effects, above and beyond receiving nothing.

Keep in mind that, for the purposes of our discussion, X can literally be *anything* within the scope of social work practice—individual therapy, group therapy, marital or couples counseling, a community-wide intervention, a local or state law, or even a national welfare policy. To give you an idea of how this design is used at a macro level, one might compare some outcome measure across two similar states, one with a certain law in effect and the other lacking that law. In this case, the differing laws represent our X or intervention or independent variable. Florida, for example, does not require motorcycle riders to wear safety helmets. Other states do require this. One could compare fatality rates for motorcycle accident victims across states, comparing those with and those without a protective helmet law, to try to investigate the contention that wearing helmets saves lives. Closer to the field of social work, some states require that abortion providers ensure that the parents of minors be notified prior to performing an abortion on that minor. Some stakeholders have questioned if these parental notification laws deter minors from seeking abortions, and they have used this posttreatment no-treatment control group design to look at abortion rates across states with and without a parental notification law.

Ideally, the period of time during which O occurs is roughly the same for the two groups. For example, if the treatment group is provided a social work service in July, with intervention lasting 3 months, then the group would be reassessed immediately posttreatment, near the end of October (when all clients had completed treatment). And, also around the end of October, the group of people who had been identified as not having received treatment (those in the no-treatment control group) would be similarly assessed. Conducting these O assessments at about the same time helps control for events in the external world that can influence client functioning, events unrelated to response to treatment or the waxing and waning of symptomatology or problem severity. Imagine if you conducted a study like this and your treatment group was assessed around September 1, 2001, and the nontreatment group was assessed in mid-September, after the terrorist attack on September 11, 2001? Clearly, your study might have been seriously compromised. Similarly, if your study was in Louisiana and your O evaluations for the two groups occurred on either side of Hurricane Katrina or the Gulf oil spill, it would be very difficult to make any legitimate comparisons in such instances. Here are some examples of using this type of research design.

Evaluating Virginity Pledges

This design, which is sometimes called the *static-group comparison design*, was used by Rosenbaum (2008) in her analysis of the effectiveness of *virginity pledges* in terms of deterring the initiation of sex and of their influence on the use of birth control. This is certainly an important issue, since the U.S. government spends (as of the time of this writing) over $200 million annually on abstinence promotion programs, some of which involve virginity pledges. Abstinence-only sex education in general, and virginity pledges in particular, are of uncertain effectiveness in preventing the initiation of sexual activity, pregnancy, or sexually transmitted diseases. In this study, derived from a large-scale national survey, 289 adolescents aged 15 years or older at the time they voluntarily completed virginity pledges were compared 5 years after taking their pledge with 645 nonpledgers, teenagers generally equivalent demographically to those who took the pledge to abstain from sex until marriage. Note that, ethically and practically, adolescents could not be randomly assigned to undertake a personal pledge to abstain from sexual intercourse, so this quasi-experimental design was an excellent method to initially evaluate such interventions. The results?

> Five years after the pledge, 82% of pledgers denied ever having pledged. Pledgers and matched nonpledgers did not differ on premarital sex, sexually transmitted diseases, and anal and oral sex variables. Pledgers had 0.1 fewer past-year partners but did not differ in lifetime sexual partners and age of first sex. Fewer pledgers than matched nonpledgers used birth control and condoms in the past year and birth control at last sex. (Rosenbaum, 2008, p. e110)

These results will be disappointing to the advocates of abstinence-only sex education and virginity pledges, and again point to the possible dangers of public policy (funding certain types of programs) getting ahead of the evidentiary curve. But the picture is admittedly mixed. For example, Martino et al. (2008), also using this design, found a protective effect for virginity pledges, comparing 12- to 17-year-olds who took a virginity pledge with those who had not, some 3 years later. About 42% of the nonpledgers had initiated intercourse at 3-year follow-up, compared to only 34% of the pledgers. The effect was modest but real.

Please note that the above examples, and others presented in this book, are being used to accurately illustrate the use of selected quasi-experimental researcher designs. They should not be interpreted to reflect comprehensive conclusions based on systematic reviews of all the relevant research evidence dealing with the possible effectiveness or ineffectiveness of the interventions being discussed. Although the summaries of the studies are accurately presented, any conclusions drawn from an individual study should *not* be presumed to reflect the value of the presented treatments as assessed by a comprehensive review of all relevant research.

Evaluating Foundation Master's of Social Work Skills Training

Social worker Dorothy Carrillo's Ph.D. dissertation used this design in a way that took advantage of a naturally occurring situation. Dorothy was assigned to instruct a class of second-year master's degree in social work (MSW) students devoted to the topic of teaching direct practice skills. In the natural course of events, Dorothy's class consisted of two types of students, 15 had earned the bachelor of social work (BSW) degree and were enrolled in the advanced standing program, wherein they could exempt the first-year foundation course in direct practice. An additional 23 students were in the traditional 2-year MSW program and had completed a first-year foundation class in direct practice skills. Thus, without any manipulation on Ms. Carrillo's part, she had two different types of students taking her class; some had completed the first-year direct practice class as a part of their MSW program, and the others had not had this course as a part of their MSW curriculum. As holders of the BSW, they were exempted from taking this course earlier.

The Council on Social Work Education permits MSW programs to exempt BSW students from taking certain foundation MSW courses, such as in direct practice, using as its rationale that selected BSW classes are redundant with first-year graduate MSW training. This was a heretofore untested assumption, and Ms. Carrillo was in a position to test it.

At the beginning of the semester, the standard practice in this class was for students to interview a simulated client who role-played being an elderly person. The students were given some background information and asked to obtain information about this pseudo-client's life history and present circumstances. These interviews were videotaped. In effect, Ms. Carrillo had a ready-made posttest-only no-treatment control group design dropped in her lap. She arranged for these videotapes, which were made very early on in the semester, to be reliably coded in terms of the student's use of selected core interviewing skills related to concepts such as facilitation, questioning/clarification, and support/empathy. One coder (a social work doctoral student) rated all 38 tapes and a reliability coder (another social work doctoral student) independently rated 13 (34%) of them as well. Inter-rater agreement on the use of the three selected interviewing skills ranged from 86% to 92%, an acceptably high level of agreement, indicating that the ratings were really of what the videotaped interviewer was doing, as opposed to the rater's purely subjective impressions. The study's purpose was to evaluate the following null hypothesis: Advanced standing and 2-year MSW program students will display equivalent use of selected foundation interviewing skills when assessed at a comparable point in their curriculum.

After the semester was over and the tapes were blindly rated, the code was broken and Ms. Carrillo could see whether the two groups of students indeed displayed similar interviewing skills or if one group was better than the other. The results (fortunately for social work educational policy) were consistent with the CSWE's policy of granting advanced standing to BSW students, exempting them from foundation MSW courses, since the BSW students and second-year MSW students *did* display similar levels on the three selected skills (see Carrillo & Thyer, 1994).

Increasing Access to Dental Care for Medicaid Preschool Children

It is important that children receive regular dental care. Many children, especially children from poor families, fail to receive such care. The state of Washington developed an Access to Baby and Child Dentistry (ABCD) program offering extended benefits to participating Medicaid-enrolled children and higher fees to dentists seeing such children. Participation in the ABCD program was voluntary, and over the course of time, some families receiving Medicaid enrolled their children in this program and some did not. After the ABCD program had been in place for a year, researchers contacted 282 parents of children aged 13–36 months, with about half the families being enrolled in the ABCD program and about half not being enrolled. Fully 43% of the children whose parents had enrolled them in the ABCS program had visited a dentist within 1 year of their being signed up, whereas only about 12% of the Medicaid children who had not been enrolled in the ABCD program had visited a dentist. In other words, enrollment in the program seemed to result in a child being 5.3 times as likely to have had at least one dental visit compared to a child not in the program. Also, the parents of ABCD-enrolled children reported that their kids were less fearful of the dentist. The program seemed very successful in promoting early dental care for children from poor families (Grembowski & Milgrom, 2000).

Promoting Positive Attitudes Toward Computer Use Among Master's of Social Work Students

The use of technology, such as computers and the Internet, has dramatically transformed social work education and practice. Like any new innovation, incorporating technology into our field met with critics, and it only moved ahead via fits and starts. Over a decade ago, some social work programs developed classes aimed at enhancing MSW students' technical skills and promoting positive attitudes related to computer use in practice. One such program was developed at the School of Social Work at Bar Ilan University in Israel (Monnickendam & Elliot, 1997). Faculty there offered direct practice students a new course devoted to computer literacy. Some direct students took the computer literacy class and some did not. Students in the administrative track did not take it either. At the end of the school term, all MSW students completed measures related to attitudes toward using computers in the human services. The design can be diagrammed as follows:

N = 34 Direct Practice Students	$X - O_1$
N = 30 Direct Practice Students	O_1
N = 32 Administrative Track Students	O_1

The results were an interesting mix. Direct practice students who took the class (depicted as X in the design) had more positive attitudes about computer use than did direct practice students who did not take the computer literacy class. This supports the hypothesis that taking such a course can indeed promote more positive attitudes about using computers. However, the administrative track students who *did not* take the computer literacy class had attitudes that were even more positive about computers than did the direct practice students who did take the class. This complicates things a bit. Plausibly, it could be contended that administrative track students had preexisting positive attitudes about technology, that the direct practice students were more touchy-feely in their approach to social work, and some presorting into direct practice or administrative tracks occurred partly on this basis before they even took the computer course. This is another nice example of taking advantage of a naturally occurring situation to imbed a quasi-experimental research design into one's evaluation work. After learning more about the designs described in this book, you will be surprised to find how many professional situations arise that lend themselves to being evaluated using them.

Moral Development of Sex Offenders
Social worker Frederick Buttell is one of the country's foremost researchers in the area of treating sex offenders who are men. Dr. Buttell adopted this design to evaluate the levels of moral reasoning evidenced by convicted sex offenders ordered into treatment. Basically, 72 male sex offenders completed a previously published, supposedly reliable and valid measure of moral reasoning, an instrument called the Defining Issues Test (DIT), a measure that presents one with a series of written moral dilemmas and asks the reader to evaluate a list of questions he or she might consider when making a decision about what to do in the depicted situation. The DIT presents six moral dilemma scenarios and results in an overall score said to be related to "principled morality, with higher scores reflective of higher levels of moral reasoning." Buttell's (2002) study was *not* a treatment outcome study; rather, it was something called a *cross-sectional survey*. In this instance, X reflected the background of being a sex offender, and O the scores on the DIT. The group lacking X was comprised of normative data on the DIT reported by the developer of this test. Dr. Buttell was thus able to compare the levels of moral reasoning exhibited by convicted sex offenders with the levels of moral reasoning evidenced by males nationwide. It was found that the sex offenders (mean age of 38 years) had significantly lower levels of

moral reasoning than did graduate students, college students, adults in general, and high school students, but scored similarly to junior high school students (as assessed against normative data for the DIT, not actual groups of clients). Buttell speculates that this low level of moral reasoning, focusing more on self-interest than on empathy, may be linked to being a sex offender and to the high rates of repeat offenses and recidivism displayed by this group. This example also illustrates how quasi-experimental designs can be used in other forms of research besides outcome studies, with cross-sectional surveys like this one being a good example.

Strengths of the Posttest-only No-treatment Control Group Design
This design is capable of answering the question "Do clients who received treatment X fare any differently compared with clients who did not receive X?," but this ability is dependent on several assumptions. First, the intervention is something that can be seen or at least determined to be present or absent. Second, the outcome measure(s) must be both reliable and valid. Third, a sufficient number of participants exists in each group (you can't reliably use this design with just a few folks in each condition). And, last, the two groups, treatment and no-treatment control group, are truly similar in all important respects, *except* that the intervention group has received the treatment while the no-treatment group has not. This last point can be a stickler.

Limitations of the Posttest-only No-treatment Control Group Design
You simply cannot assume that the two groups are similar simply because they share similar problems. You *can* conduct a statistical analysis on the members of the two groups, attempting to see if they do differ on any variables. These variables can be demographic characteristics (e.g., age, race, gender, etc.), or they can be clinical features (e.g., severity of symptoms). You do not need to analyze everything, only factors that can be plausibly deemed as important. Client's astrological signs, for example, are likely unimportant. In the Carrillo and Thyer (1994) study, Ms. Carrillo was able to show that, in terms of gender, marital status, race/ethnicity, and income, the two groups were indeed very similar. This is good, in that it argues that any differences observed during the observation period are more likely due to the treated group's exposure to treatment than to any preexisting conditions in place before the treated group received intervention. However, when Carrillo looked at age, she found a difference.

The advanced standing students' average age was 23.2 years, whereas the 2-year program students' was 29.2 years, a 6-year difference that was statistically significant. If she *had* found a difference posttraining, favoring the 2-year students, this might have been a problem since the possibility existed that the older students were somehow wiser, more seasoned in life, more mature, or perhaps had more prior social work job experience than the advanced standing students, and it was *these preexisting* factors that accounted for their superior interviewing skills performance, not the first-year foundation practice skills class that they had taken and the advanced standing students had not. However, since Carillo did not find a difference in interviewing skill ability, she was not faced with handling this possible confound. But you can see how it might arise and present problems in making a claim that intervention was responsible for such differences.

Another possibility to consider is that the null result of Carrillo's study, the finding of no difference between the MSW and BSW students' performance on interviewing skills, is that the outcome measure was too blunt or insensitive an indicator to pick up on the actually differences between the two groups. This is a common confound for any study that fails to find anticipated differences. One interpretation is that the two groups truly did not differ after training, but another is that the dependent variable, the outcome measure, is too crude. One can guard against this by choosing to use outcome measures of known reliability, validity, and sensitivity to differences and changes.

You can go to the websites of many advocacy groups that find some difference between two groups and claim that this difference exists because of some factor that separates the two groups. These claims are then used to buttress some policy position of the advocacy group. For example, you may have heard a public service announcement on the radio advocating for parents to eat more meals sitting down with their children because it has been shown that nondelinquent, non–drug-using, non–sexually active kids report having more sit-down meals with their parents than do kids who engage in delinquency, drug use, and sex. Assume that this is true (I am not claiming it is). The inferential logic is something like this:

1. A large group of kids are surveyed in terms of delinquency, sexual activity, drug use, etc.
2. Some kids engage in a high amount of such problem behavior and some do not.

3. When you examine the backgrounds of these two groups of youth, those with high- and low-delinquency status, you find that they differed in the amount of time they claimed to spend eating family-style meals.

So far, we are on solid ground. But the next steps may be logically untenable, claiming, for example:

4. Eating meals family-style will protect kids from becoming delinquent.
5. It should be a matter of policy to encourage parents to eat more family-style meals with their children, and this will reduce the risk of kids abusing drugs, committing crimes, or becoming sexually active.

Can you detect the gap in logic between step 3 and steps 4 and 5? There may be significant other preexisting differences or factors that lead to fewer family-style meals *and* a higher risk of delinquency. For example, one potential confounding factor might be having both biological parents in the home versus having only one (e.g., a single-parent home). The *real* cause might be this difference in overall parent availability for supervision, *not* the specific act of eating meals together.

While preparing this chapter, I went to the website of The Heritage Foundation (www.heritage.org), a conservative think tank that regularly produces policy papers based on contemporary social science research. They highlighted a number of studies on their site, studies which, by implication if not by explicit statement, supported generally conservative positions on various social welfare policy matters. Here are some examples:

- "Compared with peers from intact families, adolescent and young-adult women who experienced parental divorce were significantly more likely to give birth out of wedlock" (based on Martin, 2005).
- "Teens who were exposed to high levels of sexual content on television were twice as likely to become pregnant during a 3-year period than peers who had lower levels of exposure to sexual content" (based on Chandra et al., 2008).

- "Compared to adolescents who were virgins, those who
  had initiated sexual activity were 58% more likely to
  engage in delinquent behavior in the year after they had
  become sexually active" (based on Armour & Haynie,
  2007).
- "Compared with peers in intact families, children in
  blended or step families tended to have significantly lower
  GPAs and less positive engagement with school tasks
  and relationships" (based on Halpern-Meekin & Tach,
  2008).

Now, these individual studies, all using the posttest-only no-treatment
control group design in the context of a survey study, may well be sound
pieces of research. But logical and scientific problems arise if these
summarized findings (all four quotes above were taken from the Heritage
Foundation webpage on August 17, 2009) were used to justify social policies advocating something like the following:

- Since youth from families whose parents were divorced
  were more likely to give birth out of wedlock, we can drive
  down the illegitimacy rate by enacting policies that
  discourage divorce.
- Since exposure to sexual content on television promotes
  teenage pregnancy, let's exact more stringent laws censoring
  such sexual content in order to reduce teenage
  pregnancy.
- Since sexual activity in youth is associated with a much higher
  risk of subsequently engaging in crime, let's promote the teenage
  norm of sexual abstinence as a means of reducing juvenile
  delinquency.
- Since kids from divorced families have lower academic
  performance and social skills, let's try and improve the well-being
  of youth by making it more difficult to get a divorce when
  children are involved.

Although the Heritage Foundation itself is too sophisticated to draw
such explicit conclusions, causal linkages, and policy recommendations
like those four just noted above, other groups are not so constrained.

The problem is again that of uncontrolled factors that are actually caus-ally involved, rather than the particular one cited in a given study. For example, although it may well be true that greater exposure to televi-sion sexual content is associated with subsequent teenage pregnancy, the true causal factor (this is only a hypothetical example) may be lack of parental supervision. In the young, this may lead to unsupervised televi-sion watching, with the kids naturally gravitating to the more salacious shows (my own kids—aged 17, 15, 14, and 12—love *South Park*, which I consider inappropriate for them but my wife thinks is fine). Then, with puberty and even greater freedom, this lack of parental supervision pro-vides hormonally charged adolescents with more opportunities not just to *watch* sexy TV shows, but to do what comes naturally! Voila—more babies born out of wedlock. But, the causal factor is not watching TV shows; it's inadequate supervision by parents.

A more benign example of this type of fallacious reasoning can be found in the high school band program two of my sons participate in. The music programs distributed at their performances contain snippets from studies that have shown that high school students who participate in music education programs like bands are more likely to graduate from high school, to have higher GPAs, and to enroll in college more often. The implicit message is that high school music programs must be better funded in order to promote the academic attainments of teenagers. No mention is given to the possibility that the kids who gravitate to music and band may be brighter, harder-working, or come from higher socio-economic levels initially, and that these preexisting differences account for disparate outcomes between band kids and non-band high-schoolers. Once you become aware of such potential confounds and the errors in reasoning they may lead to, you will be amazed at how frequently you will encounter examples of precisely these types of errors in the media and in everyday life. Would you be surprised to read a study that found that BSW students hold more liberal and progressive values when they graduate from college than do other graduating majors? What do you think is more likely responsible for such differences—that BSW educa-tion is inherently liberalizing, or that the more liberal and progressive students gravitate to the social work major?

This inability to control for the equalization of groups on all mean-ingful factors really complicates causal inference in designs such as this and the others described later in this chapter.

The Posttest-only Comparison Group Design

Early on, Macdonald (1952) provided some suggestions relating to the evaluation of social work services that are relevant here, noting:

> I think we are ill-advised to cast about looking for no-treatment groups as control groups. We cannot keep in touch with people who are not being treated in order to learn about them and their problems. . . . I think we are better advised to examine results within the group treated, comparing subgroups who have different diagnoses or who have the same diagnoses and are treated differently. We can evaluate new methods in comparison with the old. . . ." (Macdonald, 1952, p. 137)

Although I believe that Macdonald was overly pessimistic regarding the feasibility of employing no-treatment control groups (for example, using agency wait-lists of clients is one ethical option), she was spot-on in terms of using quasi-experimental designs to evaluate clients who received differing forms of intervention, or in comparing a novel therapy with TAU.

The inferential logic of posttest-only comparison group design is relatively simple. Compare the outcomes of a group of people who received one type of intervention (X), program, or training, against the outcomes of another group who received an alternative intervention (Y). If the group X outcomes are better than the group Y outcomes, this corroborates the hypothesis that treatment X is superior on some dimension than treatment Y. If the outcomes between X and Y are no different, then this weakens the hypothesis that X is a superior treatment. This design can be diagrammed as follows:

$$X - O_1$$

$$Y - O_1$$

The design also permits more than one comparison group. For example, an intervention program for male batterers might consist of two elements, individual counseling and group counseling. In the normal course of service delivery, some referrals might get individual counseling alone, others will get group counseling alone, and a third set of clients will receive both interventions. This could be diagrammed as follows:

$$X_{\text{individual counseling alone}} - O_1$$

$$Y_{\text{group counseling alone}} - O_1$$

$$Z_{\text{combined counseling}} - O_1$$

Over, say, a 12-month period, you would likely have unequal numbers being nonrandomly assigned to one of these three groups. That is acceptable, so long as no one group's sample size falls below an acceptable limit. Clients would be enrolled throughout the year, and at some point be terminated at the conclusion of their course of treatment. The formal assessment could occur then; thus, these posttreatment assessments would occur at the same point in time procedurally, at the end of treatment for each client, but not at the same point of time chronologically, as these assessments, too, would occur throughout the year. Here are some actual published examples of social work researchers using this design.

Are Regular Faculty Better Teachers Than Adjuncts or Doctoral Students?

There is much hand wringing in contemporary academia because the proportion of teaching positions held by full-time, tenure-track faculty is declining in recent years, relative to instruction provided by community-based adjuncts hired to teach individual classes, or by doctoral students. Is this hand wringing justified? Are these lesser mortals somehow inherently less able teachers than full-time faculty? My colleagues and I decided to investigate this issue by taking advantage of the publically available course evaluations completed by students at my university. These evaluations included qualitative and quantitative sections, and we were able to retrieve these for several hundred BSW and MSW classes offered over several years. The courses were divided into those taught by regular full-time faculty, by adjuncts, and by Ph.D. students, after tossing out all those classes with fewer than ten respondents available. This design can be diagrammed as follows:

Classes Taught by Regular Faculty (N = 181)	$X - O_1$
Classes Taught by Adjuncts (N = 63)	$Y - O_1$
Classes Taught by Ph.D. Students (N = 50)	$Z - O_1$

We examined the quantitative scores on these evaluations and statistically compared the scores obtained by the three groups of instructors. Basically, we found that the full-time faculty's course evaluations were statistically the same as those earned by the adjuncts, and the evaluations earned by the adjuncts were the same as those earned by the doctoral students, but the full-time faculty had course evaluations that were statistically significantly better than those obtained by the Ph.D. students. However, the size of this difference, although statistically reliable, was quite small, and in fact practically meaningless. For all practical purposes, the three groups of instructors earned similar course evaluations. This null result suggests that, within this university and this social work program, instructional quality is not suffering because of our use of adjuncts and doctoral students. Parenthetically, this study is another example of low-hanging fruit. The data were publically available on the university's website. All we had to do was retrieve and analyze it. We did this, of course, only after obtaining our university's institutional review board approval for the study (see Thyer, Myers, & Nugent, 2011).

Do Social Workers Make Better Child Welfare Workers?

Social worker Robin Perry (2006) at Florida A & M University used this posttest-only control-group design to test the hypothesis, so widely held in the child welfare field, that having earned a professional social work degree (BSW or MSW) is superior preparation for child welfare practice than is receiving degrees in other disciplines. Working within Florida's Department of Children and Families, Perry was able to obtain the semi-annual evaluations of all child protective service (CPS) workers who were employed within the state system as of March 2002—some 2,500 employees. He randomly selected about 25% of the employees and was able to classify them as either having earned a BSW degree *or* another degree (e.g., in a field such as psychology, criminology, sociology, business, education, etc.). His outcome measure was the Career Service Evaluation Form completed semi-annually by supervisors on each worker; this form contains quantitative ratings across various important measures of worker performance. Perry grouped all the evaluation form data for the CPS workers with a BSW into one group (X), and compared their data with those performance evaluation ratings received by workers with the other educational degrees (Y). Basically, Perry found that BSWs did not score higher than CPS workers with other professional backgrounds.

Thus, his hypothesis was disconfirmed, and the claim that social work degrees make better preparation for responsible positions within child welfare is weakened. This is a rather important finding. Although disappointing for the profession of social work, it calls into question the rationale for the current practice of allocating large amounts of federal financial support specifically designed to prepare BSWs and MSWs for careers in child welfare. Perhaps such funding should be opened to students in all disciplines, social work *and* non-social work, who are prepared to commit to a career in public child welfare services? It would be premature to advocate for opening up such funding now, particularly since Perry's provocative findings have not yet been tested, much less replicated, by others; but, in science, the burden of proof rests on the person making an unusual claim. In this instance, the unusual claim is that social work training is superior to non-social work training in terms of preparing child welfare workers. The evidence in favor of this hypothesis remains rather weak.

Do School Social Worker Services Reduce Truancy?
Newsome, Anderson-Butcher, Fink, Hall, and Huffer (2008) used a posttest-only no-treatment control group design with 115 urban secondary school students in Ohio. About half received special school social work services aimed at reducing absenteeism and about half did not. The untreated half were matched as closely as possible to the treated students, but they were not assigned to treatment versus nontreatment using random assignment procedures, which makes this study a quasi-experimental design, as opposed to a true randomized controlled trial. The social worker provided an average of 14 direct or indirect interventions for each referred student, including one-on-one counseling, group counseling, phone contacts, and meetings with school personnel, parents, or outside agency staff. Intervention lasted 9 weeks, and attendance data were obtained from the school district's management information system for each student, for the 9 weeks prior to the intervention and for the 9 weeks during which it was provided. This study was approved by the human subject's IRB at both Ohio State University (to which some of the authors were affiliated), as well as by the local school district's IRB. Unfortunately, the students receiving school social work services did *not* experience a statistically significant reduction in unexcused absences relative to the no-treatment group. Thus, this report could be considered one of a treatment failure. Although personally, perhaps, and professionally

disappointing, finding out that certain forms of social work service are *not* effective in producing desired outcomes is a good thing to know, compared to not knowing.

Does Early Childhood Intervention Impact Educational Achievement and Arrest?

The interdisciplinary research team of Reynolds, Temple, Robertson, and Mann (2001), which included a social work author with a MSW, conducted a 15-year follow-up of two groups of low-income children attending public schools. A nonrandomized matched-group cohort design was used, involving 1,539 children, most of whom were African American. Nine hundred eighty-nine of the children received the Chicago Child–Parent Program, which provided comprehensive education, family, and health services, including half-day preschool at ages 3 and 4, and full-day kindergarten at elementary schools for kids aged 6–9 years. It was basically a very intensive family and educational support program. The comparison group of children received a less intensive set of services, basically kindergarten without the preschool and additional social services. The outcome measures were assessed some 15 years later, a remarkably long follow-up period, when the children averaged 20 years of age. Measures of educational attainment included high school/GED completion, grade retention (failures), and juvenile arrest records (including numbers and type of arrests). The results? The intensive intervention group had a significantly higher level of high school completion and lower rates of dropout and grade retention, all relative to the comparison group. The former also completed more years of schooling. The intensive intervention group had significantly lower rates of arrest, lower rate of multiple arrests, and fewer arrests for violent crimes. This was a remarkably ambitious and large-scale study, with an extended follow-up period, and it showed appreciable benefits for the intensive social services intervention compared to more standard options. Perhaps it is not surprising that this study was published in the *Journal of the American Medical Association*, one of the most prestigious scientific journals in the world, with the first author being a professor of social work! Can quasi-experiments conducted by social workers be of high quality, provide useful information, and appear in prestigious journals? Yes, indeed! Other examples of social workers using this design can be found in Larsen and Hepworth (1982), and in Sze, Keller, and Keller (1979).

These posttreatment-only comparison designs are exceedingly useful, but they can be markedly improved by adding formal pretreatment assessments to more rigorously ascertain whether the groups' functioning changed over time, and if posttreatment differences are observed, to help rule out the possibility that they may be attributable to existing but unknown pretreatment differences. The next section explores some common variations on using this methodological refinement.

DESIGNS WITH CONTROL GROUPS AND PRETESTS AND POSTTESTS

The Pretest–Posttest No-treatment Control Group Design

This design is used to help determine if a given intervention produces any effects above and beyond those attributable to the passage of time, concurrent history, or the experience of being assessed. A diagram depicting this design shows:

$$O_1 - X - O_2$$

$$O_1 \qquad O_2$$

We have two (or more) groups, not known to be equivalent on all possible factors, since the groups were not created using random assignment. Both groups are assessed at about the same point in time. The members of one group receive an intervention, whereas the members of the second group do not. Then, both are assessed at about the same point in time on a second occasion, after the first group receives intervention. If the treatment group changes and the no-treatment group does not, there is some modest logical justification to infer that it was the treatment, X, that produced these improvements.

In practice, with this and other designs incorporating control or comparison groups, it may be logistically difficult to accumulate enough clients at a single point in time so as to conduct the pretest assessment on everyone in both groups at roughly the same time. The pragmatic solution is often to use a *rolling enrollment protocol*, wherein new cases are added to each group over time, with perhaps months transpiring as a client is enrolled in one group, assessed, treated, then reassessed, and the information added to the dataset. Meantime, other clients who are not destined to receive X are assessed, experience a similar length of time transpiring as do clients receiving treatment, and are then reassessed. These clients' data too are banked, until sufficient numbers of clients have accumulated in each group, at which point the totality of the data are analyzed statistically. This approach is scientifically less satisfactory than measuring all participants at about the same time, since many different elements may come into play during the time period covered by rolling enrollments and assessments, elements that may change crucial features of an agency's operation, or that may broadly affect the locale, state, or nation (and hence the features of those enrolling in the project).

This pretest–posttest no-treatment control group design is a very popular approach to evaluation research. Cook and Shadish (1994, p. 566) go so far as to claim that "the most frequently employed quasi-experiment still involves only two (nonequivalent) groups and two measurement waves, one a pretest and the other a posttest measures on the same instrument." Here are some examples of evaluation research that made use of this approach.

Evaluating School Social Worker–Teacher Collaboration

School children frequently experience academic, attendance, and behavioral difficulties, and school social workers can be asked to help such children. Viggiani, Reid, and Bailey-Dempsey (2002) evaluated the outcomes of implementing a program wherein social work interns were placed in elementary school classrooms for an entire day for 2 days a week to help the teachers manage the class and resolve student difficulties before they turned into a crisis. This was done in one kindergarten and one third-grade classroom (total N = 36 children). Two comparable classes (total N = 40) did not receive the added services of the social work interns. Outcome measures related to student attendance, behavior, and grades were obtained from student report cards pre- and post-intervention. The researchers hypothesized that all three would improve in the two "treated" classrooms, compared to the two classrooms that did not receive the intervention. The treated and untreated classrooms' students were statistically comparable in terms of gender and numbers. At the end of the school year, children in the classes with the addition of the school social worker for 2 days a week had significantly improved attendance relative to the no-treatment classrooms, and achieved statistically significant improvements on 4 of 14 behavioral measures. Grades did not appear to be affected in any way. These mixed results were described by the authors as promising.

The Pretest–Posttest Alternative-Treatment Control Group Design

This design may be used to more rigorously test whether or not Treatment X produces outcomes different from those emerging from Treatment Y. The design can be diagrammed as follows:

$$O_1 - X - O_2$$

$$O_1 - Y - O_2$$

By now, you should understand what this outline means. Two groups of clients, in the natural course of events, differ in that some receive treatment X and some get treatment Y. Y may be an alternative legitimate treatment, such as TAU, or it may be a placebo treatment, something that provides exposure to the experience of being "helped," but entails something that researchers believe will not simply be innocuous but actually ineffective. If some form of pretest and posttest assessments are available, it may be possible to make some inferences about the relative value of X versus Y in terms of how selected outcome measures are impacted.

Evaluating a College-based Student Drinking Reduction Program
Abusive drinking by students is a serious problem on some college campuses. Many students are underage, and any alcohol consumption by them is illegal. Being apprehended by law officers while consuming or in possession of alcohol, or using a fake ID to gain entry into bars, can result in a criminal record. Student alcohol use is associated with problems such as DUI arrests, vehicle accidents, alcohol poisoning up to and including death, fights, a higher risk for sexual activity and unprotected sex, and so forth. Many campus administrations are trying to reduce illegal and abusive use of alcohol through various approaches. One such approach being widely touted as effective is called a *social norms marketing approach*,

wherein a campus-wide marketing campaign is used to convey accurate information about the modest amounts of alcohol actually consumed by local college students, in the hope that by making moderate drinking or alcohol abstinence be seen as the "norm," students will moderate their own alcohol intake. Faculty with the School of Social Work at San Diego State University used a pretest–posttest comparison group design to evaluate an intensive social norms drinking reduction campaign undertaken at their own university.

Students in one residence hall were exposed to the social norms campaign, and students in another residence hall received a much less intensive intervention: a 120-page booklet containing information about alcohol-related laws and policies. The social norms approach included posters, stickers, bookmarks, and notepads containing normative messages (e.g., "Seventy-five percent of students drink 0, 1, 2, 3, or 4 drinks when they party"). The social norms intervention lasted 6 weeks. A total of 476 students were exposed to the social norms approach, and 486 to the informative booklet. Pre- and posttest surveys asked students about their perception of normative drinking on their campus and about their own drinking during the last 4 weeks. The surveys were completed anonymously. Students in the two residence halls were equivalent in terms of age and class standing. The outcomes? "[S]tudents exposed to the social marketing campaign reduced their misperceptions of drinking norms but drank *more frequently* at posttest than did their counterparts in the comparison group. The campaign had *no effect* on several other drinking indicators . . . the frequency of drinking *actually increased* significantly over time within the experimental group, while declining in the comparison group" (Clapp, Lange, Russell, Shillington, & Voas, 2003, pp. 413–414, emphases added). This was certainly an unexpected finding and, of course, very disappointing.

Evaluating Two Different Methods of MSW Instruction

The opportunity to use this design occurred one semester when I was with the University of Georgia School of Social Work. I was scheduled to teach a foundation research MSW class, and a colleague was also slated to teach a different section of the same course. I usually teach using a method of instruction that places heavy reliance on using structured study questions. I rarely prepared formal lectures, and I did not use midterm exams, final exams, or term papers. My colleague taught using a different structured pedagogical strategy, one called *learning with discussion*. We both had similar syllabi in terms of course description, objectives, and the same assigned textbook. We conducted a reliable and valid assessment of the students' abilities to critique published social work research (one of the common course objectives) at the beginning of the semester. We then taught our courses using our respective and preferred method of instruction. At the beginning and again at the end of the term, we administered a comparable, equivalent assessment of their critical research skills, assessments that were blindly graded, with the two independent graders not knowing which section the student assessment paper came from or if the assessment paper was prepared at the beginning or end of the term. We then broke the code for the students' grades and time of term (beginning or end), and tabulated the pre and post-course grades for each section. Both sections of students scored equivalently during the first assessment. At the end of the semester, my students had made statistically significant improvements, whereas my colleagues' students' grades had not changed much. These results could be interpreted to mean that my method of instruction is superior to the standardized approach that she used, and of course that was the slant I placed upon them when this study was published (Thyer, Jackson-White, Sutphen, & Carrillo, 1992)! (I hope that the concept of allegiance effects occurred to you while reading the previous sentence.) Of course, we also discussed some alternative interpretations of the data and limitations of the study. By having me and the other instructor not get involved in the scoring of the critical essays, by having the essay graders blind as to which section an essay they were grading came from, or even if it was an essay completed at the beginning versus the end of the semester, we tried to control for experimenter bias/allegiance effects. By using two independent graders, with neither grader knowing how the other grader scored an essay they were reading, and calculating interrater agreement (very high), we tried to control for testing effects. Regression to the mean was not applicable in this study, student attrition (mortality) was low and comparable between the two sections, and concurrent history was at least partially controlled for by conducting the pre- and postassessments at the beginning and end of the same semester for both sections of the class. Selection bias (e.g., maybe the smarter students gravitated to one instructor vs. the other) was partially controlled for by showing that, during the pretest, the students in both sections scored comparably poorly. So, all in all, we had a reasonably tightly controlled study, even without random assignment and a true experimental design. I hope the concept of low-hanging fruit occurred to you while reading the previous paragraph.

The Switching Replications Design

This design is used to strengthen the ability to make a causal inference by trying to demonstrate, not just once but twice, that clients receiving X got better. Look over the diagram below and see if you can figure out the inferential logic behind this design:

$$O_1 - X - O_2 - O_3$$

$$O_1 - O_2 - X - O_3$$

Two groups of clients are processed a bit differently. The top group is assessed, immediately enrolled in treatment/therapy/intervention, and assessed again. During this same time period, the bottom group is similarly assessed but *does not* get treatment right away. Some time passes, and then the bottom group is assessed a second time, after which they begin the same treatment as the clients in the top group received. After treatment is completed for the second group, they are assessed a third time, as is the top group, as a form of follow-up measure, to see if treatment gains (if any) have been maintained. Ideally, following the implementation of this design, you would like to see a data pattern something like this: Both groups were essentially similar at O_1. At O_2, the treated top group would demonstrate significant improvements, and the bottom untreated group would not have improved. Then, at O_3, the bottom group would have improved following receipt of treatment X to the degree seen in the top group at O_2, while the top group would be shown to have maintained their treatment gains. In effect, this design strives for a *replicated* effect, with not just one but two demonstrations that clients improve following treatment X. The term *switching replications* refers to the fact that the top group is switched with the condition received by the bottom group initially (that of no-treatment), while the bottom group is switched to the initial condition received by the top group (namely, treatment X). This approach is also known as a *delayed treatment design* or as a *lagged-groups design*.

In the world of causal inference, science typically views results that have been replicated as more credible that one-off effects, those documented with a single demonstration. The history of behavioral and social science (and the natural and medical sciences too, for that matter), contains many reports of marvelous discoveries reported in a single study, findings that, although marvelous, could not be replicated by others. It is this experience of being fooled, so to speak, that raises replicated findings above the hoi-polloi of effects observed but a single time.

This switching replications design was used in part by clinical social worker Betsy Vonk in her evaluation of the outcomes of counseling provided to students at Emory University in Atlanta, services provided via the university's Student Counseling Center where Betsy was employed. In the normal ebb and flow of the Center's operation, not all new clients could be enrolled in counseling right away. Some, due to a lack of counselors with an open slot, had to be placed on a waiting list. In due course, those on the waiting list were contacted and asked to make an appointment for a second assessment (a reliable and valid pencil-and-paper measure of psychological symptoms), after which they could begin counseling. All clients, when treatment was terminated, were asked to complete the outcome measure again. Thus, Betsy had access to a naturally occurring dataset that conformed to the parameters of the switching replications quasi-experiment. It is classified as a quasi-experiment because the clients were not deliberately or randomly assigned to either the immediate treatment condition or to the waiting list. It happened naturally. Had assignment to the two conditions been truly random, say, on the basis of a coin toss, then Betsy's study would rise to the level of a genuine experiment. Nevertheless, at the time when she published her report on this project (Vonk & Thyer, 1999), this quasi-experimental design represented the most methodologically advanced outcome study in the field of evaluating university student counseling programs available in the published literature.

Dismantling Studies

The purpose of a dismantling study is to try to determine the relative contribution of one or more individual components of a social work intervention that contains multiple elements. Typically, one group of clients receives the "complete package" and another group receives the complete package *minus one discrete element*. The logic is that if the two groups demonstrate equivalent results, the program element that was omitted is really not necessary to the entire package's success. Alternatively, if the group that received the entire program minus the one element displays an impaired outcome, the extent of the impairment reflects the additive value of the missing element. One way of diagramming this type of study is as follows:

$$O_1 - X \quad -O_2$$

$$O_1 - X_{-1} - O_2$$

wherein X represents the complete program and X_{-1} receipt of the program with one discrete element omitted.

An example of this type of quasi-experimental design is provided in Johnson and Stadel (2007), working in the field of hospital social work. The practice issue is getting patients (or their legal guardians) to provide what are called "health care proxies" prior to their receipt of elective orthopedic surgery. A health care proxy document designates someone who can make medical decisions on the patient's behalf in circumstances wherein the patient cannot make decisions about health care on their own (e.g., in a coma). At the hospital where this study was conducted, social workers introduced the option of executing a health care proxy by one of two methods. The complete package, so to speak, involved the social worker conducting a semi-structured face-to-face interview with patients who were scheduled for surgery and their families, informing them about the concept of a health care proxy *and* giving them written information and blank health care proxies to complete and return, if they so chose. Twenty-one patients received this complete package, labeled X. An additional 36 patients were provided information about health care proxies solely by means of the written materials, without the face-to-face interviews with the social worker. This latter group represented the comparison condition, the X_{-1} group. The outcome measure was the percent of patients in each group who actually executed and turned in to the hospital a health care proxy prior to their surgery. The results? Forty-three percent (9 of 21) of the patients receiving the social work interview *and* the information completed proxies, versus only 6% (2 of 36) of those who received the information alone. This quasi-experimental evidence certainly supports the hypothesis that the combined program is superior to the information-alone intervention; to the extent that hospitals wish patients to complete health care proxies, using social workers to conduct these additional face-to-face educational interviews is an effective approach, relative to providing information alone. This is good news for those who advocate for the valued-added nature of providing social work services in health care settings. But the good news is qualified in that these interviews could likely be undertaken by non-social workers as well (e.g., by physicians, nurses, or patient representatives) and by our awareness that the nonrandom assignment of patients to the complete package versus the partial one precludes an uncritical acceptance of the causal link between complete treatment and outcome. Still, it is a good study, taking advantage of naturally occurring differences in the interventions received by clients.

At this point, we can address the two final examples of important research questions that quasi-experimental designs can address in the evaluation of social work practice.

- Question 4. *What is the status of clients who have received a novel treatment compared to those who received the usual treatment or care?*
- Question 5. *What is the status of clients who have received a novel treatment compared to those who received a credible placebo treatment?*

These questions can be better answered using the designs presented in the latter part of this chapter, than by the earlier ones presented here and in Chapter 2. What is needed to answer Question 4 is a group of clients who received the usual treatment or care, and to answer Question 5, individuals who received a placebo treatment. It may go against the grain of social work to contemplate deliberately providing an intervention known to be a placebo, but such a refinement is really necessary to come to grips with the essential question "Is what we are doing better than nonspecific influences?" Social worker Margaret Blenkner (1962) addressed this by quoting Rosenthal and Frank (1956, p. 300), who observed:

[I]mprovement under a special form of psychotherapy cannot be taken as evidence for: a) correctness of the theory on which it is based; or

b) efficacy of the specific technique used, unless improvement can be shown to be greater or qualitatively different from that produced by the patient's faith in the efficacy of the therapist and his technique. . . . To show that a specific form of psychotherapy . . . produces results not attributable to the nonspecific placebo effect it is not sufficient to compare its results with changes in patients receiving no treatment. The only adequate control would be another form of therapy in which the patient had equal faith . . . but which would not be expected by the theory of therapy being studied to produce the same effect.

Blenkner (1962, p. 58) went on to grapple bluntly with this core issue for social workers:

Are we psychologically capable of entertaining the unpleasant idea that workers can be placebos, and that our precious mystique—the worker–client relationship—may be only the ubiquitous placebo effect? Are we willing to give up our . . . prejudices long enough to find out whether it is possible that regardless of theory, school, diagnosis, client symptoms, or worker conceptualizations, if a worker has enthusiasm and conviction about his way of helping, most clients will *feel* helped and some will even *be* helped? If we are willing to do this we may finally get to the really effective factors in technique and method and begin to justify our claims to having a science-based art. (1962, p. 58, emphases in original)

If a study is conducted that shows clients fare well after they received a novel social work intervention, and a later study shows that clients who received this intervention actually improved following treatment compared to pretreatment levels of functioning, this is a good thing and consistent with the idea that the intervention "works." If further quasi-experiments show that these gains are durable and that they compare favorably with clients who received TAU, this too is a good thing to know. But our enthusiasm for this remarkable new treatment should be tempered by the knowledge that these impressive results are also consistent with the hypothesis that both the novel treatment and the established treatments produce improvements solely via placebo influences. To truly show that the novel treatment works *better* than placebo, and better than TAU, it must be compared not only against TAU, but also against a credible placebo. This requires a placebo comparison group design, perhaps formatted something like:

Novel Treatment Group	$O_1 - X - O_2$
Treatment as Usual Group	$O_1 - Y - O_2$
Placebo Treatment Group	$O_1 - Z - O_2$
No-treatment Group	$O_1 \qquad O_2$

The no-treatment control group is needed to control for history effects, the passage of time, regression to the mean, and the like. Only if the novel treatment is statistically and clinically superior to no treatment, placebo treatment, *and* to treatment as usual can we have confidence that its effects are above and beyond those of existing care, placebo influences, and the passage of time alone. Some 50 years after Blenkner (1962) issued her challenge to the profession, such a well-designed placebo-controlled study has yet to be undertaken by the social work profession. Surely, it is time.

SUMMARY

This chapter has described in the abstract a series of progressively more elaborate and sophisticated quasi-experimental designs using variations on the theme of comparing novel treatment to no treatment, to comparison treatments, and to placebo treatments. The design's abstract features were followed by presenting a series of actual, published studies illustrating their use. By adding pretreatment assessments and perhaps repeated pretests and posttests—including lengthy follow-up periods— these designs can be markedly improved upon to the point that they are capable of providing legitimate contributions to the empirical knowledge base of the human services. In some cases, these designs represent the only practical method of community-based research in environments in which it is not possible to randomly assign clients to various conditions of treatment or no treatment. In these instances, properly controlled quasi-experiments represent the highest available form of evidence that can be used to answer important questions, and these studies can find publication outlets in some of the more prestigious journals in the human services.

4

Interrupted Time
Series Designs

Intervention research can be conducted using a variety of methodological approaches. Those studies involving large numbers of participants and analyzed (usually) with inferential statistics are known as nomothetic designs. These designs typically assess clients just a few times (e.g., pre- and posttreatment), maybe with an added follow-up period or two, under varying conditions. In other words, a large number of people are studied, but not very intensively. An alternative approach is variously called *single-system research designs, single-case research designs,* or *idiographic research.* This approach involves gathering data more intensively on a very small number of people, under varying conditions.

Both approaches are seen as viable methods to produce useful knowledge about the effects of social work interventions, but the scale is different. If a nomothetic study uses a sample of clients randomly selected from a larger population of interest, apart from the capacity to generate internally valid conclusions about the effects of treatment on your sample of clients, it may be legitimate to infer the effects of that same treatment if applied to other samples from the same population, or even perhaps to the population itself. However, very few social work intervention research studies are able to obtain truly random samples of clients. Most rely on *samples of convenience,* which means that the generalizability of most nomothetic findings is compromised. This is an important point—no matter the sample size, 10, 100, or 1,000—generalizability is not legitimate unless the sample was obtained using true methods of random selection. Thus, the major method by which generalizability is inferred is via *replication*, conducting similar studies to see if initial findings can be duplicated, then expanding the variety of clients, clinicians, and settings in which the initially promising intervention is applied.

In single-system research, instead of, say, studying 30 people with one or two assessments, one person is studied on 30 occasions, perhaps with 15 being prior to treatment (a baseline phase) and 15 after treatment (the intervention phase). With proper design elements (e.g., replications with several clients, systematically removing or introducing the same treatment) it may well be possible to develop genuine causal inferences about the effects of a given intervention for a particular client or small set of clients. However, external validity is also very limited as one's "sample" of clients is typically very small and not representative (in a statistical sense) of all clients with a given condition or problem. Hence, one tries to generalize the results from initially promising single-system designs via the same technique used in nomothetic studies; namely, replications. Most social work research textbooks now contain chapters on the methodology of single-system designs (Thyer, 2010a; Thyer & Myers, 2007; Rubin & Babbie, 2008; Yegidis, Weinbach, & Myers, 2011), reflective of the acceptance of this approach since its introduction to the field of social work in the mid-1960s.

The designs featured in the present chapter reflect a hybrid form of intervention research strategy, one using the large numbers characteristic of nomothetic studies while also incorporating the large numbers of repeated assessments associated with idiographic research methods with very small numbers of clients. These designs can be quite strong, although most examples are classified as quasi-experiments since clients are not randomly assigned to varying groups or conditions. Collectively, these are labeled *interrupted time series designs*, and are very often used to evaluate large-scale social welfare policies, as well as individual program outcomes.

THE INTERRUPTED TIME SERIES DESIGN

With the interrupted time series (ITS) design, the inferential logic is relatively simple. An outcome measure assessing some variable of interest is repeatedly measured a number of times prior to the initiation of an intervention, X. Then, after X is implemented or has occurred, assessments of the outcome measure are continued. This design can be diagrammed as follows:

$$O_1 - O_2 - O_3 - O_k - X - O_{k+1} - O_{k+2} - O_{k+3} - O_{k+?}$$

with O_k referring to the total number of pretreatment assessments undertaken and $O_{k+?}$ being the final number of separate observations taken *after* the implementation of intervention X. The series of measurements taken prior to intervention is sometimes called a *baseline,* although this term is more appropriately used to refer to single-system research designs. These preintervention assessments provide us with a means of either intuitively or statistically projecting the level and slope of posttreatment measures, assuming that X did not happen. To the extent that posttreatment observations deviate from those "predicted," so to speak, on the basis of the baseline measures, we may be able to infer an actual effect from X. In single-system research, this logical inference is usually made on the basis of visually inspecting the data. However, in the ITS design, inference is usually augmented through the use of specialized inferential statistics, with one of the more common tests being called *time series analysis,* or TSA. Do not confuse TSA with time series designs; TSA is a method of statistically testing for changes in data patterns pre- and post-intervention, within the context of analyzing the outcomes of a time series design.

The most common method of TSA is known as the *univariate Box-Jenkins interrupted autoregressive integrated moving average* (ARIMA) analysis, which compares the values of some variable before the introduction of an intervention versus after that intervention. ARIMA takes into account the slope, not the just the average, of the values found in a series, and corrects for a mathematical problem known as *autocorrelation* (or *serial dependency*), wherein the value of a variable at one point in time can be used to predict the values of other variables in the series. The presence of significant autocorrelation within the time series data violates a major assumption of many parametric statistical tests; namely, that the data are independent. For example, the scores of a group of unrelated people who complete the Beck Depression Inventory (BDI) are likely not dependent— knowing one person's scores does not help predict how someone else in that group will have scored. However, if someone completes the BDI on a weekly basis for many months, knowing their score on a given date *may* help in predicting their nearby scores in the series. This violates the important property of a lack of serial dependency and thus compromises the test to some extent. Similarly, weekly or monthly state-level data (say, numbers of clients receiving food stamps) violate the assumption of independence. Knowing the numbers for one month *does* help predict scores on subsequent months. ARIMA approaches compensate for this, something that simply using a t-test or analysis of variance (ANOVA) may not do, when used to examine average changes across phases (see McDowall, McCleary, Meidinger, & Hay, 1980).

A recently proposed alternative method of inferential analysis for interrupted TSA is known as *latent growth curve modeling* (Duncan & Duncan, 2004a, b), which has the advantage of being applicable with fewer than the minimum of 50 data points recommended for use with the Box-Jenkins approach to TSA. However, this newer method does not yet seem to have been applied by social work researchers using time series designs.

When using visual analysis to attempt to make inferences, one can look for:

- Changes following the introduction of the intervention, in terms of absolute magnitude (do the data obviously change up or down right away?)
- The slope of the graphed data (a steeper slope indicates a greater rate of change, which can be important)
- The direction of the data (do the data reverse the direction taken in the baseline? That is, change from rising to falling, or vice versa)
- Does the amount of variability in the data increase or decrease following the implementation of the intervention?

Visually obvious changes in one or any combination of these potential patterns are a pretty good indication that *something* is different. This is a conservative test; thus, if you cannot simply see it, the real effect of the intervention, if any, is probably weak and not practically important. Using inferential statistics enables one to more reliability detect small changes that are not visually obvious, so researchers end up learning more about weak interventions.

Cook and Shadish (1994, p. 562) describe these types of designs as follows:

> In interrupted time series, the same outcome variable is examined over many time points. If the cause–effect link is quick acting or has a known causal delay, then an effective treatment should lead to change in the level, slope or variance of the time series at the point where treatment occurred. The test, then, is whether the obtained data show the change in the series at the prespecified point. . . . Internal validity is the major problem, especially because of history (e.g., some other outcome-causing event occurring at the same time as the treatment) and instrumentation (e.g., a change of record keeping occurring with the treatment).

Time series designs like this are not infrequently used in the investigation of psychosocial interventions provided to various groups of clients, but they are more often employed in the analysis of possible changes induced by social policy and in the field of community-wide interventions (Biglan, Ary, & Waagenaar, 2000). Their use within social work has been reviewed by Tripodi and Harrington (1979), DiNitto (1983), DiNitto, McDaniel, Ruefli, and Thomas (1986), and Bowen and Farkas (1991). These designs can be very powerful in terms of internal validity. "Although considered quasi-experimental, the ITS design has been noted as representing one of the strongest alternatives to the randomized experiment" (Duncan & Duncan, 2004a, p. 271). The following paragraphs describe some specific examples of using ITS designs as a quasi-experimental approach to evaluating social interventions.

A hypothetical example of a simple ITS design is presented in Figure 4.1. The 15 or so preintervention data points are relatively stable, and after the intervention is introduced, there is an abrupt discontinuity in the data, which is maintained over the next 15 or so data points. The more resistant to change the data could be projected to be, based on prior research or good theory, the stronger the inferences that can be made that change really did occur and that this change was due to the intervention. For example, HIV-related deaths would be a more difficult outcome to change than say, teenage attitudes toward Brittney Spears.

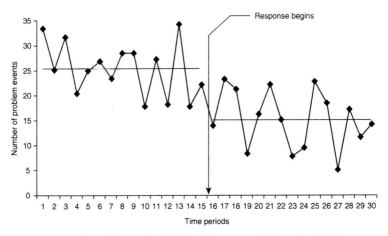

Figure 4.1. Hypothetical Example of a Simple Interrupted Time Series Design.

Server Intervention to Reduce Alcohol-related Traffic Accidence

In 1986, Oregon introduced legislation requiring specialized training for all alcohol servers (bartenders, waiters, waitresses, etc.), teaching them to recognize intoxication, how to politely stop serving intoxicated patrons, and how to encourage a customer to call a taxi, use designated drivers, etc. The intent was to reduce alcohol-related traffic accidents. By the end of 1989, when most servers had been so trained, the state found statistically significant reductions in single-vehicle nighttime traffic crashes (those with the highest percentage of alcohol involvement), which was interpreted as support for the effectiveness of this piece of social legislation (see Holder & Wagenaar, 1994).

Controversial Studies Using Time Series Analysis

Alcohol not to your taste? How about evaluating changes in laws pertaining to reporting and sentencing sexual assault? If that is of interest to you, read Schissel's (1996) TSA of such laws. Want to read something really controversial? Check out Berk, Sorenson, Wiebe, and Upchurch's study (2003); they used ITS designs to evaluate the presumptive effects of more liberalized abortion laws on homicides among young people aged 15–24 years old. Their conclusion? "We conclude that the 1990s decline in the homicide of young men is statistically associated with the legalization of abortion" (Berk et al., 2003, p. 45). These authors may be right, inferring that the decline in the numbers of people born is related to increased availability of abortion, which caused a reduction of the size of a more criminally prone age cohort. But they really can't be sure, due to the possibility of other explanations accounting for the decrease in crime. Still, the use of an ITS design is a great way to provide for initial tests of hypotheses, no matter how provocative.

Does Raising the Legal Drinking Age Reduce Teenage Traffic Accidents?

What happens when states raise or lower the minimum drinking age, in terms of alcohol-related traffic accidents among young drivers? This question lends itself very nicely to the ITS design since states already gather such accident data, and it is relatively easy to determine when the independent variable (enforcement of the new law) goes into effect. Not surprisingly, raising the minimum drinking age is clearly followed by a reduction in alcohol-related traffic accidents among young drivers (Wagenaar & Toomey, 2002). Although such a conclusion would seem both logical and self-evident, many well-intended social policies have unintended consequences, some of which are harmful, and it is always valuable to obtain actual *post-policy data* to confirm or disconfirm the anticipated effects of new policies and laws.

Does Banning Smoking in Public Buildings Reduce Psychiatric Emergency Room Visits?

Kurdyak, Cairney, Sarnocinska-Hart, Callahan, and Strike (2008) wished to evaluate the possible effects of a smoking cessation policy on visits to psychiatric emergency rooms, initially at one center in Toronto, and then when the smoking ban was implemented province-wide. Psychiatric emergency room visits at a specific hospital in Toronto were recorded from March 1, 2002 to December 31, 2006. On September 21, 2005, the specific hospital imposed a smoking ban (e.g., no smoking was allowed in or near the hospital buildings), and on May 31, 2006, the ban was imposed across the entire province for all public buildings. In a nutshell, the hospital-specific ban on smoking had no effect on psychiatric ER visits at that particular hospital, but when the smoking ban was extended province-wide to all public buildings, ER visits by individuals with a psychotic disorder dropped by over 15%. Rates of smoking are very high among individuals with a psychotic disorder, and the authors expressed the concern that this reduction might increase adverse psychiatric events (attempts at self-harm, suicide, etc.). In the authors' words: "Our findings suggest that if a smoking cessation policy is implemented in a psychiatric emergency department setting consideration must be given as to whether this will disadvantage some patient groups or populations. The smoking cessation policy may act as a barrier to crisis services in people with psychotic disorders" (Kurdyak et al., 2008, p. 782).

Do Sex Offender Registration and Community Notification Laws Reduce Sex Crimes?

Few offenses evoke as much outrage as do sex crimes. As a result, many jurisdictions have enacted mandatory registration and community notification policies for sex offenders. Sex offenders released from prison must notify law enforcement officials as to their place of residence, and law enforcement must in turn notify the community as to where registered sex offenders reside. These laws are intended to help prevent the reoccurrence of sex crimes by past offenders. Do they? Sandler, Freeman, and Socia (2008) examined this hypothesis by obtaining the criminal history files of every offender arrested for a registrable sex offense in New York state between 1986 and 2006. This involved over 160,000 different individuals and over 170,000 sex offense-related arrests. In January 1996, the state of New York enacted a Sex Offender Registration Act (SORA) requiring registration and community notification related to sex offenders, with this law serving as the study's independent variable or intervention. There were about 10 years of data available before the law was passed, and about 11 years after the enactment of the New York state SORA. A number of crime statistics were recorded, including registrable sex offenses (e.g., rape, incest, sodomy, child molestation, etc.) assessed individually by type of crime and the totals. Arrests were separated according to whether they involved a registered sex offender or an individual not previously convicted of a sex crime. The authors found no positive effect for the SORA—there were no significant effects on total sexual offending, rape, or child molestation. "This finding casts doubts upon the ability of sex offender registration and notification laws, as well as residency and occupational restriction laws, to actually reduce sexual offending" (Sandler et al., 2008, p. 297). Although disappointing, it is still good to know whether certain laws are working as intended. Considerable resources go into implementing SORA laws, resources that could perhaps be diverted to more effective law enforcement policies related to public safety and sex offenses.

The above designs are not usually sufficient to completely rule out rival hypotheses, perhaps those arising from the threats of concurrent history, the passage of time, general changes in the population of interest, and the like. Quite simply, something apart from the introduction of X may have occurred at about the same time as X was implemented, and it could be this other "something" that produced any observed changes. One way to attempt to control for such threats is found in the next design.

THE INTERRUPTED TIME SERIES DESIGN WITH A REMOVAL PHASE

This design uses inferential logic similar to that found in the switching replications design discussed earlier. Some outcome measure is repeatedly assessed, then an intervention, X, is introduced. Assessments are conducted in the same manner after X is in effect, for a given period of time, then X is *removed* and assessments continue as before. If X is truly effective, when it is introduced, there should be a change in the outcome measures. If X is genuinely responsible for any improvements (or perhaps deterioration), and X is subsequently removed, then the post-(not X) condition's data should reflect a change in the data so that the data revert to the level, slope, and variability seen during the first baseline phase, prior to the introduction of X. This design can be diagrammed as follows:

$$O_1 - O_2 - O_k - X - O_{k+1} - O_{k+2} - O_{k+n} - (\text{not X}) - O_{k+n+1} - O_{k+n+2} - O_{k+n+p}$$

Here, k refers to the final measurement taken during the first baselines, $k+n$ the final measurement taken when X is in effect, and $k+n+p$ the final measurement taken after X was withdrawn. If a sufficient number of data points are gathered for each phase of this design, the outcome measures are reliable and valid, and the effects of X are prospectively predicted to be temporary, then this is a very powerful design indeed, especially when the unit of analysis is something large, like a county, state, or nation. It is much more difficult to change large systems (think of the Titanic) than very small ones, so if effects such as those described above are observed, the internal validity of such a study is likely high, since rival explanations are pretty implausible (e.g., history, regression, maturation). Even placebo influences are unlikely when assessing large-scale systems, since placebo factors generally occur at the level of the individual. Phenomena such as mass hysteria do occur and cannot be discounted—witness the so-called "Obama effect" following President Obama's election on the generally increased level of optimism observed in the United States, even before he had undertaken any meaningful initiatives. One unpublished study found that a white-black achievement gap on a GRE-like test all but disappeared following Barak Obama's election (see Dillon, 2009). However, such powerful placebo-like influences are rarely impactful on large-scale systems, and by using this ITS design with a removal phase, placebo-like factors can usually be dismissed.

THE INTERRUPTED TIME SERIES DESIGN WITH AN EXTENDED INTERVENTION PHASE

Most of the discussion on the ITD design has assumed that the intervention is a one-time event, with potentially lingering influences. Sometimes the intervention is best construed as being applied repeatedly over a period of time, and, prospectively, perhaps being predicted to lose any influence once the intervention is discontinued. Such was the situation found in Chu, Frongillow, Jones, and Kaye (2009), in the area of improving the dietary selection of students eating at university food service operations. The study was conducted at Ohio State University's dining center for students. For 14 days pre-intervention, the researchers posted simple descriptions of each day's 12 hot entrées on the menu board and monitored which meals were chosen by the students, unobtrusively taking into account the nutritional values of each entrée (e.g., total energy, serving size, fat, protein, and carbohydrates). Then, for 14 days, the same descriptions of each entrée were posted, *along with* each entrée's nutritional information. The students' entrée selections continued to be monitored unobtrusively. In the last phase, lasting 13 days, the nutritional information was removed from the description of the entrées, leaving the students with the same information as during the first phase of the study. This study could be diagrammed as:

$$O_1 \ldots O_{14} - X_{15} \ldots X_{28} - O_{29} \ldots O_{41}$$

with 14 days of data pre-intervention (the initial baseline phase), followed by 14 days of the intervention, followed by 13 days of the baseline condition. The results?

> We observed an immediate drop in the energy content of patrons' entrée selections from the first day of posting nutrition labels for entrées at the dining center; this drop was maintained throughout the treatment period. When nutritional labels were removed, patrons reverted to selecting entrées with higher energy content relatively soon. These changes occurred without negative impact on overall sales and revenue for the dining center. (Chu et al., 2009, p. 2002)

The authors pointed to the many strengths of their study. Data were collected electronically via point-of-sale machines, so instrumentation bias was controlled for. The reversion to initial baseline patterns when the intervention was removed argues for the beneficial and causal effect of posting the nutritional information, the intervention was inexpensive to implement, and it did not reduce food service revenue. They linked their study to America's obesity epidemic and the possible value of laws mandating the posting of nutritional information on franchise restaurant menus. There appeared to be a clear functional relationship between posting nutritional information and students' choosing lower caloric value entrées. This has obvious public health implications. Whether the nutritional information would continue to exert a positive influence over a longer period of time remains open to question. It is possible that patrons would habituate to them, and the signs would have less effect on their behavior.

Researchers in North Carolina implemented a program intended to encourage low-income, older (40+ years) minority women to obtain

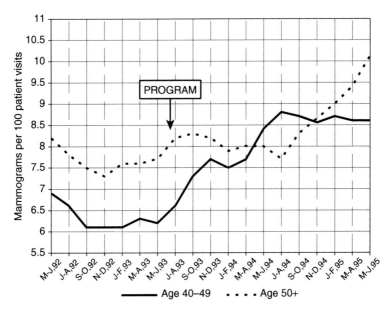

Figure 4.2. Mammograms Per 100 Patient Visit; 12 Month Moving Averages.
Source: Figure reproduced from Michielutte, Shelton, Parskett, Tatum, and Velez (2000, p. 619), with the permission of the publisher.

mammograms. A pretreatment phase looked at the numbers of mammograms obtained per 100 patient visits over about a 1-year period at a given facility, followed by about 2 years' worth of data following the introduction of a deliberate program designed to encourage mammograms. The data are depicted in Figure 4.2 and clearly show, visually, that mammograms increased after the program was implemented (see Michielutte, Shelton, Paskett, Tatum &, Velez, 2000, for a full report of this project).

THE REPLICATED INTERRUPTED TIMES SERIES DESIGN

Our confidence in the conclusions drawn from any individual study are enhanced if the effects, positive or negative, can be replicated. With ITS designs, it is sometimes possible to examine the effects of an intervention applied concurrently to two or more systems (e.g., counties, states), as in the instance when a statewide (with counties) or national (with states) policy initiative is introduced. Finding out that, following some policy becoming law, positive effects were observed in one state, such as Florida, is a good thing to know. However, Florida may be an idiosyncratic state, and the effects observed in Florida may not apply to other states. When measuring across two or more systems, when an intervention is applied to all these systems at the same time, if you observe congruent effects in both systems following the introduction of X, the confidence you have that X induced these changes is enhanced. One replication is good, two is even better, and so forth. This design may be diagrammed as:

$$\text{State A }\ O_1 - O_2 - O_3 - O_k - X - O_{k+1} - O_{k+2} - O_{k+3} - O_{k+?}$$

$$\text{State B }\ O_1 - O_2 - O_3 - O_k - X - O_{k+1} - O_{k+2} - O_{k+3} - O_{k+?}$$

Here, states A and B are measured similarly over the same time period, and intervention X (e.g., a national policy?) is introduced in both states at the same time. If both states change in similar ways following X, then we have more confidence that X caused these changes than if we tested for the effects in one state only.

This type of ITS design was used by Palmgreen, Lorch, Stephenson, Hoyle, and Donohew (2007) to evaluate the effects of the National Youth Antidrug Media Campaign (based on radio and television public service announcements), a 5-year, $1 billion initiative of the federal government to prevent and reduce drug abuse among youth. The authors obtained interview-based data on anonymously self-reported recent marijuana use among adolescents in Lexington, Kentucky, and in Knoxville, Tennessee, monthly for 42 months before the start of this new federal campaign and for 6 months after it began. In both cities, reported marijuana use significantly declined, leading the authors to conclude that the media campaign was effective and causally responsible for these decreases. In the authors' own words "We used data from a 48-month, independent sample interrupted time series project (one which tests trends before and after an intervention). . . . The interrupted time series design is one of the strongest quasi-experimental designs for inferring causal effects of an intervention" (Palmgreen et al., 2007, p. 1645).

THE REPLICATED TIME SERIES DESIGN WITH A LAGGED INTERVENTION GROUP

Another way to enhance the internal validity of an ITS is by assessing some outcome measure in two or more large-scale systems, introducing X into one system (e.g., State A) only, and seeing if hypothesized changes occur. However, X is *not* introduced into the other system(s) (e.g., State B), although these other systems continue to be monitored. If A changes and B does not, our confidence that X induced the observed changes in A is enhanced. If the same intervention X is subsequently introduced into State B, which was heretofore unchanged, and *then* State B changes in a manner similar to that observed previously in State A, then our confidence is greatly enhanced that X is causally responsible for the observed changes. This design can be diagrammed as follows:

$$\text{State A } O_1 - O_2 - O_3 - O_k - X - O_{k+1} - O_{k+2} - O_{k+3} - O_{k+?}$$

$$\text{State B } O_1 - O_2 - O_3 - O_4 - O_5 - O_6 - O_k - X - O_{k+1} - O_{k+2} - O_{k+3} - O_{k+?}$$

It is good for State B's baseline to be a good bit longer than that of State A, but there are no hard and fast rules involved as to how much longer. Sometimes data may be collected daily, weekly, monthly, or even annually. The only principle is that the additional length of time should be of sufficient duration to provide a fair appraisal as to whether or not State B's data remained stable, even after X was introduced into State A. It is not necessary that the postintervention data collection period between States A and B be identical in length, only that the available number of data points permits legitimate inferences.

THE INTERRUPTED TIME SERIES DESIGN WITH A NO-TREATMENT CONTROL GROUP

This design is an improvement over the first ITS study design described earlier is this chapter, and it improves upon this prior approach through incorporating a no-treatment control series. A sequence of observations are made of some outcome measure. Then an intervention, X, is introduced, and the series of observations are continued. As an added refinement however, a comparison group is similarly assessed during the same time period, but this second group is *not* exposed to X. This design can be diagrammed as below:

$$O_1 - O_2 - O_3 - O_k - X - O_{k+1} - O_{k+2} - O_{k+3} - O_{k+n}$$

$$O_1 - O_2 - O_3 - O_k \qquad O_{k+1} - O_{k+2} - O_{k+3} - O_{k+n}$$

The exact number of pretest observations is noted as k, simply to indicate that this number can vary from study to study, and the final number of posttest observations, $k + n$, is also open. Again, note that k and $k + n$ do not have to be the same number of observations pre- and posttreatment, but it is helpful if they are the same, in terms of inferential symmetry and treatment by statistical tests. Helpful, but not essential.

This design can be used in, say, the investigation of state policies that are implemented in one state but not in another. Some outcome measure can be tracked over similar time periods in both states, then a law or policy change is introduced into the group depicted at the top of the diagram. However, the law or policy is *not* put into effect in the bottom state. The logic is that if changes are observed post-X in the top state, but not in the bottom, the inference is strengthened that it is the law or policy that was responsible for this change.

Community Response to a Racist Murder

On June 6, 1998, James Byrd, Jr., a 49-year-old African American, was walking home after attending a family event. Three white men offered him a ride but the cloaked gesture became apparent as they assaulted, savagely beat, and chained him to their pick-up truck, eventually dragging him to his death. The trauma besetting the community grew intense in the days after the murder, as the severity of the crime quickly ignited a political, social, and media storm that gripped Jasper. (Wicke & Silver, 2009, p. 234)

This murder in Jasper, Texas, rocked the community, with virtual unanimity among the local population regarding its heinousness. Wicke and

Silver (2009) examined the community-level response to this social trauma using an ITS design with a control condition—a similar community in which the murder did not occur. Through theory and prior literature, the writers hypothesized that there would be several reactions to the murder in the areas of economic, criminal, and social indicators; specifically enhanced levels of cohesiveness and altruism; and a crumbling of racial and class barriers. Archival data were taken from public records and other reliable sources of information during the years 1995–2003, with 42 observation points prior to the murder of James Byrd, Jr. and for 66 months after. The control community, Center, Texas, was similar in terms of size, racial and ethnic composition, geography, and economics. Graphs were prepared for various outcome measures within the two communities, before and after the murder, to see if Jasper's data changed in ways following the murder not evidenced in Center. One such measure was the rate of violent crime in the two communities, and these data are presented in Figure 4.3. Apart from visual inferences, the authors used a statistical test called an *ordinary least squares regression* to see if the level and slope of the data lines changed, pre- versus posttest, and between the two communities. Violent crime did not significantly increase in the two communities during the 12 months prior to the murder in Jasper, but it did significantly

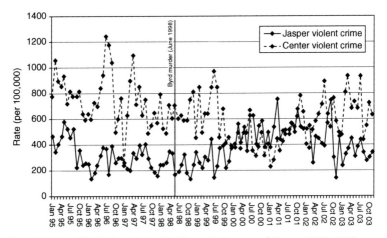

Figure 4.3. Monthly Violent Crime Incidents in Jasper and Center 1995–2003.
Source: Figure reproduced from Wicke and Silver (2009, p. 238), with permission.

increase after the first 12 months post-murder. The authors attempted to explain this rise by linking their data to prior research (e.g., Raphael, 1986) on how communities respond to disasters: initially with an altruistic response, followed by a "second disaster" as the first cohesive reactions dissipate (the community rallies together) and the original existing divisive forces among segments within the town reinstate themselves. Here, the delayed reaction (an increase in violent crime) was predicted in advance of its observed effect, which is actually more satisfactory than changes observed immediately postintervention (in this instance, the murder).

The authors' overall conclusions:

> [O]ur analysis identified several "negative" changes in Jasper in the months and years following the murder. The divorce rate increased and the housing market (as measured by the numbers of houses sold) softened; both are negative indicators of community well-being. Jasper also experienced an increase in violent crime and in its jail population. While the results seem to indicate that Jasper changed for the worse after the Byrd murder, the larger picture presented by the data suggests a remarkable degree of resilience. . . . (Wicke & Silver, 2009, p. 244)

Do Longer Bar Hours Cause More Traffic Accidents?

In 1996, the provincial government on Ontario passed a law extending the hours during which bars could remain open from 1 a.m. until 2 a.m. Vingilis et al. (2006) examined alcohol-related motor vehicle casualties and fatalities for the 4-year period prior to the passage of this Ontario law and for 3 years afterward. They compared data trends in Windsor, Ontario, with those obtained from Detroit, Michigan, located just across the river from Windsor, with easy bridge and tunnel connections between the two cities. In Windsor (with a legal drinking age of 19), a significant increase in motor vehicle-related casualties was found following the extended drinking hours. Detroit (with a legal drinking age of 21) found a decrease. No similar trends were found for other areas of Ontario or Michigan. Also, accidents in Windsor involving automobiles with Michigan license plates increased, but there were no differences in Ontario-licensed automobile accidents occurring in Detroit. The overall pattern of the data indicated that Detroit drinkers were driving to

Windsor to take advantage of the extended drinking hours in bars, as well as the younger drinking age, and that this was increasing accidents in Windsor and actually decreasing them in Detroit.

Do Mandatory Drivers' License Suspensions Reduce Drunk Driving?

This method of analysis was employed by Wagenaar and Maldonaldo-Molina (2007) to investigate the effects of suspending the drivers' licenses of drivers involved in alcohol-related crashes. Such social policies have been put into effect in 48 states, and they are intended as a deterrence policy: Don't drink and drive; if you do, you *will* lose your license. These suspension policies have been put into place in various states at various times, and this staggered pattern of implementation lent itself very nicely to using the ITS design with a no-treatment control group. These authors found that these policies do work; they are followed by statistically significant and important reductions in alcohol-related crash involvement, estimated to save about 800 lives per year in the United States. Moreover, the authors were able to show statistically that the rapidity of the punishment (time from arrest to trial and sentencing) was more of a deterrent than the severity of the post-conviction sentences.

The same approach was used by Wagenaar, Maldonaldo-Molina, Erickson, Ma, Tobler, and Komro (2007) to examine the effects of DUI fines and jail penalties on single-vehicle nighttime crash involvements, and by Seekins et al. (1988) to see if legislation requiring the use of child safety seats improved child safety when riding in automobiles.

STRENGTHENING THE TIME SERIES DESIGN

The usual suspects are involved in efforts to strengthen the internal validity of a time series design. Choose outcome measures of well-established reliability and validity. Try to ensure that the intervention was really delivered as intended and that the target group truly came into contact with it. Phases containing larger numbers of data points are more credible than those containing fewer. *Prospectively planned* ITS designs have more scientific legitimacy than do *retrospectively conducted* ones. With the former, one can develop predictive hypotheses in advance of knowing the outcomes. Such predictions are inherently "riskier" than those developed after the fact, perhaps after an examination of the data. In the latter case, such studies may be little more than a "fishing expedition." Cook and Shadish (1994, p. 562) emphasize the following:

> Plausible threats are best ruled out by using additional time series. Especially important are (a) control group time series not expected to show the hypothesized discontinuity in level, slope, or variability of an outcome; and (b) additional treatment series to which the same treatment is applied at different times so we expect the obtained data to recreate the known differences in when the treatment was made available.

Most of the ITS designs described in this chapter include variations of the above elements to strengthen our confidence that any observed changes can be legitimately attributable to the intervention. This is admittedly an inexact science in that we strive to eliminate *plausible* rival explanations, not possible but wildly implausible ones.

SUMMARY

Interrupted time series designs are widely used in the quasi-experimental appraisal of the effects of social welfare, health, and public policy interventions. They particularly lend themselves to the analysis of archival data typically maintained by city, county, and state governments, as well as data gathered at the federal level. The simpler of the ITS designs are capable of providing answers to very simple questions, whereas the more complex and controlled designs may possess sufficiently high internal validity to justify (cautious) causal inferences about the effects of interventions.

5

Evaluating and Reporting
Quasi-Experimental Studies

This concluding chapter will touch on a number of additional elements to be considered in evaluating and undertaking quasi-experimental research designs used in the evaluation of social work practice. Included will be a discussion of ways in which the data resulting from such studies may be presented and analyzed, including descriptive and inferential statistics; the interpretation of negative outcomes; contemporary editorial standards that are increasingly being used by journals to help authors structure manuscripts reporting quasi-experimental studies; and an overview of ethical principles that must be followed in the conduct of these designs.

EVALUATING THE QUALITY OF QUASI-EXPERIMENTAL STUDIES

A wide variety of published tools are available to assess the quality and susceptibility to bias in quasi-experimental studies, with one recent review locating 53 checklists and 33 scales (Sanderson, Tatt, & Higgins, 2007). Thyer (1991) presented one checklist specific to social work for use by authors in evaluating and preparing research studies, and this is reproduced in Table 5.1. Most of the guidelines contained in Table 5.1

Table 5.1 Guidelines for Assessing the Adequacy of Reports on Research

Introduction

1. Does the report appropriately cite earlier, relevant studies drawn from the social work and other disciplinary literature?

2. Does the introduction conclude with one or more explicitly stated testable hypotheses?

Methods

Clients

1. Is a clear, potentially replicable description provided of the sampling procedure used to recruit clients for the study?

2. Are salient characteristics (demographic, clinical, diagnostic, etc.) of the sample of clients described in detail to permit comparisons of this sample with those used in prior (and future) studies?

3. Is a description provided of the nature of the informed consent process used to obtain client agreement to participate in the study?

Outcome Measures

1. Did the outcome measures employed in the study possess acceptable levels of reliability and validity?

2. Were the outcome measures *clearly* pertinent to the target problem?

3. Did the outcome measures possess treatment validity?

Intervention

1. Is the intervention program (treatment) described in sufficient detail to permit replication? If not, does the author provide a source to obtain a treatment manual or more explicit description of the intervention?

2. Were measures taken to assess practitioner compliance with intended interventions? If so, were the interventions carried out as intended?

3. If blind conditions were imposed on clients or practitioners (or both), were measures taken to assess the integrity of the blind nature of the study participants?

Research Design

1. Do the authors provide a clear description of the research design employed?

2. If the clients were assigned to various conditions, is the nature of this assignment process described in sufficient detail to permit replication?

(Continued)

Table 5.1 (Continued)

3. Are pretreatment measures taken of the clients' problems, strengths, or situation? If so, were the groups of clients assigned to differing experimental conditions roughly equivalent to each other pretreatment?

Results

1. Are the results obtained from the various outcome measures consistent with one another? Is the pattern of improvement (or deterioration) clear across all outcome measures?

2. Are the results presented in the form of graphs or tables? If so, are the data comprehensible without recourse to the narrative text?

3. If the results are presented in the form of descriptive statistics, is each mean accompanied by a standard deviation?

4. If inferential statistics are employed, are the data shown to meet the assumptions the tests are based upon (e.g., normal distribution, similar standard deviations, no significant autocorrelation, etc., in the case of parametric tests)?

5. If correlational measures are employed, are the N, correlation coefficient, and alpha level reported for each such analysis?

6. If a *t*-test or analysis of variance is used, does the report of each such test contains the degrees of freedom, actual *t* or F value, and alpha level?

7. If a statistically significant difference is found, is it accompanied by an appropriate effect size?

8. If multiple inferential statistical tests are performed, are the alpha levels appropriately adjusted to account for the numbers of such tests?

9. Apart from statistically significant changes and effect sizes, is the *clinical* significance of any improvements discussed?

Discussion

1. Does the author clearly address alternative explanations (e.g., threats to internal validity) for the results, apart from the hypotheses that were tested?

2. Does the author report only conclusions supported by the data? Are speculations clearly described as such, rather than as facts?

3. Are suggestions to improve future research in this area described?

4. Are clear *applications* to practice derived from this study described, with special reference made to the unique aspects of *social work* practice?

Note: Adapted Thyer, B. A. (1991). Guidelines for evaluating outcome studies on social work practice. *Research on Social Work Practice, 1,* 88–89. Copyright 1991 by Sage Publications, Inc.

will be familiar to the reader, as they have been addressed earlier in the present volume. The rationale for each suggestion should seem evident, and this listing remains pertinent some two decades later.

Holosko (2006, pp., 452–453) also provides a checklist for use by authors who are preparing an article manuscript for submission to the journal *Research on Social Work Practice*, a portion of which is reproduced here:

Method
A. Sample
   - Are the techniques used in the sample selection process specified?
   - Is the time frame for sampling specified?
   - If there are other unique features of the sample, are they mentioned?
B. Design
   - Is the type of study design mentioned?
   - Is the time frame to complete the study mentioned?
C. Data Collection
   - Do you specify where and how data were collected?
   - Do you mention the ethical considerations of data collection, including whether institutional review board (IRB) approval was obtained or why it was not necessary?
D. Outcome Measures
   - Are all outcome measures used in the study specified and referenced, as appropriate?
   - Do you comment on the reliability and/or validity of the outcome measures?
E. Intervention
   - Is the intervention described in sufficient detail to permit replication, or are citations provided to primary sources fully describing the intervention?

Results
A. Statistics
   - Are all statistics used to analyze the data mentioned?
   - Do all inferential tests include levels of significance and/ or are effects sizes or proportions of variance accounted for (if appropriate)

These questions are intended to be answered in a yes or no manner, with authors asked to go back and address any issue that is not responded to in the affirmative. Making sure that all of this information is included in any research write-up of the results of a quasi-experimental study will go far toward ensuring some consistency in reporting the essential information needed to properly understand and appraise a given investigation.

Additional guidelines regarding the preparation of social work articles can be found in Thyer (2002, 2008), Schilling et al. (2005) and in Holden et al. (2008). However, for practical purposes, contemporary social work researchers contemplating designing, writing up, and attempting to publish a quasi-experiment can focus on only two major sets of criteria, the STROBE statement and the Journal Article Reporting Standards produced by the American Psychological Association (APA).

THE STROBE STATEMENT

STROBE stands for *Strengthening the Reporting of Observational Studies in Epidemiology.* "The STROBE statement was developed to assist authors when writing up analytical observational studies, to support editors and reviewers when considering such (quasi-experimental) articles for publication, and to help readers when critically appraising published articles" (von Elm et al., 2007, p. 801). In the general field of health care, the term "observational study" is often used in lieu of quasi-experimental study, but the logic remains the same when it comes to evaluating interventions. Observational studies are construed as having several methods, one of which is known as the *cohort study.* Here is how one text describes these designs:

> A cohort study follows a group of people from one point in time to another and observes changes that occur during that period. The study can be retrospective . . . or prospective. . . . Cohort studies may use routine data or data specially collected for the purpose of the study, or both. . . . A cohort study is one in which subjects who . . . receive a particular treatment are followed over time. They may be compared with another group . . . without treatment. . . . Cohort studies can be very powerful. . . . This type of research is useful for studying: the outcome of treatment where a randomized controlled trial is impossible . . .

different approaches to service delivery and management when these cannot be tested by a randomized controlled trial. . . . In addition, cohort studies are also a useful means of studying "natural experiments" . . . where different patterns of care exist in similar settings as a result of history or tradition. (Moore & McQuay, 2006, p. 163)

So, the term "cohort study" is used to describe what in health care is commonly called an *observational study*. This latter term is used to indicate that there was no deliberate manipulation of treatment assignments, which is characteristic of randomized controlled trials (RCTs). Wherever the STROBE statement refers to an observational study, just think of it meaning a quasi-experimental design. All cohort studies are observational (or quasi-experimental, if you prefer) designs, but not all observational (or quasi-experiments) are cohort studies.

Another variety of observational study is called a *case–control study*. In this approach, clients who have one outcome (e.g., recovery from severe alcoholism) are compared with clients who did not recover from alcoholism. Careful case histories are taken to try to ascertain if any distinct factors can be used to figure out what may have been responsible for these disparate outcomes. If, for example, it was found in a large sample of *former* heavy drinkers that most had become active participants in Alcoholic's Anonymous (AA), and that in a demographically similar group of heavy drinkers who did not stop drinking very few had joined AA, the tentative hypothesis might be drawn that AA involvement leads to sobriety. You can see why this example would be considered very tentative evidence in terms of making any casual inferences because of the possibility of uncontrolled confounding factors.

A real-life example occurred to test the hypothesis, widely prevalent at one point, that certain infant vaccinations triggered the development of autistic disorder. Researchers in Denmark (where medical records are very well maintained) examined the incidence of autism in 440,655 youth who had received the vaccinations in question and compared them to 96,648 nonvaccinated youth. In the former, the percent with autism was 0.06, and in the latter 0.055, a negligible and non–statistically significant difference. In this case, the case–control study was powerful evidence indeed to disconfirm the hypothesis that infant vaccination causes autistic disorder (see Moore & McQuay, 2006, p. 170). It is my impression that case–control observational (e.g., quasi-experiments) designs are rarely used by social work researchers, relative to cohort-type observational studies.

Social workers undertaking a quasi-experiment would be well advised to be familiar with the STROBE statement to be sure that no important features are omitted from consideration in either the study's design or in the write-up of the final report or journal manuscript. A large number of journals (primarily biomedical in nature) have adopted the STROBE statement as a portion of their editorial policy, and the applications of this checklist to behavioral and social science research, including social work studies, are obvious and compelling.

The STROBE statement is supported by a website (www.strobe-statement.org) that goes into the details of these recommendations and provides a rationale for each. To date, no social work journal has appeared to incorporate the STROBE statement into its editorial policy. This does not diminish the usefulness of the guidelines, however, which are reported in their entirety in Table 5.2.

Table 5.2 STROBE Statement—Checklist of Items that should be Included in Reports of Observational Studies

	Item No	Recommendation
Title and abstract	1	(a) Indicate the study's design with a commonly used term in the title or the abstract
		(b) Provide in the abstract an informative and balanced summary of what was done and what was found
Introduction		
Background/ rationale	2	Explain the scientific background and rationale for the investigation being reported
Objectives	3	State specific objectives, including any prespecified hypotheses
Methods		
Study design	4	Present key elements of study design early in the paper
Setting	5	Describe the setting, locations, and relevant dates, including periods of recruitment, exposure, follow-up, and data collection

(*Continued*)

Table 5.2 (Continued)

Participants	6	(a) *Cohort study*—Give the eligibility criteria, and the sources and methods of selection of participants. Describe methods of follow-up
		Case–control study—Give the eligibility criteria, and the sources and methods of case ascertainment and control selection. Give the rationale for the choice of cases and controls
		Cross-sectional study—Give the eligibility criteria, and the sources and methods of selection of participants
		(b) *Cohort study*—For matched studies, give matching criteria and number of exposed and unexposed
		Case–control study—For matched studies, give matching criteria and the number of controls per case
Variables	7	Clearly define all outcomes, exposures, predictors, potential confounders, and effect modifiers. Give diagnostic criteria, if applicable
Data sources/ measurement	8*	For each variable of interest, give sources of data and details of methods of assessment (measurement). Describe comparability of assessment methods if there is more than one group
Bias	9	Describe any efforts to address potential sources of bias
Study size	10	Explain how the study size was arrived at
Quantitative variables	11	Explain how quantitative variables were handled in the analyses. If applicable, describe which groupings were chosen and why
Statistical methods	12	(a) Describe all statistical methods, including those used to control for confounding
		(b) Describe any *methods* used to examine subgroups and interactions
		(c) Explain how missing data *were* addressed
		(d) *Cohort study*—If *applicable*, explain how loss to follow-up was addressed
		Case–control study—If applicable, explain how matching of cases and controls was addressed
		Cross-sectional study—If applicable, describe analytical methods, taking account of sampling strategy
		(e) Describe any sensitivity analyses

(*Continued*)

Table 5.2 (Continued)

Results

Participants	13*	(a) Report numbers of individuals at each stage of study—e.g., numbers potentially eligible, examined for eligibility, confirmed eligible, included in the study, completing follow-up, and analyzed
		(b) Give reasons for nonparticipation at each stage
		(c) Consider use of a flow diagram
Descriptive data	14*	(a) Give characteristics of study participants (e.g., demographic, clinical, social) and information on exposures and potential confounders
		(b) Indicate number of participants with missing data for each variable of interest
		(c) *Cohort study*—Summarize follow-up time (e.g., average and total amount)
Outcome data	15*	*Cohort study*—Report numbers of outcome events or summary measures over time *Case–control study*—Report numbers in each exposure category, or summary measures of exposure *Cross-sectional study*—Report numbers of outcome events or summary measures
Main results	16	(a) Give unadjusted estimates and, if applicable, confounder-adjusted estimates and their precision (e.g., 95% confidence interval). Make clear which confounders were adjusted for and why they were included
		(b) Report category boundaries when continuous variables were categorized
		(c) If relevant, consider translating estimates of relative risk into absolute risk for a meaningful time period
Other analyses	17	Report other analyses done—e.g., analyses of subgroups and interactions, and sensitivity analyses

Discussion

Key results	18	Summarize key results with reference to study objectives

(*Continued*)

Table 5.2 (Continued)

Limitations	19	Discuss limitations of the study, taking into account sources of potential bias or imprecision. Discuss both direction and magnitude of any potential bias
Interpretation	20	Give a cautious overall interpretation of results considering objectives, limitations, multiplicity of analyses, results from similar studies, and other relevant evidence
Generalizability	21	Discuss the generalizability (external validity) of the study results
Other information		
Funding	22	Give the source of funding and the role of the funders for the present study and, if applicable, for the original study on which the present article is based

*Give information separately for cases and controls in case–control studies and, if applicable, for exposed and unexposed groups in cohort and cross-sectional studies.

Note: An Explanation and Elaboration article discusses each checklist item and gives methodological background and published examples of transparent reporting. The STROBE checklist is best used in conjunction with this article (freely available on the websites of *PLoS Medicine* at http://www. plosmedicine.org/, *Annals of Internal Medicine* at http://www.annals.org/, and *Epidemiology* at http://www.epidem.com/). Information on the STROBE Initiative is available at www.strobe-statement.org.

As with the guidelines found in Table 5.1, it is hoped that the suggestions provided by STROBE's checklist of items are self-evident. Just as even the most experienced pilots complete a checklist prior to taking off in an airplane, social work authors and research consumers can benefit from a careful review of the STROBE standards prior to submitting an article for publication.

JOURNAL ARTICLE REPORTING STANDARDS

Social work research will be more directly impacted by the new guidelines appearing in the sixth edition of the *Publication Manual of the American Psychological Association* (American Psychological Association [APA], 2009, pp. 247–253), since most social work journal *do* follow the APA's publication guidelines. Several sets of documents are included in the

APA's new *Journal Article Reporting Standards* (JARS). One set of reporting standards includes information recommended for inclusion in all new data-based manuscripts (pp. 247–248), and a second set includes reporting standards for studies using nonrandom assignment of participants to experimental groups (p. 250); for example, in quasi-experiments.

The general recommendations are broken out by the section of the manuscript: for example, Title and title page, Abstract, Introduction, Method (Participant Characteristics, Sampling Procedures, Sample Size, Power and Precision, Measures and Covariates, Research Design), Results (Participant flow, Recruitment, Statistics and data analysis, Ancillary analyses), and Discussion. Additional reporting standards for studies using nonrandom assignment of participants to experimental groups (e.g., quasi-experiments) are presented in the Methods section and involve providing details as to the assignment method (e.g., unit of assignment, as in individuals, groups, communities), Procedures used to help minimize potential bias, Masking (e.g., whether or not those assessing the outcomes were aware of the condition assignments), and Statistical Methods (e.g., statistical methods used to compare study groups on primary outcomes).

It is an advance for the field to have such recommended standards clearly established, as this will aid in the reporting and understanding of the design and conduct of quasi-experimental studies. To the extent that social work journal editors rigorously adhere to the latest publication standards found in the APA's *Publication Manual* (and they should, for consistency's sake), social work researchers will be guided by these new standards and write up their quasi-experiments in a manner consistent with these guidelines. The APA actually provides a very useful, free multimedia tutorial on preparing papers in APA style (see http://www.apastyle.org/learn/tutorials/basics-tutorial.aspx), although it does not cover the specifics of the JARS. Basically, every social work researcher should acquire a personal copy of the APA's *Publication Manual* and learn its guidelines well. This is an essential skill for any researcher.

THE COALITION FOR EVIDENCE-BASED POLICY GUIDELINES

The Coalition for Evidence-based Policy has issued guidelines titled *Which Comparison-Group ("Quasi-experimental") Study Designs Are*

Most Likely to Produce Valid Estimates of a Program's Impact (see http://
coalition4evidence.org/wordpress/wp-content/uploads/2009/11/
Validity-of-comparison-group-designs-updated-Nov09.pdf). These offer
the following standards for appraising the credibility of a given quasi-
experiment in terms of its ability to yield credible answers:

- *A number of careful investigations have been carried out to
  address this question.* In other words, more than a single
  quasi-experimental has been conducted to answer this question,
  and similar conclusions have been arrived at.
- *The comparison-group designs most likely to produce valid results
  contain all of the following elements:*
  (i)   The program and comparison groups are highly similar in
        observable preprogram characteristics, including:
- *Demographics* (e.g., age, sex, ethnicity, education, employment,
  earnings)
- *Preprogram measures of the outcome the program seeks to improve*
  (at the beginning of the study, the groups are roughly equivalent
  in terms of their scores on the outcome measures)
- *Geographic location* (both studies obtain participants from the
  same general area)
  (ii) Outcome data are collected in the same way for both
        groups
        (e.g., the same survey administered at the same point to
        both groups)
  (iii) Program group and comparison group members are likely
        to be similar in motivation
  (iv) Statistical methods are used to adjust for pretreatment
        differences between the two groups
- *Preferably, the study choses the program and comparison groups
  "prospectively" (i.e., before the program is administered)*
- *The study follows the same practices that a well-implemented
  RCT follows in order to produce valid results (other than the
  actual random assignment)*: For example, the study should
  have adequate sample size, use valid outcome measures,
  prevent cross-overs to or contamination of the comparison
  group, have low sample attrition, use an intent-to-treat analysis,
  and so on.

The similarities among the JARS, the STROBE statement, and the guidelines provided by Thyer, Holosko, and the Coalition for Evidence-based Policy, are all highly congruent, with few contradictory recommendations. Each can be useful in appraising the adequacy of a written report of the design and conduct of a quasi-experimental study. Given the wide currency of the *APA Style Manual*, however, I believe the JARS standards to be the single most useful resource in this regard.

REPORTING RESULTS

Basically, quantitative data may be presented in two ways: visually via tables, graphs, and figures; and numerically via descriptive and inferential statistics. Both approaches have their strengths and weaknesses, and can be seen as complementary approaches, not competing ones. Various sources describe how descriptive statistics should generally be reported (not specific to quasi-experimental designs). For example, Thyer (1991) suggested:

> Whenever descriptive statistics are employed, they should be reported in their entirety. It is common for articles to include information about means (averages) but to omit the accompanying standard deviation. A mean without a standard deviation does not allow the reader a clear understanding of the variation present in the data, and it precludes other scholars from conducting replication or secondary analyses of the data. It is common for some analyses to not include all of the clients present in a particular group. For example, there may have been dropouts from the study or the client failed to complete all outcome measures. Thus, a report of the exact numbers of clients should also accompany each mean value and standard deviation, as well as any data presented in the form of percentages. (p. 84)

It is important to pay particular attention to presenting relevant demographic information on your sample(s) of clients. Their mean age, races/ethnicities, diagnoses, gender, marital status, and other germane characteristics should be reported, as this information is crucial to any scientific investigation. It also aids other researchers in determining if different studies made use of client samples that were relatively similar or widely disparate from each other.

The above suggestions are a good start, but the APA *Publication Manual* (2009) is perhaps the best resource you have in terms of learning the conventions of presenting results. Here are some of the more pertinent guidelines contained in this manual:

> In the results section, summarize the collected data and the analysis performed on those data relevant to the discourse that is to follow. Report the data in sufficient detail to justify your conclusions. Mention all relevant results, including those that run counter to expectation; be sure to include small effect sizes (or statistically nonsignificant findings) when theory predicts large (or statistically significant ones). Do not hide uncomfortable results by omission. Do not include individual scores or raw data, with the exception, for example, of single-case designs or illustrative examples.... When reporting the results of inferential statistical tests or when providing estimates of parameters or effect sizes, include sufficient information to help the reader fully understand the analyses conducted and possible alternative explanations for the outcomes of those analyses. Because each analytic technique depends on different aspects of the data and assumptions, it is impossible to specify what constitutes a "sufficient set of statistics" for every analysis. However, such a set usually includes at least the following: the per-cell sample sizes; the observed cell means (or frequencies of cases in each category for a categorical variable); the cell standard deviations, or the pooled within-cell variance.... For inferential statistical tests (e.g., t, F and X^2 tests), include the obtained magnitude or value of the test statistic, the degrees of freedom, and the probability of obtaining a value as extreme or more extreme than the one obtained (the exact p value), and the size and direction of the effect. When point estimates (e.g., sample means or regression coefficients) are provided, always include an associated measure of variability (precision), with an indication of the specific measure used (e.g., the standard error). (APA, 2009, pp. 32–33)

Few things are more frustrating for a reader than looking for some important feature (say, the racial makeup of the clients in a given study) and not being able to find it. Or, for a researcher wishing to undertake a meta-analysis of a given report, to find that the standard deviations or sample sizes are not included along with the mean values for a given variable. Appropriately including relevant demographic and outcomes information versus obsessively reporting irrelevant minutia in tedious detail can be a difficult balancing act. Further guidance can be found in reviewing particularly well done studies in areas relevant to the one you are undertaking or reviewing, and learning from the models presented by these published articles.

INTENT-TO-TREAT VERSUS EFFICACY SUBSET ANALYSIS

In social work research, the conventional practice has been to analyze outcomes based on who actually receives a treatment. For example, if in a pretest–posttest study, 100 clients are initially assigned to receive a treatment, and 80 of the original 100 participants remain for the posttest assessment (e.g., 20 dropped out), the common technique is to look at the average score pretest (with n = 100), compared to posttest (when n = 80). One may hope, ideally, that the group mean at posttest is statistically improved versus the pretest mean, and one may judge this as reflecting the possible positive effects of intervention. A problem with this method is that the drop-outs may alter the posttest mean scores in ways *unrelated* to the possible effects of treatment. For example, if the most impaired clients tended to be more likely to drop out, the group means at posttest could look much improved, when in reality the changes in the average score are really due to the most impaired clients being omitted from the posttest analyses. This approach is known as *efficacy subset analysis* (although the term is not widely used) and, again, is the most common way in which social work interventions are evaluated. A problem with this approach is that it introduces bias into the statistical analysis and inflates the likelihood of making a type I error (concluding that treatment exerted an effect, when in reality it did not).

One recommended way to compensate for this problem is to include *all* participants at each assessment, regardless of whether they received the intervention or not. This is called an *intention-to-treat* analysis, and is attempted by obtaining the same outcome measures from those who dropped out from treatment as from clients who completed treatment (Lachin, 2000). In other words, in an intention-to-treat analysis, even if 20 clients had dropped out from treatment at posttest, the social work researchers would try very hard to get them to complete the posttreatment assessments, and to then include these data along with those obtained from those who successfully engaged in treatment and completed intervention. Thus, the pre- and posttest comparisons involved 100 and 100 persons, not 100 and 80, respectively.

The more common approach to the problem of dropouts is for the researchers to compare salient demographic and outcome measures between those who completed treatment and those who dropped out. If there are no statistically significant differences between the two groups, the problem of attrition is considered to have been addressed, and it is assumed that the completers did not differ from the dropouts in any meaningful way. Another way is to impute missing data, using any of a variety of methods of statistical legerdemain. The more Calvinistic research methodologists consider these approaches (retrospectively comparing completers vs. noncompleters, or imputing missing data) to be a less than satisfactory resolution of the problem, however, and urge adoption of intent-to-treat analysis as the most rigorous solution. If this approach is followed, then one can analyze the data both ways, using the intent-to-treat approach (including all original clients) or via an efficacy subset analysis (limited to those who actually completed treatment). An intent-to-treat analysis is a much more conservative approach to analyzing the effects of an intervention. For example, receipt of treatment may have many effects in addition to those directly assessed by the outcome measures. Treatment could cause terrible side effects, be psychologically very grueling, or cause a great deal of family or spousal discord. This could be missed if the outcome measures solely looked at presenting symptoms or problems, such as group mean scores on the Beck Depression Inventory (BDI), or illicit drugs consumed. By including treatment dropouts in the outcome analyses, the researcher will likely obtain a more complete picture of how people react to a given intervention, not simply how those who were able to complete it reacted to it symptomatically. To my knowledge, no social work outcome study has yet to include an intent-to-treat analysis as a part of its evaluation design. It is likely that such intent-to-treat analyses will be introduced and eventually become common within the social work outcomes literature. Recall that most social work journals follow the APA's *Publication Manual*. This guide now clearly states:

In studies reporting the results of experimental manipulations or interventions, clarify whether the analysis was by intent-to-treat. That is, were all participants assigned to conditions included in the data analysis regardless of whether they actually received the intervention, or were only participants who completed the intervention satisfactorily included? Give a rationale for the choice. (APA, 2009, p. 35)

INTERPRETING NEGATIVE OUTCOMES

Research that fails to reject the null hypothesis, or which fails to find a predicted difference (e.g., a given treatment was not followed by meaningful improvements, or the treatment group did not improve its functioning more than the nontreatment control or comparison group) is often seen as a disappointment by the researchers. This may occur because of one's personal investment in a project or a desire to see the research hypotheses corroborated. We have a natural tendency to want to see positive results, results that truly do make a difference in people's lives, and when this does not happen, we are disappointed. The consumers of research—social work practitioners, administrators, policy-makers, and clients—all wish to find results with a difference, something they can take away and perhaps apply to their agency-based practice or policy, or use as guidance in seeking out genuinely effective therapies. This is, of course, understandable. From the viewpoint of the behavioral or social scientist however, keep in mind that the purpose of research is to reveal the truth, to discover lawful relationships in nature and among human beings. Social work research is not intended so much to *prove* a particular point as it is to simply discover what the point is, what exists. Ideally, research is not driven by a quest to prove that a given hypothesis is true, but rather to determine what the results *are*, positive, negative, or neutral. It is more objective to state that the research question is "How do clients who receive rectification therapy (RT) fare posttreatment, compared to clients who received treatment as usual (TAU)?" as opposed to "Clients who receive RT will display statistically and clinically greater improvements, compared to clients who received TAU." (As you'll recall from Chapter 1, rectification theory is an imaginary treatment for juvenile delinquency.)

When faced with a negative result, for example a finding that a given therapy did not prove to be effective, one can examine the study to help determine the possible reasons for this outcome. There are several possibilities. One is that, truly, the therapy really does not work.

This is the default position, since most therapies do not really prove helpful, relative to no treatment, to credible placebo treatments, or in the long run. In other words, the null hypothesis usually *is* the true state of affairs. However, any study whose conclusions support the null hypothesis should be carefully examined to make sure that it *really is* a good study, a well designed and fair appraisal. This is because any poorly designed study can find no differences, and one's task, when interpreting a finding of no difference, is to critically appraise the quality of the study to be sure it has a reasonable chance of actually finding any differences, if they existed. This brings up the other possibility alluded to above; namely, that the study was so poorly designed and conducted that its finding of no difference cannot be trusted as legitimate.

TYPE I AND TYPE II ERRORS

When drawing conclusions from an outcome study, one may make a true conclusion or a false conclusion. If treatment really works, and you conclude from a study that it does work, this is a true conclusion. If treatment does not really work, and you conclude that it does not really work, this is a true conclusion as well. However, if a treatment *really does not* work, but on the basis of your study you conclude that it does work, this is an incorrect conclusion, and this type of mistake has been labeled a type I error. If treatment *really does* work, and you conclude on the basis of a study that it does not work, this incorrect conclusion is called a type II error. When one commits a type I error— claiming that something worked but it really did not—one unfairly promotes ineffective treatments. When one commits a type II error—saying something did not work when it really dids—then genuinely effective treatments can be overlooked or prematurely discarded. Both mistakes are problematic. The diagram below helps explain these concepts further.

Through using a conventional alpha level of $p < .05$, roughly speaking about 1 in 20 scientific conclusions will consist of a type I error (claiming a difference exists when it really does not). Science tries to reduce the perpetuation of type I errors via replication. If you conclude, on the basis of a study with one statistically significant difference on an outcome measure between a treatment and control group, that treatment is more effective than the control condition, you have a 1 in 20 chance of being wrong.

	Reality	
	Treatment Does Not Work	*Treatment Works*
You conclude that treatment works.	Type I Error	True Conclusion
You conclude that treatment does not work.	True Conclusion	Type II Error

If someone replicates this study, the chance of obtaining two similarly wrong conclusions is .05 × .05, or .0025, a dramatically smaller risk, and this clearly shows why single studies should be replicated before a finding of an effect (e.g., treatment X "works") should be accepted as legitimate. The chance of three type I errors like this is .05 × .05 × .05, or .000125, a very small risk indeed. The importance of replication has been asserted by Ziman (1978, p. 56): "The results of repetitions of the same experiments are fundamental to the creation of any body of knowledge."
And by Thomas (1975, p. 278):

> The results of replication may be essentially positive, in which case confidence in the reliability of the procedures used is greatly increased. Indeed, each successful, positive replication increases plausibility multiplicatively, because the chance occurrence of such results becomes much more improbable with each additional replication. The same may be said, of course, for replicated failures.

Going back further, we can turn to Chapin (1949, p. 135), who generously claimed:

> For only by replication in numerous similar studies may we escape from the dilemma of whether the obtained differences were due to the non-randomness of the samples, or to the fact that they were drawn from different universes. . . . Should the same results be found on many trials, then generalization from even non-random samples to a universe might be valid and justified. (p. 135)

> And

> [T]hrough the replication of experimental design studies, which attempt to measure the effectiveness of specific means–ends schemes planned to

attain specific goals, it may be possible to develop a systematic mosaic of nonrandom samples that will possess a degree of representativeness to compensate for lack of randomization,and thus to supply a basic representativeness upon which reliable scientific generalizations may rest. (p. 139)

The mathematics linking type I and type II errors dictates that when the likelihood of one type of error declines, the other goes up, and vice versa. If you use a more stringent alpha level to determine statistical significance (reducing the possibility of committing type I error), you make it more difficult to "find" differences, and you may overlook real effects. The risk of type I errors is that "findings" are discovered that are really false. In intervention research, this means that some therapies are said to be effective when they are really not. The danger of type II errors is that effective treatments may be ignored. However, type II errors are in some ways *less problematic,* because any true effects "missed" are liable to be real, reliable in a statistical sense, but pragmatically small, exerting little clinical impact. Given two groups of sufficient size, a treatment group and a no-treatment group, a difference of 1% favoring the treatment will be determined to be statistically significant, and indeed, it will be real in a probabilistic sense. However, an intervention that reduces clients' average scores on something like the BDI by 1% is unlikely to be a clinically useful treatment, even if the effect is genuine. Thus, a true effect could be claimed from the study (treatment X statistically significantly reduces BDI scores), but it would be a type I error, claiming a true effect when one does not actually exist (that is clinically useful). Indeed, our journals are filled with individual studies (maybe 1 in 20?) that reached statistical significance, but in reality represent type I errors.

When a type II error occurs, when we miss a true effect, it is usually because the effect is small and clinically unimportant. Thus, in the world of intervention research, type II errors are less problematic in developing a scientific knowledge base of meaningfully effective treatments than are the plethora of type I errors, wherein teeny effects are artificially elevated to importance when they are merely statistically reliable.

One common design problem that can yield an incorrect conclusion that a given treatment is ineffective is using too few clients to adequately support the statistical analysis (e.g., an underpowered study). Dattalo (2007) provides an excellent overview on this topic. Other obstructions to finding differences may involve the use of inappropriate or insensitive outcome measures. For example, the Michigan Alcoholism Screening Test-Revised (MAST) is a 22-item client self-report instrument designed to detect alcohol abuse. Some of the items consist of questions whose positive answers will be insensitive to change, such as:

6. Have you ever attended a meeting of Alcoholics Anonymous?
___ Yes
___ No
7. Have you ever gotten into physical fights when drinking?
___ Yes
___ No
17. Have you ever gone to anyone for help about your drinking?
___ Yes
___ No

A MAST score is based on the total of yes answers. You can see how questions using the words "Have you ever . . ." would not change pre- and posttest results. If a researcher used the MAST as a pretest and post-test measure in a quasi-experimental study, even if treated clients became completely sober, many of their responses to the MAST items would not change. If participants' scores on the MAST did not change between the pre- and posttest (after treatment), one could conclude, perhaps erroneously, that the treatment was ineffective due to this lack of change. In reality, however, the measure was simply incapable of picking up on any real changes in drinking habits.

Other possible flaws that can result in failing to find an effect of treatment would be issues such as the therapist being incompetent to perform the intervention he is charged with providing; the clients failing to attend enough sessions or to otherwise adequately engage in treatment; or perhaps a blurring of treatment conditions, wherein some clients are assigned to receive treatment X only and others treatment Y only, but in the actual conduct of treatment the therapists inadvertently or deliberately (perhaps for what they considered to be sound clinical reasons) provided elements of Y to clients assigned to condition X, or vice versa. This contamination would also result in the finding of no differential effect between the two groups and the erroneous conclusion that X and Y do not vary in their effectiveness.

Thus, when faced with a null finding, an important task is to critically review the article itself and see if the study was adequately designed.

If it is not, then it is useless because its negative findings cannot be relied upon, since you to not know if they are a legitimate conclusion or a type II error. But if the study is methodologically rigorous, then the negative findings are more likely to reflect the true state of affairs; namely, that the treatment does *not* really work. And this is a good thing to know.

How can it be a good thing to know that certain interventions or practices *do not* work? Look over the examples below and ask if these studies with negative results actually advanced the human services in positive directions:

- Comprehensive summaries of the outcomes literature on social casework were published by Fischer (1973, 1976), Segal (1972), and Grey and Dermody (1972), finding that the available research indicated that, for the most part, professional social work services provided no positive effects, and some cases provided negative ones. Over the next couple of decades, this led to a surge in better-designed outcome studies, many of which documented more positive results.
- In the face of widespread and inaccurate reports that early childhood vaccinations caused autistic disorder, leading to measurable declines in vaccinations and increases in vaccine-preventable childhood diseases, comprehensive reviews of this quasi-experimental evidence were published clearly showing no credible link between autistic disorder and childhood vaccinations (Smeeth et al., 2004; Demicheli et al., 2008).
- A comprehensive review of antidepressant drug trials, co-authored by a licensed clinical social worker, found that these powerful medications were not useful in the treatment of mild to moderate depression, but were useful only in the most severe cases, and that they are widely overprescribed (Turner, Matthews, Linardatos, Tell, & Rosenthal, 2008). This important study appeared in the prestigious *New England Journal of Medicine*.
- Although medications are widely prescribed for the treatment of persons suffering from anorexia nervosa (AN), a large-scale review of the available studies found that "Pharmacotherapy provides little benefit in the treatment of AN at present" (Crow, Mitchell, Roerig, & Steffen, 2009, p. 1).

- Facilitated communication (FC) is a widely used treatment to try to help persons with severe autism and other developmental disorders communicate via typing on a keyboard. A "facilitator" holds the client's hand over the keyboard as the client supposedly pecks out words and sentences. Many thousands of persons were trained in and provided this therapy. Careful investigations revealed that the facilitators were unconsciously guiding the typing, and that it was not being done by the client. It was a manifestation of the *Ouija board effect*, not an effective therapy (Herbert, Sharp, & Guidano, 2002). Leading professional organizations have called for a ban on the clinical use of FC.
- One supposedly crucial component of treatment in the popular psychotherapy called *eye movement desensitization and reprocessing* (EMDR) includes having the client use her eyes to track the therapist's finger as it is waved back and forth in front of the client. Considerable time and training go into doing these eye movements "correctly." Dismantling studies of EMDR provided with and without these supposed crucial eye movements have shown that they have no effect on outcomes (e.g., Carrigan & Levis, 1999), thus undercutting the neurophysiological basis said to be responsible for EMDR's effects.
- So-called *reparative therapy* attempts to convert gay men or lesbians to a heterosexual orientation. The National Association of Social Workers (NASW) has determined that, thus far, the available evidence indicates that reparative therapy does not work. Because of this, as well as because of issues related to respect for diversity and wanting to avoid pathologizing gay and lesbian orientations, the NASW has issued a position statement claiming that the practice of reparative therapy by social workers is unethical and should not be provided to clients. Similar statements have been issued by other human service organizations. Is it important to be aware of the outcome studies demonstrating that reparative therapy does not work? Obviously.
- Considerable health care resources, public and private, go into providing clients with the treatment known as acupuncture, which consists of inserting thin needles into precise positions on the body called *meridians*. Much research shows that people who receive legitimate acupuncture feel better. However,

a considerable number of experiments have been conducted comparing real acupuncture, involving the accurate placement of the needles into the correct meridians, versus fake acupuncture, in which the needles are placed into randomly chosen spots. Typically, both groups of patients improve equally, suggesting that acupuncture is essentially a powerful placebo treatment (Novella, 2011). Is it important to know if acupuncture exerts specific effects, other than placebo influences? Obviously.

The bottom line here is that research with negative outcomes or with findings of no difference can be quite important and valuable. This perspective is emphasized in Holden et al. (2008, p. 68), who stated that "Neither reviewers nor editors should consider studies reporting negative results as inherently inferior to studies reporting positive results. It is the conceptualization and conduct of the study, combined with the interpretation and write up of the results that are important—not the direction of the results."

Quasi-experiments with negative results can serve to head off an ultimately unproductive line of research. This is why federal requests for proposals for large research grants frequently ask that investigators include any pilot data in the results of their grant application. Suppose one wished to do a large-scale randomized controlled clinical trial of RT as a treatment for juvenile delinquency, and it was proposed to test the effectiveness of RT by comparing its results against TAU for adjudicated kids within the community. The outcome measure is recidivism, which would be examined at 3, 12, and 24 months following the termination of treatment. The proposed study could be diagrammed as:

$$\text{R} \quad N = 100 \quad X_{RT} - O_{1(3\,months)} - O_{2(12\,months)} - O_{3(24\,months)}$$

$$\text{R} \quad N = 100 \quad X_{TAU} - O_{1(3\,months)} - O_{2(12\,months)} - O_{3(24\,months)}$$

Note that with the relatively large sample size there is no real need for any pretreatment measures. And with the lengthy follow-up periods, this would be seen as a very strong design to evaluate the relative effectiveness of RT versus TAU—but also a *very* expensive one. If there were no prior evidence that RT produces any positive results, much less that it is any better than TAU, federal (and other) funders might be reluctant to spend the hundreds of thousands of dollars it could take to carry out this complex randomized controlled experiment. Remember, the default hypothesis most likely to be true *is* the null hypothesis—there will be no differences across time within groups or between groups during the various follow-up periods. Given this, the grant is unlikely to be funded. It is simply not a good bet for the funders.

Now imagine that the above grant proposal was accompanied by pilot data with positive results from a pre-experimental or quasi-experimental study, maybe one looking as simple as this:

$$N = 100 \quad X_{RT} - O_{1(3\,months)} - O_{2(12\,months)} - O_{3(24\,moths)}$$

Here, we have a single imaginary group of 100 youth who received RT. Further imagine that the recidivism rate at 3 months was 4%; 6% at 12 months; and 7% total at 24 months. Whoa! These are remarkably low recidivism rates for any intervention applied in the field of juvenile justice, and for them to remain low for 2 full years posttreatment would be unheralded in the annals of delinquency research. With very strong results like this, when dealing with an intractable problem, the need for a no-treatment control group or for a comparison treatment condition is less stringent. Pilot data with strong results like this, even in the context of a simple posttreatment-only group design, really augments the legitimacy of one's request for sizable funding to conduct an evaluation of far greater methodological rigor (and cost). This illustrates one of the strengths of quasi-experimental studies.

Take the converse. You are a researcher interested in examining the effects of RT on recidivism rates among juvenile delinquents, and you do the simple pre-experimental posttest-only study noted above and find that recidivism rates are 70% at 3 months, 80% at 12 months, and 85% at 24 months. Even without a control group, these rates would be seen as quite high, and certainly not supportive the hypothesis that RT is an effective intervention to reduce recidivism among delinquents. Faced with this disappointing information, you may well be inclined to drop further investigations into RT for juvenile offenders, and to forego any effort to design and seek funding for a large-scale RCTs. This is another strength of quasi-experiments—they can serve as a filter or screen, useful in weeding out the obviously ineffective and useless. By doing so, one can stop pursuing lines of inquiry that will ultimately prove to be a dead end (thus saving lots of time, energy, and professional disappointment). "A study not worth doing is not worth doing well" (Holland, 1997, p. 2585).

Tremendously powerful interventions need neither control groups nor statistical analysis to judge their effects. Also, issues that are well recognized as being relatively intractable, those that respond little or not at all to placebo influences, that do not change with the passage of time, that are not prone to maturation effects, and that tend to be relatively steady-state, do not require control or comparison conditions to be usefully researched. Some examples might include individuals diagnosed with obsessive-compulsive disorder (OCD), autistic disorder, severe Down syndrome, or schizophrenia of the paranoid type. Now, this is not to say that the natural history of these conditions suggests that the picture is completely hopeless, but it must be admitted that the vast majority of persons with these conditions, reliably diagnosed, are unlikely to dramatically improve absent something akin to a miracle (which *can* happen, occasionally). So, for example, if one conducted a pretest–posttest study with lengthy follow-up periods for 100 persons with one of these disorders (say, OCD); found well-established, severe, and unabated psychopathology lasting for years; then provided these individuals with RT and found that immediately posttreatment and at 1 and 2 years later, not a single person met the diagnostic criteria for OCD and for all intents and purposes seemed "cured," this could be a Nobel-prize-winning study. No statistics and no control groups would be needed. Holland expressed it this way:

> One example of a trial that should not be a randomized controlled trial is when the initial results are so striking and the database of prior experience so uniform that the conclusion is inescapable. . . . Where the observation represents a sea change, based on unmistakable objectivity . . . the wisdom and experience of the observer reach the goal sooner and with a shorter causality list. (Holland, 1997, p. 2585)

In a satirical article titled *Parachute Use to Prevent Death and Major Trauma Related to Gravitational Challenge: A Systematic Review of Randomized Controlled Trials,* Smith and Pell (2003) facetiously pointed out that no RCTs existed demonstrating that using parachutes saves the lives of people falling out of airplanes. Their point is that with obviously powerful interventions, there is no need for RCTs or quasi-experimental studies to demonstrate the value of the approach. Regrettably, for research purposes, such clear-cut situations are relatively rare in the human services. Many of the psychosocial problems we address via intervention research wax and wax in severity, and clients have a distressing habit of sometimes getting better all on their own, without any professional intervention (e.g., stopping smoking and abusive drinking, losing weight, overcoming phobias or unemployment, leaving abusive relationships and developing much more productive lives). This is good for the persons concerned but makes the task of drawing legitimate causal inferences about the effects of treatment much more difficult for the poor researcher.

One tool that researchers have to help detect small but reliable effects of interventions is known as *inferential statistics*, the use of various statistical tests to determine if the results obtained from a study significantly deviate from those expected by chance or random variation in the data alone. With quasi-experimental studies, the usual purpose of inferential statistics is to derive conclusions about the clients seen in *our* particular research project, and not to try to generalize any results to larger populations of interest. For example, if you conduct a pretest–posttest study on an Individual Development Account program for 50 poor families that you were able to recruit from within your local community due to their convenience, it is most likely that your 50 families are not somehow "representative" of all poor people in your area. Therefore, you cannot legitimately (in a scientific sense) extrapolate any conclusions from your study to all local poor people. But you can use inferential statistics to tell you if the mean amount of savings for your 50 families significantly increased following the program. If you find out that it has, and the savings are meaningful—not merely statistically significant—as a practical matter, you could be tempted to apply this same program to other local poor people and see if the positive findings can be replicated. If this happens, each successful replication enhances your confidence that, yes indeed, you do have an intervention that helps the poor save, but this enhanced generalizability is based on successful replications with different groups of poor people, not from conducting the original study on a representative sample of the local poor.

REPORTING RESULTS

Let's begin with simple descriptive statistics, since these are the most appropriate way of describing the results of very simple studies. In the case of the posttest-only design $(X - O_1)$, the group of clients (individuals, families, couples, organizations, communities, etc.) is exposed to an intervention and systematic data are obtained on client functioning following receipt of the intervention. However, no pretreatment measures are formally taken. An example of this might be a group of middle schoolers who received the Drug Abuse Resistance Education (DARE) program, and then, some years later, their drug use is assessed. Here, the data can be presented in a very simple descriptive manner. If, 5 years later, 100% scored negative on a drug screening, this would be evidence consistent with the hypothesis that the DARE program did help protect kids from using drugs. If 95% scored positive for drug use, we could be pretty sure DARE was not very useful in this regard. With less extreme results, interpretation is more difficult because this design offers no group to compare against the youth who received DARE. If 35% of the kids who received DARE turned up positive for drug use, is this a relatively good or bad result? Lacking information about the extent of drug use from comparable kids who did not get DARE, it is difficult to tell if DARE is protective or not. To some extent, such a determination is a judgment call.

We may be able to evaluate the results of a given program offered in the context of a posttest-only design if very strong public claims have been made for the expected results of this program. For example, one authority has claimed that EMDR is effective in reducing and even eliminating military combat-related posttraumatic stress for 85% or more of patients after only a few sessions. This is a very strong, even remarkable, claim, one that may sound too good to be true. If a posttest-only study was done with military combat veterans, and posttreatment posttraumatic stress disorder (PTSD) rates were found to be much higher than 15%, the strong claims made by EMDR's proponents would be weakened.

An example of the purely descriptive analysis of a posttest-only study is provided in Thyer (1988). I had adopted a new method of instruction that I called *teaching without testing*. Basically, it involves having my students bring their written answers to detailed study questions to each weekly class they had with me, with the study questions being based on that week's particular assignment. During class, I would call upon individual students for their answers to particular questions, often digressing to elaborate on some point or another and facilitating class discussion of each question. I graded each week's assigned set of questions and opted to not use a mid-term or final examination or term paper assignment, since the students were apparently working very hard every week. My impression was that this was a better method of promoting learning than using tests or term papers. Student had to read the assigned material each week, write out the content, and then engage in discussion about it during class. This made it very difficult to escape coming into close contact with the course materials. I used this method in several bachelor's degree, master's degree, and doctoral-level classes and, at the end of each term, asked the students to anonymously answer some questions about my method of instruction. The general results are depicted in Table 5.3:

Table 5.3 Percentage of Students (N = 40) Who "Strongly Agreed" or "Agreed" with the Anonymous Survey's Questions.*

79% "I found answering the study questions an excellent way to learn the course content."

88% "Answering the study questions helped me to keep up to date in my readings."

85% "I found answering the study questions a better learning tool than having to prepare for mid-term and final examinations."

94% "I found answering the study questions a better learning tool than having to write a term paper."

65% "I devoted more time studying my class readings in this course than in my other courses."

37% "I attended this class more regularly than my other classes."

*Reproduced from Thyer (1988, p. 51).

This looks good, but you can readily see the limitations of this type of descriptive analysis. The students' favorable endorsements may have been influenced by their desire to please me, even though I tried to minimize this by keeping their appraisals anonymous. However, if I had gotten really bad appraisals, that too would have been really informative, basically telling me to change my method of teaching. As it was, this preliminary positive endorsement led me to conduct future quasi-experimental studies on my own teaching using this method of instruction.

A more recent example of taking a purely descriptive approach to analyzing the results of a posttest-only study is reported by DeWalt et al. (2009), who evaluated a goal-setting intervention in the area of patient self-management of diabetes. The brief 15-minute structured intervention was intended to help patients with diabetes establish small, realistic, but meaningful goals in helping them manage their diabetes, in areas such as diet, exercise, blood glucose monitoring, medication adherence, and insulin use. The patient chose an area on which to focus and was helped to create an action plan intended to lead to healthy behavior change. Follow-ups occurred some 3–4 months following the intervention, and patients were asked if they remembered the action plan and whether they had achieved the behavioral goal. Of an initial 250 patients who received the intervention, 20 did not complete the study, which is fairly low attrition. One set of purely descriptive results are presented in Table 5.4 (from Dewalt et al., 2009, p. 221):

Table 5.4 Number of Subjects Who Achieved and Sustained a Given Number of Goals

Number of Times Goals Achieved/ Behavior Sustained	Frequency	Percent
0	17	7
1	44	19
2	92	40
3	76	33
Total	229	

Other information was provided in this study, but the core analysis, the extent to which patients reported positive behavioral changes following the goal-setting intervention, was presented purely descriptively. The researchers were pleased with this result, inasmuch as the intervention was low-cost, brief, and seemingly resulted in patient changes. Although this level of analysis may seem rather low-grade ore for scientific investigations, keep in mind that such studies are best seen as preliminary or pilot work that serves as a precursor to more sophisticated investigations.

We can also compare the outcomes of a posttest-only study with those expected on the basis of chance along. This was the approach used by Albright and Thyer (2010) in their simple test of the validity of the national examination used in most states to license clinical social workers (the LCSW exam). These authors obtained a copy of the LCSW sample or practice test, a test said to be similar in difficulty and content to the real test. This sample LCSW test was completed by 59 first-year MSW students. However, the actual questions were blanked out, leaving only the four possible answers to each question visible, and the students were told to pick the correct response. They knew this was a study on the guessability of the LCSW exam. Now, with four possible options per item, but only one correct one, it could be predicted that the average score would be about 25% correct. In reality our students answered on average 52% of the questions correctly, more than double the score expected by chance alone.

Now Albright and Thyer could have simply reported these data descriptively, as above, but this could have left lingering the possibility that perhaps these students scored so much higher on the basis of chance alone; maybe these students were particularly lucky. A simple inferential test can be used in situations like this, a method called the *Z test*. The Z test is used when you have a sample of clients who score some given value on a particular measure, and this value can be known or predicted from the larger population of interest. The Z test statistic can tell you if the obtained score is significantly different from the predicted score, and it is often used in standardized tests of this nature. In this case, the obtained score is the average of how our 59 students scored, or 52%. The expected population score is 25%: how well "everyone" should score when guessing randomly. The Z test is calculated using the following formula:

$$Z = (X - m)/SE$$

Where X is the mean of the sample to be standardized, m (mu) is the population mean, and SE is the standard error of the mean. SE = s/SQRT(n), where s is the population standard deviation and n is the sample size (see http://changingminds.org/explanations/research/analysis/z-test.htm). The value of Z tells you how much the sample score differs from the population mean, in terms of standard deviation units. With the Z score in hand, one looks up a Z table in a statistics book or online and determines if the result is statistically significant. If it is, then you know that the results are unlikely (usually at the. 05 level) to be due to chance. In other words, a real effect is present, and in the case above, yes, the 59 MSW students scored significantly better than chance. Therefore, the sample test (a proxy for the real exam) is very guessable, and hence may not be a legitimate evaluation of one's ability to practice social work safely. This type of study, using blanked-out questions from sample tests, has been used in a variety of areas to examine the validity of standardized tests. Other examples within social work include the validity of the GRE as an admissions requirement for MSW programs (Donohue & Thyer, 1992), the School Social Work Examination (Johnson, Thyer, Daniels, Anderson, & Bordnick, 1996), the Academy of Certified Social Workers examination (Thyer & Vodde, 1994), and the advanced practice examination also used to license social workers at a lower level than the LCSW (Randall & Thyer, 1994). All these studies used the posttest-only design and the Z test as an inferential statistic.

Another method of analysis was used by Thyer, Sowers-Hoag, and Love (1986) in their analysis of how BSW and MSW student perceptions of field instruction quality varied according to gender mix. At the end of an internship, all students completed a standardized measure evaluating their field experience. Over the course of a number of semesters, students received their primary supervision from a supervisor of a given gender, and we were interested in seeing if the students' perception of the quality of their field experience varied by their own gender and that of their supervisors. When we did this study, we had post-internship supervision satisfaction scores for 413 students. This posttest-only design, including the numbers of students per group and their mean satisfaction score (with the standard deviation for each mean), could be diagrammed as below:

Because we had data that was scored using an interval scale, the appropriate inferential test is one called a *one* (time period) *by four* (groups) *analysis of variance* (ANOVA). Basically, we found no meaningful differences across the four groups of students and supervisors. Thus, suggestions that had appeared in prior literature indicating that students

# of Students	Type of Supervision They Received	M Score (SD)
N = 217	W Female Student/Female Supervisor – O_1	68.4 (8.6)
N = 122	X Female Student/Male Supervisor – O_1	63.9 (11.6)
N = 30	Y Male Student/Female Supervisor – O_1	63.0 (10.0)
N = 44	Z Male Student/Male Supervisor – O_1	64.6 (9.4)

be placed on the basis of gender with supervisors of the same gender in order to achieve an optimal internship experience were not supported by our data.

The situation is a bit more complicated in the case of the pretest–posttest design $[O_1–X–O_2]$, with the choice of test also being dependent upon the nature of the data being collected. In both descriptive and inferential statistics, data can be roughly grouped into the following methods of measurement:

- **Categorical** (also known as nominal) data, classifies one's data into groups according to some identifiable feature. Descriptively, one might think of variables such as gender (male, female), race (white, black, Hispanic, Asian, etc.), food stamp status (yes or no), or religion (Protestant, Catholic, Jewish, Muslim, Hindu, etc.). Examples drawn from outcome research might include a binary categorization of *Cured* versus *Not Cured*, *Positive* versus *Negative* (think of drug screening results), *Pass* versus *Failed* (think of school performance), etc. For the purposes of data analysis, numbers may be assigned to categorical data (e.g., for entry into a database), with say 1 = male and 2 = female, or 1 = Protestant, 2 = Catholic, 3 = Jewish, 4 = Muslim, and 5 = Hindu. However, these numbers have no mathematical meaning; for example, a female (scored as a 2) is somehow not twice the value of a male (scored as a 1). Nor would it make sense to calculate the average gender or religion of your clients using the above coding schemes. Categorical data are usually reported in terms of numbers and percentages, not means and standard deviations.
- **Ordinal** data occurs when values are ordered in ranks that represent some sort of meaningful hierarchy, as in first place,

second place, and third place; college status (freshman, sophomore, junior, senior); or levels of impairment (highly impaired, moderately impaired, mildly impaired). Knowing the *order* of something provides more information than does simply knowing a category because it also conveys a sense of hierarchy. But the order does not provide information as to the magnitude of differences. A first-place horse can lead the second-place horse by a nose, a length, or by several lengths. Knowing that one was in first place and the other in second tells you about their order, but not the extent of their differences. Ordinal data are usually reported in terms of numbers and percentages, and their preferred measure of central tendency is the *mode* (most common value in a series) or *median* (the midpoint in a range of values).

- **Interval** data can be used to categorize values as well as place them in a hierarchy, but they convey still more information since the values assigned have a mathematical meaning in relation to each other, with differences representing meaningful and consistent distinctions. Examples include clients' weights, heights, or cholesterol levels, or a student's SAT score or her score on some scale, test, or measure whose range of values does not include a meaningful zero value. One cannot weight zero pounds, have zero height, or even earn a zero score on the SAT (if you take it you have some sort of non-zero score). The values of something measured on an interval scale have arithmetic meaning in relation to each other. Someone weighing 200 pounds weighs twice as much as someone who weighs 100 pounds. One student's SAT score of 1,000 is 100 points below the score of a student who scored 1,100, and 100 points above the score of a student with a 900 score. The intervals are basically equivalent to each other. The preferred measures of central tendency for interval data are the mode, mean, or *arithmetic mean*, with the latter being the most commonly used one in inferential statistics.
- **Ratio** data possess all of the attributes of interval data, except that the scaling system possesses a meaningful zero value, representing the complete absence of the attribute. The number of children a client has, the number of crimes committed or hospitalizations

experienced, or the amount of money in the bank reflect examples of data that can be analyzed using ratio scales. The value of each could be zero. The central tendency of a variable measured on a ratio scale may include the mode, median, or arithmetic mean (e.g., average). In physics, the Kelvin scale, which includes a zero value reflecting the complete absence of warmth, is an example of a ratio level of measurement. However the Celsius temperature scale is an example of an interval measure, since, although it does include a value of zero, this number was arbitrarily set because it represents the value at which water freezes, not the complete absence of temperature. Cold as it is, water at 0° Celsius retains warmth/temperature and can grow colder still.

Now, in returning to the example of the one-group pretest–posttest design, in order to decide what statistic to use, we must determine on what level of measurement to scale the outcome value. Let take as an example psychiatric patients who are admitted for inpatient treatment and, upon admission, are asked to complete a measure of psychiatric symptomatology that yields scores with the interval level of measurement. Then, when they are about to be discharged, they complete the same measure. The social work researcher wishes to test the hypothesis "Clients who are treated on our unit will display statistically significantly lower levels of psychiatric symptomatology on discharge, relative to their scores on admission." This is a good hypothesis. It can be falsified (clients might on average grow worse), and it is directional, calling for changes in one direction only (they will get better, not worse). A directional hypothesis is a riskier hypothesis in that it is easier to falsify, compared to a nondirectional one ("I predict that clients will *change* on average over the course of their treatment on this unit.") A directional hypothesis that also asserts a certain level of change ("Clients will improve, on average, by at least 5 points") is even riskier than a purely directional one that lacks an additional prediction as to the extent of change.

In the case of the one-group pretest–posttest design ($O_1 - X - O_2$), the appropriate test to see if scores have significantly changed between the two assessments is called the *paired sample t-test* (also called the pairwise *t*-test), if you have an outcome measure that is scaled as an interval or ratio measure. It is called *paired* because the two sets of scores are from the same group of people. This test basically examines the mean (average) score at pretreatment, compares it to the average score at posttreatment, and lets you know, with a certain level of probability, if the observed difference is likely due to chance or to some other nonrandom factor. It does not tell you what *caused* any differences. It is highly unlikely that the pretest and posttest scores will be exactly the same—people do change, and random and systematic errors occur in measurement—so the mean scores will very likely differ. The question for the researcher is, "Is this difference due to chance or not?" If the *t*-test does fall below a certain threshold of probability (the convention is the .05 level, meaning less than 1 chance in 20 that the difference was due to random factors, the data's natural variability, or chance), the null hypothesis is rejected, and you can assume that *something else* is responsible for the observed changes. This something else may be the treatment, but, as we have seen, it may be due to a number of other factors, such as threats to internal validity, those confounding variables described earlier that may really have caused these changes, not the treatment. So, a statistically significant *t*-test does not mean that *treatment* caused any improvements (or deterioration for that matter), only that true changes did occur and treatment *may* have been the reason.

Back in the day before safety belt use was required by law in most states, I used this design (a pretest–posttest design) to evaluate changes in my students' seat belt use by offering them extra credit in class if they would sign a safety belt use pledge, agreeing to wear their safety belts each time they drove in a car, in return for some extra credit. However, according to the contract, if I ever saw them, during the course of the semester, riding in a car and appearing to be unbuckled, they agreed to accept a final grade of F in the class! Thirty-five of forty students signed the pledge at the beginning of the term and provided anonymous estimates of the percent of time they wore their safety belts when driving (about 83% [SD = 29%]). At the end of the term, anonymous belt use was reported to be 94% (SD = 17%). The paired sample *t*-test result was [$t(34) = -2.02$; $p < .05$]. (The astute reader will have noted that I should have reported the *exact* p value here.) Because the *t*-statistical was significant at the <.05 level, I could conclude that my students' safety belt use *did increase* over the term, which is consistent with the hypothesis that the safety belt pledge had an effect. However, I could not be certain that the increase was the result of the agreement they signed, since other factors could have been responsible. For example, during the term, there might have been a horrible and well-publicized local accident involving college students who died because they were not using their safety belts and it was this publicity that actually caused my students to increase their safety belt use. Or, maybe the state passed a mandatory safety belt use law, and this policy change was really responsible for their greater reported seat belt use. Basically, one has no way of knowing if it was intervention (the pledge) that caused the change, but we do know safety belt use increased, and that is a good thing. One student told me at the end of the term that after she signed her pledge she coaxed her boyfriend into wearing his safety belt also. During the term, he was in a serious car accident in which his car was demolished, and both he and the highway patrol officer attributed his survival to his wearing his safety belt. This is a satisfying bonus to my undertaking this small project (Thyer, 1987).

A more recent example of this design and the use of the paired-sample t-test is the analysis undertaken by Jones, Chancy, Lowe, and Risler (2010), who looked at the possible effectiveness of residential treatment on sexually abusive youth. On intake, all youths (ages 9–18) completed a reliable and valid measure of psychosocial functioning called the Child and Adolescent Assessment of Functioning Scale (CAFAS), and they completed this measure again at discharge (average length of stay was 30 months). A total of 58 youth had pretest and posttest scores available for analysis. Jones et al. (2010, p. 177) posed the following research question: "Do youths' functional impairment scores and sexual interest scores *change* from intake to discharge from a residential treatment program?" (It would have been stronger, scientifically, to not just ask this question, but also to pose the more risky directional prediction included in the hypothesis: "Do CAFAS scores statistically significantly *improve* over the course of treatment?")

Mean CAFAS scores at pretest for the 58 youth were about 145 points (SD = 39) and at discharge 74 points (SD = 46). With the CAFAS, lower scores imply higher functioning; thus it was found that this change of some 70 points in a positive direction was statistically significant, when examined by the paired-sample t-test. Jones et al. cannot conclude that the treatment program caused these changes. They may be due to maturation (teenagers were tested over a 30-month period) or to the passage of time alone. Again, inferential tests can detect reliable differences, not the source of those differences.

This same design and statistic was used by Parrish and Rubin (2011) in their analysis of the effectiveness of continuing education (CE) programs they offered on the topic of evidence-based practice. These writers provided a series of CE workshops, and assessments involved having participants complete a reliable and valid measure called the Evidence-based Practice Process Assessment Scale (EBPAS) at the beginning of the workshop and again some 3 months after it was concluded. Delaying assessment for 3 months provided a more valid evaluation of the workshops' effectiveness since you could look at long-term retention, not knowledge only retained immediately after the conclusion of the training. For all participants, combined across four different workshops, the mean EBPAS score pretraining was about 27 points (SD = 7), and 3 months after the 7-hour training program it was about 32 points (SD = 7), with higher scores indicating greater knowledge. The t-test $[t(57) = -3.4; p <. 001]$ was significant, demonstrating that these improvements were not due to chance. These authors properly did not make any unwarranted causal inferences; that is, they did not state that they could be sure these improvements were *caused* by the workshop they provided, but they did provide a good discussion of rival explanations and why they believed a case could be made for ascribing the changes to the workshops attended. For example, the pretest–posttest design does not usually control for the threat to internal validity called maturation. However, given that their workshops were only 7 hours in length, the follow-up period was only 3 months, and all participants were adults, it is pretty unlikely that maturation is a viable rival explanation. Allen Rubin is one of social work's most distinguished researchers, and it speaks to the value of the quasi-experimental pretest–posttest design and paired-sample t-test that this approach was used by him and his colleague to evaluate CE training. Simple designs *do* have value in answering simple questions, and sometimes it is very important to answer simple questions first.

If an outcome measure is categorical or ordinal in nature, then a different test statistic should be used to analyze the results of a pretest–posttest design. Take the case of a study that compared the outcome of 57 patients with panic disorder who received either panic control training (a cognitive behavior therapy), alprazolam (an antianxiety medication), waiting list control (no treatment), or a placebo medication (Klosko, Barlow, Tassinari, & Czerny, 1990). There were several categorical outcome measures assessed posttreatment including end-state functioning (e.g., cured vs. not cured) and the complete absence of experiencing further panic attacks. These results are summarized in Table 5.5, along with the associated chi-square (X^2) analysis. Overall, the study's results generally favored the behavioral therapy on a number of outcome measures.

Table 5.5   Selected Categorical Outcome Measures Reported by Klosko et al. (1990)

	Cured	Experienced Zero Panics
	N(%)*	N(%)**
Alprazolam (N = 16)	8(50%)	8(50%)
Placebo (N = 11)	5(45.5%)	4(36.4%)
Panic Control Training (N = 15)	11(73.3%)	13(86.7%)
Waiting List (N = 15)	2(20%)	5(33.3%)

* X^2 (3, N = 57) = 8.62, $p < .05$.
** X^2 (3, N = 57) = 10.42, $p < .02$.

Here, the use of the inferential test helpfully augments simply eyeballing the data.

Jainchill, Hawke, and Messina (2005) used chi-square analyses to examine possible differences in outcomes among male and female adjudicated adolescents who received treatment in a therapeutic community (TC). At 5 years post-TC treatment, the follow-up sample included 70 males and 51 females who were assessed on an array of psychosocial, criminal, and drug use variables. Very simply put, this study could be diagrammed as follows:

$$N = 70 \quad \text{males} \quad X - O_1$$

$$N = 51 \quad \text{females} \quad Y - O_1$$

Among the statistically significant differences that appeared 5 years after TC treatment were included (among many variables assessed) whether the clients was arrested for drug possession, drug sales, or property crimes. These outcomes are broken down by gender and presented in Table 5.6.

Table 5.6 Selected 5-year Categorical Outcomes Following Therapeutic Community Treatment for Drug Abuse

	Males (N = 70)	Females (N = 51)
Involved in Drug Possession	63%	34%*
Involved in Drug Sales	56%	18%**
Involved in Property Crimes	29%	10%***

*$X^2 = 6.97, p < .01$
**$X^2 = 14.45, p < .001$
***$X^2 = 4.23, p < .04$
From Jainchill, Hawke, & Messina, 2005, p. 984.

For each variable, it appears that males are more likely have engaged in selected illegal activities 5 years following TC treatment, compared to female clients.

Suggested inferential tests suitable for each type of quasi-experimental design are noted in Table 5.7. There are other appropriate ones that can be used, and those mentioned are presented as one suggested course of analysis, not the sole appropriate or definitive approach to statistical inference with these designs. They are, however, those most commonly employed.

EFFECT SIZES

It is now widely recognized that in studies with a sufficiently large sample size, very small differences can be shown to be statistically significant, which only means that the difference is reliable or not likely (within a certain probability) due to random variation in the data. It does not refer to the clinical importance of the changes or differences observed. An effect size (ES) should accompany any report of a statistically significant difference as it provides more of an estimate of the meaningfulness of any difference or change. One measure of ES that may be familiar to the reader is associated with reporting Pearson correlations of paired quantitative data, correlations that can range from −1 to +1. The correlation, r, when squared, yields a measure called the *coefficient of determination*, and it estimates the proportion of variance shared by the two measures. If two measures are correlated +.40, the coefficient of

Table 5.7 Chart of Designs/Diagrams Outlining Design Categories, Objectives, Statistics Used

Pre-Experimental Designs

1. The Posttest-Only Single Group Design

$$X - O_1$$

This design controls for virtually no threats to internal validity. Its data are usually presented descriptively. Inferential statistics (e.g., Z-test) may be applied if there are known values for the outcome measure available on a larger population of interest.

2. The Pretest–Posttest Single Group Design

$$O_1 - X - O_2$$

This design controls for very few threats to internal validity. Its data can be discussed descriptively and analyzed using inferential tests, such as the paired-sample t-test if the outcome measure is scaled as an internal or ratio variable, or the X^2 test if the data are categorical or ordinal.

3. The Pretest–Posttest Single-Group Design with Repeated Pretests

$$O_1 - O_2 - X - O_3$$

This design may partially control for regression to the mean. Interval/ratio outcomes can be evaluated using the analysis of variance for repeated measures (ANOVA), and categorical/interval scaled data can be analyzed using a one (groups) by three (time periods) X^2 test.

4. The Pretest–Posttest Single-Group Design with Repeated Posttests

$$O_1 - X - O_2 - O_3$$

This design may partially control for relapse or improvements that are temporary.

Interval/ratio outcomes can be evaluated using the ANOVA, and categorical/interval scaled data analyzed using the X^2 test.

Quasi-Experimental Designs, with a Control or Comparison Condition

1. The Posttest-Only No-Treatment Control Group Design

$$X - O_1$$
$$O_1$$

(*Continued*)

Table 5.7 (Continued)

This design may partially control for the passage of time, concurrent history, and maturation. Interval/ratio scaled outcome measures may be evaluated using the t-test for independent samples, comparing posttreatment group means, and the X^2 test applied to the frequency data of categorical or ordinal variables. This design can also involve more than one control or comparison group.

2. The Pretest–Posttest No-Treatment Control Group Design

$$O_1 - X - O_2$$

$$O_1 \qquad O_2$$

This design may partially control for the passage of time, regression to the mean, concurrent history, the existence of pretreatment differences between groups, and maturation. Interval/ratio scaled measures may be analyzed using the two (groups) by two (times) ANOVA, and categorical/ordinal scale data using a two (groups) by two (times) X^2 test.

3. The Pretest–Posttest Alternative Treatment Comparison Group Design

$$O_1 - X - O_2$$

$$O_1 - Y - O_2$$

Where X indicates a group that received an experimental intervention, and Y indicates a group that received some alternative treatment, treatment as usual, or a placebo intervention. This design may partially control for placebo effects, social desirability factors (wanting to please the therapist), concurrent history, and existence of pretreatment differences between the two groups. Use a two (groups) by two (times) repeated measures ANOVA for interval/ratio data, or a two by two X^2 test for categorical/ordinal data.

4. The Pretest–Posttest Alternative Treatment/No Treatment Control Comparison Design

$$O_1 - X - O_2$$

$$O_1 - Y - O_2$$

$$O_1 \qquad O_2$$

This design may partially control for the passage of time, concurrent history, social desirability factors, regression to the mean, and pretreatment differences among the groups. Interval/ratio level data may be analyzed using a two (times) by three (groups or condition) ANOVA, with a similar X^2 test applied to categorical/ordinal data.

(*Continued*)

Table 5.7 (Continued)

Note: Each of the above quasi-experimental designs may be modified by using more than one pretest assessment period, more than one posttest assessment, or both, typically strengthening the basic design's internal validity.

Time Series Designs

1. The Posttreatment-Only Time Series Design

$$X - O_1 - O_2 - O_3 - O_k$$

This design takes a very large number of posttreatment assessments after an intervention has been introduced. It controls for very few threats to internal validity, and its results are usually graphed and interpreted visually.

2. The Simple Interrupted Time Series Design

$$O_1 - O_2 - O_k - X - O_{k+1} - O_{k+2} - O_{k+n}$$

These designs typically have a large number of pretests and posttests. O_k indicates the final pretest assessment, O_{k+1} indicates the first posttreatment assessment, and O_{k+n} the last posttreatment assessment. Time series designs with very large numbers of data points may be analyzed with a test statistic known as time series analysis, for which a minimum of 50 data points per phase is recommended, pre- and postintervention. This design may control for regression to the mean, maturation, and repeated testing.

3. The No-Treatment Control Group Interrupted Time Series Design

$$O_1 - O_2 - O_k - X - O_{k+1} - O_{k+2} - O_{k+n}$$

$$O_1 - O_2 - O_k \qquad O_{k+1} - O_{k+2} - O_{k+n}$$

Two similar groups (states, counties, organizations) are repeatedly assessed on some variable of interest. The top group receives an intervention (X) after a number of assessments, and the bottom group does not. This design controls for regression, maturation, repeated testing, concurrent history, and the passage of time. Use time series analysis to investigate changes within this design and for other forms of interrupted time series data.

determination is .40 × .40, or .16. This means that up to 16% of the variance in one measure can be predicted from the other. If you have two variables with a Pearson correlation of .80, then from .80 × .80, we know that at most .64% of the variance in one measure can be predicted from the other. In the social sciences, ES around .10–.20 are called small, those >.20–.35 as medium, and those >.35 as large.

Generally speaking, measures of ES when looking at differences (not correlations) provide an estimate of the extent to which the average member of the experimental treatment group is better (or worse) off compared to the average member of the comparison (TAU, no-treatment, placebo control condition) group, as expressed in standard deviation units. An ES of .30 favoring RT over a no-treatment control group would mean that the average RT client was .30 standard deviation (SD) units better off than persons who did not receive treatment; an ES size of .80 would mean that the treated clients were, on average, .80 SDs better off than those not treated, etc. Typically ES in social work intervention research is rather small, reflecting that our interventions are not exceptionally potent; however, given the intractability of many of our clients' problems, reliable small gains may be important to demonstrate. Simply knowing an ES by itself not a sufficient measure of importance. It must be interpreted within the context of the overall study design. Foe example, an ES of .30 favoring RT clients versus untreated clients is not as impressive as is effect size of .30 favoring treated RT clients versus placebo-treated or clients who received TAU. For many problems, most therapies are capable of yielding some small benefits, comparing to getting nothing. The more robust comparison is to compare experimental treatment versus TAU or placebo. Also, outcome measures that are labile, or of weak reliability and validity, may lend themselves to yielding stronger ES than do those obtained from studies using more rigorous measures.

Effect sizes may be calculated for all inferential statistical tests, with one known as Cohen's d being the most commonly used for t-tests. It is calculated by taking the difference between the two means (pre- versus post, or between two groups posttreatment), divided by the pooled standard deviation of the data. A similar effect size for use with t–tests is called Hedge's g. For ANOVAs and multiple regression results, another test may also be used, called Cohen's f^2, whereas for X^2 tests, a measure called Cramer's phi is appropriate. There is a large literature on the importance of calculating ES and of including this information in statistical reporting. The *Publication Guidelines* (APA, 2009) of the American Psychological Association now requires it, as do an increasing number of journals (e.g., *Research on Social Work Practice*). A number of articles can be found in the social work (Hudson, Thyer, & Stocks, 1985; LeCroy & Krysik, 2007) and related literatures (Cohen, 1994) that address the topic, and common statistical software programs include options for reporting ES.

Effect size information is also very important when attempting to systematically review a number of studies evaluating the effects of a given treatment. If sufficient primary statistical information is included in an original study, other researchers will be more able to aggregate the results of relevant studies using a technique called *meta-analysis* to arrive at conclusions made possible through combining a larger number of small studies. Littell, Corcoran, and Pillai (2008) provide a good review of designing and conducting systematic reviews and meta-analyses, with the latter being based on ES calculations.

ETHICAL CONSIDERATIONS IN THE DESIGN AND CONDUCT OF QUASI-EXPERIMENTS

As members of a profession, social workers, including researchers, are guided by various codes of ethics. The code of ethics promoted by the NASW (2008) is among the more widely recognized, but other social work organizations (e.g., the Clinical Social Work Association), other interdisciplinary groups that individual social workers may choose to affiliate with, in addition to or in lieu of the NASW (e.g., the Association for Behavior Analysis – International, or the American Evaluation Association), and various state licensing boards, may also promulgate specific codes of ethics. So, although the NASW code of ethics is not the sole appropriate standard that may cover a social worker's activities, it will be referred to here due to its widespread acceptance. The NASW COE standards relating to evaluation and research appear in Table 5.8.

It is clear that conducting research, especially evaluation research related to practice and policy, is an expected role of professional social workers. Whenever possible, clients should provide informed consent, without penalty or deprivation, prior to their being enrolled in a research project, and underage or otherwise impaired individuals should have their consent provided by an appropriate proxy (e.g., parent, guardian *ad litem*, etc.). Clients must be able to withdraw their participation at any time during a project, and must be protected from undue risk of harm. Information gathered from clients must be protected and treated respectfully and confidentially, not promiscuously disclosed to others unconnected with the research project. Data must be reported honestly.

Table 5.8 National Association of Social Workers Code of Ethics Standards
Pertaining to Evaluation and Research Activities

(a) "Social workers should monitor and evaluate policies,
the implementation of programs, and practice interventions.
(b) Social workers should promote and facilitate evaluation and research
to contribute to the development of knowledge.
(c) Social workers should critically examine and keep current with emerging
knowledge relevant to social work and fully use evaluation and research
evidence in their professional practice.
(d) Social workers engaged in evaluation or research should carefully
consider possible consequences and should follow guidelines developed
for the protection of evaluation and research participants. Appropriate
institutional review boards should be consulted.
(e) Social workers engaged in evaluation or research should obtain
voluntary and written informed consent from participants, when
appropriate, without any implied or actual deprivation or penalty for refusal
to participate; without undue inducement to participate; and with due
regard for participants' well-being, privacy, and dignity. Informed consent
should include information about the nature, extent, and duration of the
participation requested and disclosure of the risks and benefits of
participation in the research.
(f) When evaluation or research participants are incapable of giving
informed consent, social workers should provide an appropriate explanation
to the participants, obtain the participants' assent to the extent they are able,
and obtain written consent from an appropriate proxy.
(g) Social workers should never design or conduct evaluation or research
that does not use consent procedures, such as certain forms of naturalistic
observation and archival research, unless rigorous and responsible review
of the research has found it to be justified because of its prospective
scientific, educational, or applied value and unless equally effective
alternative procedures that do not involve waiver of consent are not feasible.
(h) Social workers should inform participants of their right to withdraw
from evaluation and research at any time without penalty.
(i) Social workers should take appropriate steps to ensure that participants
in evaluation and research have access to appropriate supportive services.
(j) Social workers engaged in evaluation or research should protect
participants from unwarranted physical or mental distress, harm, danger,
or deprivation.
(k) Social workers engaged in the evaluation of services should discuss
collected information only for professional purposes and only with people
professionally concerned with this information.
(l) Social workers engaged in evaluation or research should ensure the
anonymity or confidentiality of participants and of the data obtained from
them. Social workers should inform participants of any limits of
confidentiality, the measures that will be taken to ensure confidentiality,
and when any records containing research data will be destroyed.

(Continued)

Table 5.8 (Continued)

(m) Social workers who report evaluation and research results should protect participants' confidentiality by omitting identifying information unless proper consent has been obtained authorizing disclosure.
(n) Social workers should report evaluation and research findings accurately. They should not fabricate or falsify results and should take steps to correct any errors later found in published data using standard publication methods.
(o) Social workers engaged in evaluation or research should be alert to and avoid conflicts of interest and dual relationships with participants, should inform participants when a real or potential conflict of interest arises, and should take steps to resolve the issue in a manner that makes participants' interests primary.
(p) Social workers should educate themselves, their students, and their colleagues about responsible research practices."

Reprinted from the National Association of Social Workers (1999, Section 5.02).

These are all sensible standards, and there is seemingly little to quibble about. However, the devil is in the details.

When data are gathered retrospectively and anonymously, perhaps obtained from state or federal agencies, the principle of informed consent for participation in research is largely a moot point. In many instances, the data collected and analyzed in time series designs are not even derivable down to the level of individuals. It is not people who are directly being measured but more conceptual phenomena such as accidents, visits, numbers of births, high school dropouts, etc. It may even be possible that formal institutional review board (IRB) approvals are not necessary for such studies, if you are not interacting with human beings or gathering personally identifiable information. This may also be the case if you are making use of data that are publicly available, as such studies too may be exempt from IRB oversight. However, if a researcher is employed at an institution that receives federal funding, it always a wise policy to check with the chair of the local IRB regarding the possibly exempt status of your project. In the case of IRB oversight, the best policy is to get permission first, not seek forgiveness afterward. IRBs can be very touchy on this issue (see Holosko, Thyer, & Danner, 2009).

When it might be technically possible to obtain informed consent from research participants but is impractical, the IRB may grant you a dispensation from tracking down individuals whose data comprises the variables you are analyzing. This can be especially useful when the data may be years old and locating individuals would be very difficult. This dispensation is more likely to be granted if the data are innocuous, not sensitive; if your sample of clients is not a protected group (e.g., prisoners, pregnant women, minorities of color, children), if the risks are otherwise low, and the identity of respondents is either not known or will be kept confidential.

Generally speaking, according to federal policy, conducting a quasi-experimental evaluation of practice or policies will be considered research, *if* the project meets *both* of the following standards:

1. The project involves a systematic investigation, *and*
2. The design, goal, purpose, or intent of the project is to contribute to generalizable knowledge.

Generalizable knowledge is interpreted by the federal government to mean that the researcher plans to publish his or her results in a journal or present it at a professional or academic meeting or conference. This is an important caveat: If your purpose in conducting an evaluation is solely to develop an internal report for an agency or organization, perhaps with the intent of improving the agency's services, with no plans to distribute the report publicly, then the project does not rise to the threshold of the federal definition of research, and no external oversight or approval from a Human Subjects Protection board is required. You can do all the quasi-experimental evaluations you wish, so long as you have no intent (and do not eventually) to publish or present them publicly. Technically, such projects are not research!

A *human subject* is a living person from whom an investigator/researcher obtains data (1) through intervention or other interaction with them or (2) through identifiable personal information (e.g., name, address, social security number, etc.). *Intervention* refers to the physical methods by which data are collected, and any type of manipulation of the client or his or her environment for the purposes of the research. *Interactions* includes communication or interpersonal contact between the researchers and the clients. What these features include is fairly clear, but what they exclude is often overlooked. For example, data related to deceased individuals may not be technically construed as research, but could be the source of information comprising a quasi-experimental study.

Data gathered by others, say agency staff, and provided to the researcher with the data de-identified (no personal information provided) could conceivably not be called doing research. Analyzing publicly available data, from state databases for example, lacking personal information (say, mortality statistics before and after some new policy is enacted) would not be engaging in research, according to federal guidelines. There is no personal information, and you are not interacting with human beings. Even if personal information is gathered, it is conceivable that the activity may not be construed as research in certain circumstances. For example, my local paper publishes color mug shots of people arrested in our community on a weekly basis. I could use these photos (which are *very* personal) of real live people in some sort of research project, for example to examine if white or black felons received disparate sentences for the same type of crime, or to see if males with beards or facial tattoos committed different types of crimes than do clean-shaven men. Earlier, I described how I accessed individual teacher's course evaluations from my university's publicly available website and looked for possible differences in teaching effectiveness. In that case, although I technically did not need to gain approval from my university's IRB, I chose to do so, just in case any irate person questioned my using this perhaps sensitive information.

Even if one does not belong to a professional association that promotes a particular code of ethics or is a licensed social worker, a part of being a professional social worker consists of adhering to ethical practices. This includes persons who conduct research such as quasi-experiments. The principle of "First, do not harm" is of paramount importance, as are the general values of respecting clients, protecting privacy, obtaining informed consent when appropriate (with provision for withdrawing such consent without any penalty), and beneficence (hopefully, clients or the field will benefit in some manner, from your study). Quasi-experimental outcome studies, because they involve interventions provided to real live clients, must be based on an ethical bar set higher than more benign and less intrusive forms of research (e.g., surveys, correlational investigations). One of the most infamous studies ever conducted in the United States was the Tuskegee Study of the natural history of untreated syphilis involving low-income African American men in the rural south. This could be construed as a quasi-experimental study, a posttest-only time series analysis lasting decades. It was a social worker, Peter Buxtun, who served as the whistle-blower on this project and forced its eventual termination and the provision of treatment (and financial compensation) to the participants and their families. (see http:// en.wikipedia.org/wiki/Peter_Buxtun). Even relatively unsophisticated quasi-experimental designs can be the context for unethical studies. It is crucial that social workers undertake quasi-experiments in a manner consistent with the highest ethical standards. This requires familiarity with appropriate codes of ethics and due consideration of these ethical standards from the inception of any such study.

THE FUTURE OF SOCIAL WORK AND QUASI-EXPERIMENTAL RESEARCH

Across the social sciences, we see that a far greater proportion of quasi-experiments are published relative to true RCTs, and that this distribution holds true within the social work disciplinary literature devoted to empirically evaluating the outcomes of practice. Our field has made use of such designs since the early part of the 20th century, and they form an important core body of research investigating what has worked, and not worked, in serving clients effectively. Several predictions may be ventured:

1. Social work will continue to make comparatively extensive use of quasi-experimental designs, although they, like empirical research as a whole, will remain a minor form of disciplinary scholarship.

2. Recognizing that the weaker of these designs pose significant limitations in terms of permitting true causal inferences, those that are published will include more stringent cautionary language so that readers will avoid exaggerating the results or extend causal claims beyond those legitimately permitted by the data. Rubin and Parrish (2007) documented the degree to which problematic phrases involving causal inferences are found in published experimental and quasi-experimental social work outcome studies. Rubin himself honestly noted his own mistakes in this area, citing a specific example, and vowed to be more conservative in his future writing. With a noble example like that, we can hope that journal editors as well as authors will be more vigilant in excising unjustifiable claims ("Treatment X *caused*

clients to get better") from articles before they appear in print. More conservative language might say something like "The results of this study are *consistent* with the hypothesis that treatment X caused the clients to get better."

3. Large-scale funded quasi-experiments may come under increasing pressure to be registered. For many years, RCTs have been encouraged, and in some cases required by funders, to be registered with a system sponsored by the World Health Organization (see www.clinicaltrials.gov). Listing on this clinical trials registry encourages transparency in design and reporting, aids in recruiting research participants, and serves as a large-scale database of experimental intervention research. Over 80,000 studies from over 150 countries are on the ClinicalTrials.gov registry, most of which are drug trials for various medical conditions. However, thousands of trials are listed in the general area of mental health, and over 400 appear when "psychotherapy" is used as a search keyword. This is a great resource for psychosocial intervention researchers, as well as pharmaceutical investigators. It has been recently suggested that a similar separate registry be specifically developed for quasi-experimental studies (Staff, 2010). However, it should be noted that almost 14,000 quasi-experimental studies are already listed on www.clinicaltrials.gov. Whether a new registry for quasi-experiments is developed or not, it seems likely that the public registration of quasi-experimental outcome studies of psychosocial interventions on such trial registries will become increasingly common in the years to come, especially if governmental funding sources require this as a precondition of receiving research dollars.

SUMMARY

Pre-experimental and quasi-experimental research designs are major investigatory tools in the evaluation of the outcomes of social work practice and in beginning enquiries into the causal effects of specific psychosocial interventions. These designs provide excellent ways to get credible answers to some simple questions facing each practitioner, administrator, and policy analyst. The designs reviewed in this chapter range from the simple and parsimonious to the complex and elegant. Each possesses strengths and limitations and should not be accepted for use without a full consideration of a given design's potential to provide the answers to the questions being posed by the social worker.

Some of these designs were used in the very earliest published evaluations of the effects of social work, and they remain in widespread use today. In this volume, I have tried to portray the essential features of the major varieties of quasi-experiments, the inferential logic behind them, and to present an array of examples of their use. I have highlighted many such studies authored by social workers that appeared in some of the highest-quality scientific journals, to illustrate the utility and acceptance of these designs within the scientific toolbox we all have access to. All social workers, at a minimum, should be able to recognize these designs, understand their logical foundations, and provide an informed critique of contemporary research that makes use of them. Some social workers will find it within the scope of their professional activities to actually undertake using some of these designs in the evaluation of their own practice. This book was written to encourage such efforts, as such studies will promote the empirical foundations of our discipline, as envisioned over a century ago by many of our founders.

Glossary

Alpha level Alpha is the probability of making a type I error (rejecting the null hypothesis when the null hypothesis is true) when using an inferential statistical test. Most inferential tests set alpha at or less than .05.

ANOVA A parametric inferential statistic that examines differences between the means of three more groups in a study, groups exposed to different independent variables (e.g., treatment vs. no treatment), or longitudinally at least three times for a single group (e.g., pretest, posttest, and at follow-up).

Assessment/Treatment interaction Changes in a study's outcome measures induced by an interaction between the assessment procedures used and interventions received. This is may be a threat to the internal validity of a study.

Attrition/mortality Clients sometimes drop out of a research study before it is completed, and this drop out is known as attrition or mortality. This may be a threat to the internal validity of a study since the participants remaining at the study's conclusions are only a subset of the individuals who began the study.

Beneficence A primary ethical concern of social research. It refers to both doing no harm to people you are studying and, at the same time, promoting a common good for individuals in the research community because of your study. Its origin in present-day social research in America can be traced back to the Belmont Report.[*]

---

[*] *Terms with an asterisk were reproduced with permission from M. J. Holosko and B. A. Thyer (2011). Pocket glossary for commonly used research terms. Thousand Oaks, CA: Sage.*

Categorical data Data (variables) that differ only in kind, not in amount or degree. Nominal data are categorical: for example, female versus male, true versus false.*

Causal inference Drawing conclusions about the effects of an independent variable by ruling out rival explanations apart from the intervention under investigation.

Chi-square test A nonparametric test of statistical significance, appropriate when the data are in the form of frequency counts. It compares frequencies actually observed with expected frequencies to see if they are statistically different.*

Cohen's d A widely used measure of effect size.

Cohort study An observational (e.g., quasi-experimental) study in which a defined group of people (the cohort) is followed over time. The outcomes of people in subsets of this cohort are compared, to examine those who were exposed or not exposed (or exposed at different levels) to a particular intervention or other factors of interest.*

Comparison group A group of clients in a study who receive treatment as usual, partial treatment, or a placebo treatment. Changes observed in a comparison group can be "subtracted" from changes observed in the group of clients who received "real" treatment, to help determine the effects of "real" treatment absent changes induced by receiving the usual treatment, placebo treatment, or partial treatment.

Control group A group of clients in a study who do not receive any formal intervention. This is used to control for various threats to internal validity such as the passage of time, concurrent history, and regression to the mean. Changes observed in the control group can be "subtracted" from changes observed in the treatment group, to help determine the "real" effects of the treatment, absent changes induced by non–treatment-related factors.

Demographic features Background information relating to statistical characteristics of a study's groups (e.g., age, gender, race, income, etc.).

Dependent variables What is measured in a study, and what is affected during the study. The dependent variable (e.g., outcome measure) responds to the independent variable (e.g., treatment or intervention). It is called dependent because it depends on the independent variable.*

Descriptive statistics Numbers used to describe the basic features of sample data in a study. They provide simple summaries about the sample and its measures; for example, mean, median, mode, variance, or standard deviation. Descriptive statistics are given at the beginning of most quantitative studies' data analysis processes.* Sample descriptive statistics should include information such as a group's gender distribution, age, race, ethnicity, socioeconomic status, and diagnosis (if relevant).

Differential attrition   Occurs when clients drop out from participation in a study to varying degrees across groups (e.g., treatment versus no-treatment). Thus, at the end of the study, the proportions of clients remaining in each group may differ, making it difficult to draw any inferences about the effects of treatment. This may be a threat to the internal validity of a study.

Diffusion/contamination of treatments   This occurs when a comparison group learns about a research program from other program participants, thus preventing the control and experimental groups from remaining distinct. This may be a threat to the internal validity of a study.*

Differing treatment credibility   This may occur when clients receiving differing treatments (e.g., real treatment vs. placebo therapy) perceive that the treatment they are receiving may be more or less believable (e.g., effective). More credible treatments may exert more powerful placebo effects than less believable interventions. This may be a threat to the internal validity of a study.

Dismantling study   An outcome study in which one group of clients receives a "complete" treatment package, and their results are compared to clients who receive a subset of the complete treatment. Differential outcomes may be ascribed to the absent components of complete treatment.

Effect sizes   An index used to indicate the magnitude of an obtained change, result, or relationship between time 1 and time 2 observations. Cohen's d is the most commonly used statistic to compare mean score differences. Approximately speaking, effect sizes (ES) can be small, $<.03$; medium, $+.05$; or large, >0.75.* Each time a statistically significant difference is reported, its associated ES should be included.

Effectiveness study   A study evaluating a treatment, conducted under clinically representative or real-life conditions. It is usually used in the later stages of evaluating a new intervention.*

Efficacy study   A study conducted under conditions of maximum experimental control (e.g., carefully screened clients, highly trained therapists using detailed treatment manuals).* Such studies maximize potential internal validity at the expense of external validity (e.g., generalizability to real-life practice). Interventions found useful using efficacy studies should be replicated in effectiveness studies in real world settings.

Efficacy subset analysis   Examining various subgroups of participants who received a given intervention to ascertain any possible differences in outcomes (e.g., Do females respond more or less than males?).

Evaluation study   A systematic inquiry to describe or assess the intervention impact of a specific program or intervention on individuals by determining its activities and outcomes. These can be evaluations of practice or programs.*

Experimental design   A research study in which one or more independent variables are systematically varied by the researcher to determine their effects on dependent variables.* Randomized experiments randomly assign participants to various treatment, control, or comparison groups.

F test A statistical test of the equality of the variances of two or more populations. The test compares the differences between groups and within groups over time. It is used in analysis of variance inferential tests (ANOVA).*

Human subject A living human being from whom data involving personally identifiable information is obtained in the context of a research study. The term *participant* is now preferred over the word *subject*, and outcome studies of social work often use the more accurate term *client.*

Hypothesis A tentative, testable assertion regarding the occurrence of certain behaviors or events; a prediction of study outcomes. It is used to determine how independent and dependent variables can be tested and written in either null or directional form. It is based on literature, theory, or observation of a phenomena. It forms the basis of experiments designed to establish plausibility, association, prediction, or causality.*

Independent variable The variable that affects or is presumed to affect the dependent variable under study and is included in the research design so that its effect can be determined. This is sometimes called the *experimental, manipulated,* or *treatment variable,* or in outcome studies, the *treatment* or *intervention.**

Inferential logic The process of drawing conclusions from a research study using the principles of logic, specifically those pertaining to inductive and deductive reasoning.

Institutional Review Board (IRB) A committee designated to approve, monitor, and review biomedical and behavioral science involving humans, with the aim of protecting the rights and welfare of the research participants. It is a federal requirement in universities, large organizations, hospitals, and so on.*

Intention-to-treat analysis A method of evaluation for randomized trials in which all participants randomly assigned to one of the treatments are analyzed together, regardless of whether they completed or received that treatment, in order to preserve randomization.* This approach may also be used in with non-randomized quasi-experimental studies.

Interrupted time series design Longitudinal research in which ongoing repeated measurements of the outcomes are made and treatment is introduced at some point, while measurements continue as before.*

Interval data Variables scaled using a system that produces rank ordering and equal distances. Interval data lack an absolute zero point.

Instrument change Occurs when changes in obtained measures are due to the instrument calibration or changes in observers, judges, or interviewers (e.g., greater sensitivity with practice, or less observer attentiveness after repeated observations). This may be a threat to the internal validity of the findings of a study.*

JARS Journal Article Reporting Standards, guidelines contained within the *Publication Manual of the American Psychological Association* pertaining to the writing up and analysis of research reports. Many journals now require submitted manuscripts to be in compliance with the JARS.

Maturation The possibility that results are due to changes that occur in participants as a direct result of the passage of time, human developmental processes, or fatigue, and that may effect their performance on the dependent variable. This may be a threat to the internal validity of the findings of a study.*

Meta-analysis A systematic review that uses quantitative methods of published research interventions and studies to synthesize and summarize the results of a large number of research studies on one particular topic. This allows aggregate claims about interventions and their effects to be made and offers empirical suggestions about best practices or interventions. The unit of analysis in meta-analysis is the effect size found in different studies.*

Multiple posttreatment assessments The process of repeatedly and formally assessing a study's outcome measures at several (not just one) points in time following exposure to an intervention. These can be used to help establish the long-term effects of any treatment.

Multiple pretreatment assessments The process of repeatedly and formally assessing a study's outcome measures at several (not just one) points in time before clients receive treatment. These can be used to help establish any trends in the data (e.g., are the clients getting better, worse, or is functioning stable) prior to treatment.

Multiple treatment interference The carryover or delayed effects of prior experimental treatments when individuals receive two or more experimental treatments in succession. This may be a threat to the internal validity of the findings of a study.*

n The number of people in a sample.

N The number of people in a population.

Nonparametric tests A body of statistical tests used when the data represent a nominal (categorical) or ordinal level scale, or when the assumptions required for parametric tests cannot be met. This class of tests do not hold the assumptions of normality.*

Objectivity A presumed lack of bias or prejudice.*

One-group posttest-only design A pre-experimental design involving one group that is given a test after treatment is given. It attempts, therefore, to evaluate a program's outcomes when no available comparison group and no pretest data are available (or needed, as in a client satisfaction study).*

One group pretest–posttest design A pre-experimental design involving one group that is pretested, exposed to a form of treatment, and then posttested.*

Ordinal data Assigning numbers to variables, presenting the rank ordering (first, second, third, etc.) of the entities measured. This is the second level of measurement, one up from the first, nominal, or categorical.*

Outcome measures Specific standardized or nonstandardized benchmarks used to assess whether the intervention or program resulted in any changes.* Also known as *dependent variables.*

Outcomes research Research to measure practice or program effectiveness. Such studies examine what has changed as a result of the intervention being offered.*

Parametric tests Inferential statistical tests based upon the assumption that the data are normally distributed.

Passage of time Changes in client functioning that may occur during the natural course of events, unrelated to treatment. Because many client problems/issues naturally wax and wane over time, time itself may be a threat to a study's internal validity.

Pearson correlation A common index of correlation appropriate when the data represent either interval level or ratio scales. It takes into account each and every pair of scores and produces a coefficient (*r*) between 0.00 and plus or minus 1.00. A positive *r* indicates that, as one variable goes up or down, so does the other. Negative or inverse *r* indicates that as one variable goes up, the other goes down.*

Placebo influences An inactive treatment or procedure, literally meaning "I do nothing." The placebo effect (usually a positive or beneficial response) is attributable to the participant's or experimenter's expectation that the treatment will have an effect.*

Posttest-only control/comparison group design A research design involving at least two groups of participants. One group receives a treatment, the other receives no treatment, placebo treatment, or an alternative treatment condition. This design is quasi-experimental if the groups are formed naturally. It is an experiment if the groups are formed using random assignment.*

Pre-experimental research design A research design that involves studying only a single group of participants, either posttreatment only, or pre- and posttreatment. No control or comparison groups are used.*

Pretest–posttest no-treatment control group design A study wherein one group of clients is assessed, receives an intervention, and is reassessed. Their results are compared to a comparable group of clients who were assessed, not treated, and then reassessed. It is an attempt to control various threats to internal validity, such as passage of time, concurrent history, and regression to the mean.

Pretest–posttest alternative treatment comparison design A study wherein one group of clients is assessed, receives an intervention, and is reassessed. Their results are compared to a comparable group of clients who were assessed, who then receive an alternative treatment (e.g., treatment as usual, placebo care), and are then reassessed. It is an attempt to control various threats to internal validity, such as passage of time, concurrent history, regression to the mean, placebo influences, and expectancy bias.

Quasi-experimental design A type of research design in which the treatment and control or comparison groups are not created using random assignment procedures. It does involve the manipulation of an independent variable and the specification of a test hypothesis.*

Random assignment A method analogous to tossing a coin to assign clients to treatment groups. The experimental treatment is assigned if the coin lands on heads, and a conventional, control, or placebo treatment is given if the coin lands on tails.*

Random selection A sample selected in such a way that every member of the population has an equal chance of being selected.*

Randomized controlled trial (RCT) An outcome study wherein participants are randomly allocated to an experimental group or a control or comparison group and followed over time on the variables or outcomes of interest. RCTs are capable of high levels of internal validity.*

Ratio data The highest measurement scale that, in addition to being an interval scale, also has an absolute zero in the scale.*

Regression to the mean A statistical phenomenon that can make natural variation in repeated data look like real change. It happens when unusually large or small measures tend to be followed by measurements that are closer to the mean. This may be a threat to the internal validity of the findings of a study.*

Replication Conducting a measurement, experiment, or study again; the second instance may be a repetition of the original study using different participants. If the study is repeated and produces the same findings, this enhances the validity and generalizability of the findings.*

Selection bias This occurs with differential selection of participants for comparison groups. Score differences, consequently, can be attributed to pretreatment differences among groups. This may be a threat to the internal validity of a study.*

Single-system research design A study conducted with one person, family, group, or system to explore the results of an intervention targeting specific outcomes. Typically, repeated measures of client functioning are taken prior to intervention, during intervention, and perhaps after the intervention is discontinued. These designs are a form of *idiographic research*—studies involving small numbers of participants—as opposed to nomothetic research involving large numbers of participants. Also known as single-participant, single-subject, or N = 1 research.*

Social desirability bias The tendency of people to answer questions in ways that are typically acceptable in a particular culture. This will generally take the form of over-reporting good behavior and underreporting bad behavior.*

STROBE An explicit set of methodological standards for quasi-experimental studies. The acronym stands for *STrengthening the Reporting of OBservational* *studies in Epidemiology.* Many journals now require that submitted manuscripts be consistent with these standards.

Switching replications design A outcome study wherein one group of clients receives an intervention and a second, comparable group does not receive the intervention. The outcomes are then assessed. The second group then receives the same intervention, and is assessed to see if they responded to the intervention in a way similar to the first treatment group.

Systematic review A review of clearly formulated questions that uses systematic and explicit methods to identify, select, and critically appraise relevant research and to collect and analyze data from the studies that are included in the review.*

t test A parametric inferential statistical test used to examine the differences between the means of two groups (an independent samples *t* test) or the mean values on some outcome measure obtained from the same group on two occasions (e.g., before and after treatment), a paired sample *t* test.

Therapist bias/allegiance effects A possible confound in an outcome study wherein one or more therapists delivering experimental or other interventions possesses more or less adherence to each of these treatments. If this differential allegiance is reflected in how they interact with clients, this may bias the outcomes of the study. This is a possible threat to the internal validity of an outcome study.

Treatment fidelity Specific checks placed in a study to confirm that the manipulation of the independent variable occurred as planned. It includes such things as treatment definitions specified, implementer training, treatment manuals written, supervision of treatment agents, sampling for consistency, proper utilization of data collection strategies, and so on.*

Type I error A conclusion that a treatment or intervention works when it actually does not. The risk of a type I error is often called *alpha*. In a statistical test, it describes the chance of rejecting the null hypothesis when it is in fact true. It is also called a false positive.*

Type II error A conclusion that there is no evidence a treatment works when it actually does work. The risk of a type II error is often called *beta*. In a statistical test, it describes the change of not rejecting the null hypothesis when it is in fact false. The risk of a type II error decreases as the number of participants in a study increases. It is also called a false negative.*

References

Abel, E. M., & Greco, M. (2008). A preliminary evaluation of an abstinence-oriented empowerment program for public school youth. *Research on Social Work Practice, 18*, 223–230.

Albright, D. L., & Thyer, B. A. (2010). A test of the validity of the LCSW examination: *Quis custodiet ipsos custodes? Social Work Research, 34*, 229–234.

American Psychological Association. (2009). *Publication Manual of the American Psychological Association* (6th ed.). Washington, DC: Author.

Armour, S., & Haynie, D. L. (2007). Adolescent sexual debut and later delinquency. *Journal of Youth and Adolescence, 36*, 141–152.

Bales, K. (1996). Lives and labours in the emergence of organised social research, 1886–1907. *Journal of Historical Sociology, 9*, 113–138.

Barlow, D. H. (2010). Negative effects from psychological treatments: A perspective. *American Psychologist, 65*, 13–20.

Bausell, R. B. (2007). *Snake oil science: The truth about complementary and alternative medicine.* New York: Oxford University Press.

Berk, R. A., Sorenson, S. B., Wiebe, D. J., & Upchuch, D. M. (2003). The legalization of abortion and subsequent youth homicide: A time series analysis. *Analysis of Social Issues and Public Policy, 3*, 45–64.

Biglan, A., Ary, D., & Waagenaar, A. C. (2000). The value of interrupted time-series experiments for community intervention research. *Prevention Science, 1*, 31–49.

Blenkner, M. (1962). Control-groups and the placebo-effect in evaluative research. *Social Work, 7*, 52–58.

Booth, C. (1902–1903). *Life and labour of the people of London.* London: Macmillan.

Bordnick, P. S., Elkins, R. L., Orr, T. E., Walters, P., & Thyer, B. A. (2004). Evaluating the relative effectiveness of three aversion therapies designed to reduce craving among cocaine abusers. *Behavioral Interventions, 19*, 1–24.

Bowen, G. L., & Farkas, G. (1991). Application of time-series designs to the evaluation of social services program initiatives: The recycling fund concept. *Social Work Research and Abstracts, 27*(3), 9–15.

Brandell, J. R., & Varkas, T. (2010). Narrative case studies. In B. A. Thyer (Ed.). *Handbook of social work research methods* (2nd ed., pp. 376–396). Thousand Oaks, CA: Sage Publications.

Buttell, F. P. (2002). Exploring levels of moral development among sex offenders participating in community-based treatment. *Journal of Offender Rehabilitation, 34*(4), 85–95.

Campbell, D. T., & Stanley, J. C. (1963). *Experimental and quasi-experimental designs for research.* Chicago: Rand-McNally.

Capp, H., Thyer, B. A., & Bordnick, P. S. (1997). Evaluating improvement over the course of adult psychiatric hospitalization. *Social Work in Health Care, 25,* 55–66.

Carrigan, M. H., & Levis, D. J. (1999). The contributions of eye movements to the efficacy of brief exposure treatment for reducing fear of public speaking. *Journal of Anxiety Disorders, 13,* 101–118.

Carrillo, D. F., Gallant, J. P., & Thyer, B. A. (1993). Training M.S.W. students in interviewing skills. *Arete, 18*(1), 12–19.

Carrillo, D. F., & Thyer, B. A. (1994). Advanced standing and two-year program M.S.W. students: An empirical investigation of foundation interviewing skills. *Journal of Social Work Education, 30,* 278–288.

Chandra, A., Martno, S. C., Collins, R. L., Elliott, M. N., Berry, S. H., Kanouse, D. E., & Mui, A. (2008). Does watching sex on television predict teen pregnancy? Findings from a national Longitudinal Survey of Youth. *Pediatrics, 122,* 1047–1054.

Chapin, F. S. (1917). The experimental method and sociology. *The Scientific Monthly, 4,* 133–144.

Chapin, F. S. (1949). The experimental method in the study of human relations. *The Scientific Monthly, 68,* 132–139.

Chen, S. Y., Jordan, C., & Thompson, S. (2006). The effect of cognitive behavioral therapy (CBT) on depression: The role of problem-solving appraisal. *Research on Social Work Practice, 16,* 500–510.

Chu, Y. H., Frongillo, E. A., Jones, S. J., & Kaye, G. L. (2009). Improving patrons' meal selections through the use of point-of-selection nutritional labels. *American Journal of Public Health, 99,* 2001–2005.

Clapp, J. D., Lange, J. E., Russell, C., Shillington, A., & Voas, R. B. (2003). A failed norms social marketing campaign. *Journal of Studies on Alcohol, 64,* 409–414.

Cnaan, R., & Tripodi, S. (2010). Randomized controlled experiments. In B. A. Thyer (Ed.). *Handbook of social work research methods* (2nd ed., pp. 205–220). Thousand Oaks, CA: Sage.

Cohen, J. (1994). The earth is round ($p < 0.05$). *American Psychologist, 49,* 997–1003.

Colosetti, S. D., & Thyer, B. A. (2000). The relative effectiveness of EMDR versus relaxation training with battered women prisoners. *Behavior Modification, 24,* 719–739.

Cook, T. D., & Campbell, D. T. (1979). *Quasi-experimentation: Design and analysis for field settings.* Boston: Houghton-Mifflin.

Cook, T. D., & Shadish, W. R. (1994). Social experiments: Some developments over the past 15 years. *Annual Review of Psychology, 45,* 545–580.

Copp, H. L., Bordnick, P. S., Traylor, A. C., & Thyer, B. A. (2007). Evaluating wraparound services for seriously emotionally disturbed youth: Pilot study outcomes in Georgia. *Adolescence, 42,* 723–732.

Council on Social Work Education. (2008). *Educational Policy and Accreditation Standards.* Alexandria, VA: Author. Available at *http://www.cswe.org/File. aspx?id=13780.*

Crolley, J., Roys, D., Thyer, B. A., & Bordnick, P. S. (1998). Evaluating outpatient behavior therapy for sex offenders: A pretest-posttest study. *Behavior Modification, 22,* 485–501.

Crow, S. J., Mitchell, J. E., Roerig, J. D., & Steffen, K. (2009). What potential role is there for medication treatment in Anorexia Nervosa? *International Journal of Eating Disorders, 42,* 1–9.

Dattalo, P. (2007). *Determining sample size: Balancing power, precision, and practicality.* New York: Oxford University Press.

Davis, L. V. (1994). Rejoinder to Dr. Marsh. In W. Hudson & P. S. Nurius (Eds.). *Controversial issues in social work research* (pp. 73–74). Boston, MA: Allyn & Bacon.

Davis, R. M. (2008). British American Tobacco ghost-wrote reports on tobacco advertising bans by the Advertising Association and J. J. Boddewyn. *Tobacco Control, 17,* 211–214.

DeAngelis, C. D., & Fontana, P. B. (2008). Guest authorship, mortality reporting, and integrity in Rofecoxib studies reply. *JAMA, 300,* 905–906.

Demicheli, V., Jefferson, T., Rivetti, A., & Price, D. (2008). *Vaccines for measles, mumps and rubella in children. Cochrane Database of Systematic Reviews, 4,* Art. No. CD004407. DOI: 10.1002/14651858.CD004407.pub2.

de Schmidt, G. A., & Gorey, K. M. (1997). Unpublished social work research: Systematic replication of a recent meta-analysis of published intervention effectiveness research. *Social Work Research, 21,* 58–62.

DeWalt, D. A., Davis, T. C., Wallace, A. S., Seligman, H. K., Bryant-Shilliday, B., Arnold, C. L., Freburger, J., & Shillinger, D. (2009). Goal setting in diabetes self-management: Taking the baby steps to success. *Patient Education and Counseling, 77,* 218–223.

Devine, E. T. (1908). Results of the Pittsburgh Survey. *Proceedings of the American Sociological Society, 3,* 85–92.

Diehl, D., & Frey, A. (2008). Evaluating a community-school model of social work practice. *School Social Work Journal, 32*(2), 1–20.

Dillon, S. (22 January 2009). Study sees an Obama effect as lifting Black test takers. *The New York Times,* A15. Accessed May 10, 2010, from *http://www.nytimes.com/2009/01/23/education/23gap.html.*

DiNitto, D. (1983). Time-series analysis: An application to social welfare policy. *Journal of Applied Behavioral Science, 19,* 507–518.

DiNitto, D. M., McDaniel, R. R., Ruefli, T. W., & Thomas, J. B. (1986). The use of ordinal time-series analysis in assessing policy inputs and impacts. *Journal of Applied Behavioral Science, 22,* 77–93.

Donohue, B., & Thyer, B. A. (1992). Should the GRE be used as an admissions requirement by schools of social work? *Journal of Teaching in Social Work, 6,* 33–40.

DuBois, W. E. B. (1899). *The Philadelphia Negro.* Philadelphia. PA: University of Pennsylvania.

Duncan, T. E., & Duncan, S. C. (2004a). A latent growth curve modeling approach to pooled interrupted time series data. *Journal of Psychopathology and Behavioral Assessment, 26,* 271–278.

Duncan, T. E., & Duncan, S. C. (2004b). An introduction to latent growth curve modeling. *Behavior Therapy, 35,* 333–363.

Epstein, W. M. (1990). Rational claims to effectiveness in social work's critical literature. *The Social Science Journal, 27,* 129–145.

Fischer, J. (1973). Is casework effective? A review. *Social Work, 18,* 5–20.

Fischer, J. (1976). *The effectiveness of social casework.* Springfield, IL: Charles C. Thomas.

Freud, S. (1962/1894). Obsessions and compulsions. In J. Strachey (Ed.). *The standard edition of the complete psychological works of Sigmund Freud* (Vol. 3, p. 81). London: Hogarth Press.

Geron, S. M., & Stetekee, G. S. (2010). Applying for research grants. In B. A. Thyer (Eds.). *Handbook of social work research methods* (2nd ed., pp. 619–630). Thousand Oaks, CA: Sage Publications, Inc.

Gordon, M. (1973). The social survey movement and sociology in the United States. *Social Problems, 21,* 284–298.

Gorey, K. M., Thyer, B. A., & Pawluck, D. E. (1998). Differential effectiveness of prevalent social work practice models. *Social Work, 43,* 269–278.

Grembowski, D., & Milgrom, P. M. (2000). Increasing access to dental care for Medicaid preschool children: The Access to Baby and Child Dentistry (ABCD) program. *Public Health Reports, 115,* 448–459.

Grenier, A. M., & Gorey, K. M. (1998). The effectiveness of social work with older people and their families: A meta-analysis of conference proceedings. *Social Work Research, 22,* 60–64.

Grey, A. L., & Dermody, H. E. (1972). Reports of casework failure. *Social Casework, 53,* 534–543.

Halpern-Meekin, S., & Tach, L. (2008). Heterogeneity in two-parent families and adolescent well-being. *Journal of Marriage and Family, 70,* 435–451.

Harrison, D. F., & Thyer, B. A. (1988). Doctoral research on social work practice. *Journal of Social Work Education, 24,* 107–114.

Herbert, J. D., Sharp, I. R., & Guidano, B. A. (2002). Separating fact from fiction in the etiology and treatment of autism: A scientific review of the evidence. *The Scientific Review of Mental Health Practice, 1,* 23–43.

Herron, W. G., & Sitkowski, S. (1986). Effect of fees on psychotherapy: What is the evidence? *Professional Psychology: Research and Practice, 17,* 347–351.

Hogarty, G. E. (1989). Meta-analysis of the effects of practice with the chronically mentally ill: A critique and reappraisal of the literature. *Social Work, 34,* 363–373.

Holden, G., Thyer, B. A., Baer, J., Delva, J., Dulmus, C. N., & Shanks, T. W. (2008). Suggestions to improve social work journal editorial and peer-review processes: The San Antonio response to the Miami Statement. *Research on Social Work Practice, 18,* 66–71.

Holder, H. D., & Wagenaar, A. C. (1994). Mandated server training and reduced alcohol-involved traffic crashes: A time-series analysis of the Oregon experience. *Accident Analysis & Prevention, 26,* 89–97.

Holland, J. F. (1997). Clinical trials in cancer. *Clinical Cancer Research, 3,* 2585–2586.

Holosko, M. J. (2006). A suggested author's checklist for submitting manuscripts to *Research on Social Work Practice. Research on Social Work Practice, 16,* 449–454.

Holosko, M. J. (2010). What types of designs are we using in social work research and evaluation? *Research on Social Work Practice, 20,* 665–673.

Holosko, M. J., Thyer, B. A., & Danner, J. E. (2009). Ethical guidelines for designing and conducting evaluations of social work practice. *Journal of Evidence-based Social Work, 6,* 1–13.

Hudson, W. W., Thyer, B. A., & Stocks, J. T. (1985). Assessing the importance of experimental outcomes. *Journal of Social Service Research, 8*(4), 87–98.

Hyun, M. K., Lee, M. S., Kang, K., & Choi, S. M. (2008). Body acupuncture for Nicotine Withdrawal Symptoms: A randomized placebo-controlled trial. *Complementary and Alternative Medicine, 7,* 233–238.

Jainchill, N., Hawke, J., & Messina, M. (2005). Post-treatment outcomes among adjudicated adolescent males and females in modified therapeutic community treatment. *Substance Use & Misuse, 40,* 975–996.

Johnson, P. A., Thyer, B. A., Daniels, M., Anderson, R., & Bordnick, P. S. (1996). Is the school social worker examination valid? *Arete, 20*(2), 1–5.

Johnson, Y. M., & Stadel, V. L. (2007). Completion of advance directives: Do social work preadmission interviews make a difference? *Research on Social Work Practice, 17,* 686–696.

Jones, C. D., Chancey, R., Lowe, L. A., & Risler, E. A. (2010). Residential treatment for sexually abusive youth: An assessment of treatment outcomes. *Research on Social Work Practice, 20,* 172–182.

Keller, D. P., Schut, L. J., Puddy, R. W., Williams, L., Stephens, R. L., McKeon, R., & Lubell, K. (2009). Tennessee lives count: Statewide gatekeeper training for youth suicide prevention. *Professional Psychology: Research and Practice, 40,* 126–133.

Klosko, J. S., Barlow, D. H., Tassinari, R., & Czerny, J. A. (1990). A comparison of alprazolam and behavior therapy in treatment of panic disorder. *Journal of Consulting and Clinical Psychology, 58,* 77–84.

Knaevelsrud, C., & Maercker, A. (2007). Internet-based treatment for PTSD reduces distress and facilitates the development of a strong therapeutic alliance: A randomized controlled trial. *BMC Psychiatry, 7,* 13.

Knaevelsrud, C., & Maercker, A. (2010). Long-term effects of an internet-based treatment for posttraumatic stress. *Cognitive Behaviour Therapy, 39,* 72–77.

Kurdyak, P., Cairney, J., Sarnocinska-Hart, Callahan, R. C., & Strike, C. (2008). The impact of a smoking cessation policy on visits to a psychiatric emergency department. *Canadian Review of Psychiatry, 53,* 779–782.

Lachin, J. M. (2000). Statistical considerations in the intent-to-treat principle. *Controlled Clinical Trials, 21,* 167–189.

Larsen, J., & Hepworth, D. H. (1982). Skill development of helping skills in undergraduate social work education: Model and evaluation. *Journal of Education for Social Work, 18,* 66–73.

LeCroy, C. W., & Krysik, J. (2007). Understanding and interpreting effect size measures. *Social Work Research, 31,* 243–248.

Levinson, D. R. (2010). *Most Medicaid children in nine states are not receiving all required preventive screening services.* Washington, DC: Department of Health and Human Services, Office of the Inspector General. Accessed May 25, 2010, from *http://oig.hhs.gov/oei/reports/oei-05-08-00520.pdf.*

Ligon, J., & Thyer, B. A. (2000). Client and family satisfaction with brief community mental health, substance abuse, and mobile crisis services in an urban setting. *Crisis Intervention, 6,* 93–99.

Lilienfeld, S. O. (2007). Psychological treatments that cause harm. *Perspectives on Psychological Science, 2,* 53–70.

Littell, J. H., Corcoran, J., & Pillai, V. (2008). *Systematic reviews and meta-analyses.* New York: Oxford University Press.

Lowry, F. (Ed.). (1939). *Readings in social casework: 1920–1938*. New York: Columbia University Press.

Macdonald, M. E. (1953). Some essentials in the evaluation of social casework. *Journal of Psychiatric Social Work, 22*(3), 135–137.

Martin, V. (2005). The consequences of parental divorce on the life course outcomes of Canadian children. *Canadian Studies in Population, 32,* 29–51.

Martino, S. C., Elliott, M. N., Collins, R. L., Kanouse, D. E., & Berry, S. H. (2008). Virginity pledges among the willing: Delays in first intercourse and consistency in condom use. *Journal of Adolescent Health, 43,* 341–348.

McDowall, D., McCleary, R., Meddinger, E. E., & Hay, A. J. (1980). *Interrupted time series analysis*. Thousand Oaks, CA: Sage.

Michielutte, R., Shelton, B., Paskett, E. D., Tatum, C. M., & Velez, R. (2000). Use of an interrupted time-series design to evaluate a cancer screening program. *Health Education Research, 15,* 615–623.

Monnickendam, M., & Elliot, E. J. (1997). Effects of a practice-centered, cognitive-oriented computer course on computer attitudes: Implications for course content. *Social Work and Social Sciences Review, 6,* 175–185.

Moore, A., & McQuay, H. (2006). *Bandolier's little book of making sense of the medical evidence*. New York: Oxford University Press.

Myers, L. L., & Rittner, B. (2001). Adult psychosocial functioning of children raised in an orphanage. *Residential Treatment of Children and Youth, 18*(4), 3–21.

National Association of Social Workers. (2008). *Code of Ethics*. Washington, DC: NASW Press.

Nezu, A. M., & Nezu, C. M. (2008). *Evidence-based outcome research: A practical guide to conducting randomized controlled trials for psychosocial interventions*. New York: Oxford University Press.

Novak, I., Cusick, A., & Lowe, K. (2007). A pilot study on the impact of occupational therapy home programming for young children with cerebral palsy. *American Journal of Occupational Therapy, 61,* 463–468.

Newsome, W. S., Anderson-Butcher, D., Fink, J., Hall, L., & Huffer, J. (2008). The impact of school social work services on student absenteeism and risk factors related to school truancy. *School Social Work Journal, 32*(2), 21–38.

Novella, S. (2011). What is acupuncture? *The Skeptical Inquirer, 35*(4), 28–29.

Ottenbacher, K. J. (1997). Designing and interpreting clinical studies. In M. Fuhrer (Ed.), *Assessing medical rehabilitation practices* (pp. 233–256). Baltimore, MD: Paul H. Brookes.

Pabian, W., Thyer, B. A., Straka, E., & Boyle, P. (2000). Do the families of children with developmental disabilities obtain recommended services? A follow-up study. *Journal of Human Behavior in the Social Environment, 3*(1), 45–58.

Palmgreen, P., Lorch, E. P., Stephenson, M. T., Hoyle, R. H., & Donohew, L. (2007). Effects of the Office of National Drug Control Policy's marijuana initiative campaign on high-sensation-seeking adolescents. *American Journal of Public Health, 97,* 1644–1649.

Parrish, D. E., & Rubin, A. (2011). An effective model for continuing education training in evidence-based practice. *Research on Social Work Practice, 21,* 77–87.

Perry, R. E. (2006). Do social workers make better child welfare workers than non-social workers? *Research on Social Work Practice, 16,* 392–405.

Pharis, M. E. (1976). Ten reasons why I am not bothered by outcome studies which claim to show psychotherapy is ineffective. *Clinical Social Work Journal, 4,* 58–61.

Pignotti, M. (2005). Thought Field Therapy Voice Technology vs. random meridian point sequences: A single-blind controlled experiment. *The Scientific Review of Mental Health Practice, 4*(1), 72–81.

Pignotti, M. & Thyer, B. A. (2009). Why randomized clinical trials are important and necessary to social work practice. In H-W. Otto, A. Polutta, & H. Ziegler (Eds.), *Evidence-based practice: Modernizing the knowledge base of social work* (pp. 99–109). Farmington Hills, MI/Opladen, Germany: Barbara Budrich Publishers.

Randall, E. J., & Thyer, B. A. (1994). A preliminary test of the validity of the LCSW examination. *Clinical Social Work Journal, 22,* 223–227.

Raphael, B. (1986). *When disaster strikes: How individuals and communities cope with disaster.* New York: Basic Books.

Raskin, M., Johnson, G., & Rondestvedt, J. W. (1973). Chronic anxiety treated by feedback-induced muscle relaxation: A pilot study. *Archives of General Psychiatry, 28,* 263–267.

Reid, W. J., & Hanrahan, P. (1982). Recent evaluations of social work: Grounds for optimism. *Social Work, 27,* 328–340.

Reid, W. J., & Shyne, A. W. (1969). *Brief and extended casework.* New York: Columbia University Press.

Residents of Hull House. (1895). *Hull-House maps and papers; A presentation of nationalities and wages in a congested district of Chicago, together with comments and essays on problems growing out of the social conditions.* New York: Crowell.

Reynolds, A. J., Temple, J. A., Robertson, D. L., & Mann, E. A. (2001). Long-term effects of an early childhood intervention on educational achievement and juvenile arrest: A 15-year follow-up of low-income children in public schools. *JAMA, 285,* 2339–2346.

Richards, K. V., & Thyer, B. A. (2011). Does Individual Development Account participation help the poor? A review. *Research on Social Work Practice, 21,* 348–362.

Rogers, C. R. (1933). A good foster home: Its achievements and limitations. *Mental Hygiene, 17*, 21–40.

Rosenbaum, J. E. (2008). Patient teenagers? A comparison of the sexual behavior of virginity pledgers and matched nonpledgers. *Pediatrics, 123*, e110–e120.

Rosenthal, D., & Frank, J. D. (1956). Psychotherapy and the placebo effect. *Psychological Bulletin, 53*, 294–302.

Royse, D., Thyer, B. A., & Padgett, D. (2010). *Program evaluation: An introduction* (5th ed.). Belmont, CA: Brooks/Cole/Cengage.

Rubin, A., & Babbie, E. R. (2008). *Research methods for social work* (6th ed.). Belmont, CA: Thomson.

Rubin, A., & Parrish, D. (2007). Problematic phrases in the conclusions of published outcome studies: Implications for evidence-based practice. *Research on Social Work Practice, 17*, 334–347.

Salloum, A. (2008). Group therapy for children after homicide and violence: A pilot study. *Research on Social Work Practice, 18*, 198–211.

Sanderson, S., Tatt, I. D., & Higgins, J. P. T. (2007). Tools for assessing quality and susceptibility to bias in observational studies in epidemiology: A systematic review and annotated bibliography. *International Journal of Epidemiology, 36*, 666–676.

Sandler, J. C., Freeman, N. J., & Socia, K. M. (2008). Does a watched pot boil? A time-series analysis of New York state's Sex Offender Registration and Notification law. *Psychology, Public Policy, and Law, 14*, 284–302.

Schilling, R., Baer, J. C., Barth, R., Fraser, M., Herman, D., Holden, G. et al. (2005). Peer review and publication standards in social work journals: The Miami Statement. *Social Work Research, 29*, 119–121.

Schissel, B. (1996). Law reform and social change: A time-series analysis of sexual assault in Canada. *Journal of Criminal Justice, 24*, 123–138.

Schneider, D. J., May, G., Carithers, T., Coyle, K., Potter, S., Endahl, J., Robin, L., McKenna, M., Debrot, K., & Seymour, J. (2006). Evaluation of a fruit and vegetable distribution program–Mississippi, 2004–05 school year. *Journal of the American Medical Association, 296*, 1833–1834.

Segal, S. P. (1972). Research on the outcome of social work therapeutic interventions: A review of the literature. *Journal of Health and Social Behavior, 13*, 3–17.

Seekins, T., Fawcett, S. B., Cohen, S. H., Elder, J. P., Jason, L. A., Schnelle, J. F., & Winett, R. A. (1988). Experimental evaluation of public policy: The case of state legislation for child passenger safety. *Journal of Applied Behavior Analysis, 21*, 233–243.

Shadish, W. R. (2011). Randomized controlled studies and alternative designs in outcome studies: Challenges and opportunities. *Research on Social Work Practice, 21*, 636–643.

Shadish, W. R., Clark, M. H., & Steiner, P. M. (2008). Can nonrandomized experiments yield accurate answers? A randomized experimental comparing random to nonrandom assignment. *Journal of the American Statistical Association, 103*, 1334–1343.

Shadish, W. R., Cook, T. D., & Campbell, D. T. (2002). *Experimental and quasi-experimental designs for generalized causal inference.* New York: Houghton Mifflin.

Shadish, W. R., Galindo, R., Wong, V., Steiner, P. M., & Cook, T. D. (2011). A randomized experiment comparing random and cutoff-based assignment. *Psychological Methods, 16*, 179–191.

Shadish, W. R., Matt, G. E., Navarro, A. M., & Phillips, G. (2000). The effects of psychological therapies under clinically representative conditions: A meta-analysis. *Journal of Consulting and Clinical Psychology, 126*, 512–529.

Shadish, W. R., & Ragsdale, K. (1996). Random versus nonrandom assignment in controlled experiments: Do you get the same answer? *Journal of Consulting and Clinical Psychology, 64*, 1290–1305.

Shipton, B., & Spain, A. (1981). Implications of payment of fees for psychotherapy. *Psychotherapy: Theory, Research and Practice, 18*, 68–73.

Smeeth, L., Cook, C., Fombonne, E., Heavey, L. Rodrigues, L. C., Smith, P. G., & Hall, A. J. (2004). MMR vaccination and pervasive developmental disorders: A case-control study. *The Lancet, 364*, 963–969.

Smith, G. C. S., & Pell, J. P. (2003). Parachute use to prevent death and major trauma related to gravitational challenge: Systematic review of randomized controlled trials. *BMJ, 327*, 1459–1461.

Smith, G. S., Thyer, B. A., Clements, C., & Kropf, N. P. (1997). An evaluation of coalition building training for aging and developmental disabilities service providers. *Educational Gerontology, 23*, 105–114.

Solomon, P., Cavanaugh, M. M., & Draine, J. (2009). *Randomized controlled trials.* New York: Oxford University Press.

Spinelli, M. (1997). Interpersonal psychotherapy for depressed antepartum women: A pilot study. *American Journal of Psychiatry, 154*, 1028–1030.

Staff. (2010). Should protocols for observational research be registered? *The Lancet, 375*, 348.

Stewart, R. E., & Chambless, D. L. (2009). Cognitive-behavioral therapy for adult anxiety disorders in clinical practice: A meta-analysis of effectiveness studies. *Journal of Consulting and Clinical Psychology, 77*, 595–606.

Sze, W. C., Keller, R. S., & Keller, D. B. (1979). A comparative study of two different teaching and curricular arrangements in human behavior and social environments. *Journal of Education for Social Work, 15*, 103–108.

Thomas, E. J. (1975). Uses of research methods in interpersonal practice. In N. A. Polansky (Ed.), *Social work research* (revised edition, pp. 254–283). Chicago: University of Chicago Press.

Thomlison, R. J. (1984). Something works: Evidence from practice effectiveness studies. *Social Work, 29,* 51–56.

Thyer, B. A. (1987). Contingency contracting to promote automobile safety belt use by students (letter). *The Behavior Therapist, 10,* 150, 160.

Thyer, B. A. (1988). Teaching without testing: A preliminary report of an innovative technique for social work education. *Innovative Higher Education, 13,* 47–53.

Thyer, B. A. (1991). Guidelines for evaluating outcome studies on social work practice. *Research on Social Work Practice, 1,* 76–91.

Thyer, B. A. (2002). How to write up a social work outcome study for publication. *Journal of Social Work Research and Evaluation, 3,* 215–224.

Thyer, B. A. (2008). *Preparing research articles.* New York: Oxford University Press.

Thyer, B. A. (Ed.) (2010). *Handbook of social work research methods.* Thousand Oaks, CA: Sage Publications, Inc.

Thyer, B. A. (2011). LCSW examination pass rates: Implications for social work education. *Clinical Social Work Journal, 39,* 296–300. DOI: 10.1007/s10615-009-0253-x.

Thyer, B. A., Jackson-White, G., Sutphen, R., & Carrillo, D. F. (1992). Structured study questions as a social work teaching method. *Innovative Higher Education, 16,* 235–245.

Thyer, B. A., & Myers, L. L. (2007). *A social worker's guide to evaluating practice outcomes.* Alexandria, VA: Council on Social Work Education.

Thyer, B. A., Myers, L. L., & Nugent, W. R. (2011). Do regular social work faculty earn better student course evaluations than adjunct faculty or doctoral students? *Journal of Teaching in Social Work, 31,* 365–377.

Thyer, B. A., Sowers-Hoag, K. M., & Love, J. P. (1986). The influence of field instructor-student gender combinations on student perceptions of field instruction quality. *Arete, 11*(2), 25–30.

Thyer, B. A., & Vodde, R. (1994). Is the ACSW examination valid? *Clinical Social Work Journal, 22,* 105–122.

Thyer, B. A., Vonk, M. E., & Tandy, C. C. (1996). Are advanced standing and two-year MSW program students equivalently prepared? An empirical investigation. *Arete, 20*(2), 42–46.

Tripodi, T., & Harrington, J. (1979). Uses of time-series designs for formative program evaluation. *Journal of Social Service Research, 3*(1), 67–78.

Turner, E. H., Matthews, A., Linardos, E., Tell, R. A., & Rosenthal, R. (2008). Selective publication of antidepressant trials and its influence on apparent efficacy. *The New England Journal of Medicine, 358,* 252–260.

Videka-Sherman, L. (1988). Meta-analysis of research on social work practice in mental health. *Social Work, 33,* 325–338.

Viggiani, P. A., Reid, W. J., & Bailey-Dempsey, C. (2002). Social worker-teacher collaboration in the classroom: Help for elementary students at risk. *Research on Social Work Practice, 12,* 604–620.

Vingilis, E., McLeod, A. L., Seeley, J., Mann, R., Voas, R., & Compton, C. (2006). The impact of Ontario's extended drinking hours on cross-border cities of Windsor and Detroit. *Accident Analysis and Prevention, 38,* 63–70.

Von Elm, E., Atlman, D. G., Egger, M., Pocock, S. J., Gotzsche, P. C., & Vandenbrouche, J. P. (2007). The Strengthening and Reporting of Observational Studies in Epidemiology (STROBE) statement: Guidelines for reporting observational studies. *Epidemiology, 18,* 800–804.

Vonk, E. M., & Thyer, B. A. (1999). Evaluating the effectiveness of short-term treatment at a university counseling center. *Journal of Clinical Psychology, 55,* 1095–1106.

Vonk, M. E., Zucrow, E., & Thyer, B. A. (1996). Female MSW students' satisfaction with practicum supervision: The effect of supervisor gender. *Journal of Social Work Education, 32,* 415–419.

Waber, R. L., Shiv, B., Camon, Z., & Ariely, D. (2008). Commercial features of placebo and therapeutic efficacy. *JAMA, 299,* 1016–1017.

Wagenaar, A. C., & Maldonaldo-Molina, M. M. (2007). Effects of drivers license suspension policies on alcohol-related crash involvement: Long-term follow-up in forty-six states. *Alcoholism: Clinical and Experimental Research, 31,* 1399–1406.

Wagenaar, A. C., Maldonaldo-Molina, M. M., Erickson, D. J., Ma, L., Tobler, A. L., & Komro, K. A. (2007). General deterrence effects of U.S. statutory DUI fine and jail penalties: Long-term follow-up in 32 states. *Accident Analysis and Prevention, 39,* 982–994.

Wagenaar, A. C., & Toomey, T. L. (2002). Effects of minimum drinking age laws: Review and analyses of the literature from 1960 to 2000. *Journal of Studies on Alcohol, Supplement No. 14,* 206–225.

Welner, A. Welner, Z., & Fishman, R. (1979). Psychiatric adolescent inpatients: Eight- to ten-year follow-up. *Archives of General Psychiatry, 36,* 698–700.

Whitt-Glover, M. C., Hogan, P., Lang, W., & Heil, D. P. (2008). Pilot study of a faith-based physical activity program among sedentary Blacks. *Preventing Chronic Disease, 5*(2), A51.

Wicke, T., & Silver, R. C. (2009). A community responds to collective trauma: An ecological analysis of the James Byrd murder in Jasper, Texas. *American Journal of Community Psychology, 44,* 233–248.

Wilson, J. M., Wallace, L. S., & DeVoe, J. E. (2009). Are state Medicaid application enrollment forms readable? *Journal of Health Care for the Poor and Underserved, 20,* 423–431.

Wolf, D. B., & Abell, N. B. (2003). Examining the effects of meditation techniques on psychosocial functioning. *Research on Social Work Practice, 13,* 27–42.

Wood, W. G. (1982). Do fees help heal? *Journal of Clinical Psychology, 38,* 669–673.

Yegidis, B., Weinbach, R. W., & Myers, L. L. (2011). *Research methods for social workers* (7th ed.). New York: Allyn and Bacon.

Yoken, C., & Berman, J. S. (1984). Does paying a fee alter the effectiveness of treatment? *Journal of Consulting and Clinical Psychology, 52,* 254–260.

Ziman, J. (1978). *Reliable knowledge: An exploration of the grounds for belief in science.* Cambridge: Cambridge University Press.

Zite, N. B., Philipson, S. J., & Wallace, L. S. (2007). Consent to Sterilization section of the Medicaid-Title XIX form: Is it understandable? *Contraception, 75,* 256–260.

Index

acupuncture, 14
Addams, Jane, 3
Analysis of Variance (ANOVA), 110, 158
APA Publication Manual, 140
ARIMA, 109
Assessment/treatment interactions, 64
Association for Behavior
    Analysis International, 171
autocorrelation, 109

baseline, 109
behavioral approach test, 64
Buxtun, Peter, 176

categorical data, 159
causal knowledge, 17
Chapin. F. Stewart, 5
client attrition, 48
Clinical Social Work Association, 171
Coalition for Evidence-based
    Policy Guidelines, 137–139
Code of Ethics, 10, 172
coefficient of determination, 166
Cohen's *d*, 170
Cohen's *f²*, 170
cohort study, 131
concurrent history, 61
Council on Social Work Education, 10, 81
Cramer's *phi*, 170
Cross-sectional survey, 84

delayed treatment design, 100
dependent variable, 26
design, 8
differential attrition, 61
differing treatment credibility, 67
diffusion/contamination of treatments, 71
dismantling studies, 101–103

Educational Policy and
    Accreditation Standards, 10
effect sizes, 140, 166, 169–171
effectiveness studies, 31
efficacy studies, 31
efficacy subset analysis, 141–143
epidemiological studies, 21
experimental designs, 56
experimental method, 6
extended intervention phase, 116

Fischer, Joel, 6

generalizable knowledge, 20
ghost authorship, 72

Habitat for Humanity, 11
Hedge's *g*, 170
Heritage Foundation, 87, 88
Hull House, 3
human subject, 174
hypothesis, 8

idiographic research, 107
independent variable, 26
individual development accounts, 37
inferential logic, 108
inferential statistics, 27, 153
Institutional Review Board (IRB), 93, 173
instrument change, 65
intent-to-treat analysis, 141–143
interactions, 174
interrupted time series design, 108
interval data, 160
intervention, 174

Journal Article Reporting Standards
   (JARS), 131, 136–137
*Journal of the American Medical
   Association (JAMA)*, 55, 94

lagged groups design, 100
lagged intervention group, 120
latent growth curve modeling, 110
LCSW, 12, 32
LCSW exam, 157–158
life satisfaction, 42

Macdonald, Mary, 7
maturation, 59
mortality/attrition, 60
multiple pretreatment assessments, 52
multiple treatment interference, 63

National Association of Social Workers
   (NASW), 10, 25, 171
negative outcomes, 143–144
nomenclature, 26
nomothetic research, 27, 39
nonblind assessments, 62
nonparametric tests, 28
no-treatment control group, 120
no-treatment control group interrupted
   time series design, 169

observational study, 131
one-group pretest-posttest
   design, 43–55
ordinal data, 159–160
ordinary least squares regression, 122
orphanages, 35
Ouija board effect, 149

paired-sample *t*-test, 161
parametric tests, 27
participants, 27
passage of time, 59
philosophical assumptions, 25
pilot data, 22
placebo effects, 57
placebo factor, 13
pre-experimental designs, 9, 56
pretest-posttest alternative
   treatment control group
   design, 97, 168
pretest-posttest alternative treatment/
   no-treatment control comparison
   design, 168
pretest-posttest no-treatment control
   group design, 95–97, 168
pretest-posttest single group
   design, 167
pretest-posttest single group design
   with repeated posttests, 167
pretest-posttest single group design
   with repeated pretests, 167
postest-only comparison
   design, 90–95
posttest-only no-treatment control
   group design, 78–89, 167
posttest-only single group
   design, 34–42, 167
post-treatment assessments, 40
posttreatment-only time series
   design, 168

quality of life, 42
quasi-experimental designs, 9, 56

randomized controlled trials
   (RCTs), 16, 20, 23, 56
ratio data, 160–161
regression to the mean, 58
removal or withdrawal
   phase, 53, 115
replicated interrupted time-series
   design, 118
replication, 107
research grants, 21
Research on Social Work Practice, 17,
   120, 170
Rogers, Carl, 4

sample of convenience, 107
selection bias, 69
serial dependency, 109
Sex Offender Registration Act, 114
simple interrupted time series design, 169
single-case research designs, 107
single-system research designs, 107
Social Work Research, 17
statistical power, 40
STROBE Statement, 131–136
switching replications design, 100

therapeutic relationship, 13
therapist bias/allegiance effects, 72

Thought-Field Therapy, 14
time-series analysis, 112
time-series design, 50
treatment as usual (TAU), 27, 97, 104, 143, 150, 151, 170
treatment fidelity, 73
treatment group, 29
true experiments, 9
Type I error, 144–146
Type II error, 144–146

univariate Box-Jenkins integrated moving average, 109

CPSIA information can be obtained at www.ICGtesting.com
Printed in the USA
BVOW010346040112

279486BV00004B/3/P

9 780195 387384